Liturgy For Living

Liturgy *for* Living

Revised Edition

Written by
Charles P. Price and Louis Weil

MOREHOUSE PUBLISHING

First edition © 1979 the Seabury Press, Inc.
Revised edition © 2000 by Morehouse Publishing

Morehouse Publishing
P.O. Box 1321
Harrisburg, PA 17105

Morehouse Publishing is an imprint of Church Publishing, Inc.

Cover design by Corey Kent.

Library of Congress Cataloging-in-Publication Data

Price, Charles P., 1920–
    Liturgy for living / written by Charles P. Price and Louis Weil, with the assistance of a group of editorial advisors under the direction of the Church's Teaching Series Committee.—Rev. ed.
        p. cm.
    Includes bibliographical references and index.
    ISBN 0-8192-1862-6 (alk. paper)
    1. Episcopal Church—Liturgy. 2. Episcopal Church. Book of common prayer (1979) I. Weil, Louis, 1935– II. Title.
    BX5940 .P74 2000
    264'.03'009—dc21

                                                                    00-060930

ISBN: 0-8192-1862-6

Printed in the United States of America
    07 08 10 9 8 7 6

To the memory of
Charles Philip Price
4 October 1920–13 October 1999
Priest, professor, and friend

Preface

The late Urban T. Holmes, dean of the seminary at Sewanee, Tennessee, conceived the idea of asking Charles P. Price and me to coauthor the volume on the liturgy for the second Church's Teaching Series. Dean Holmes was at that time my colleague on the faculty at Nashotah House. His intention was to demonstrate to the Episcopal Church at large that the liturgical movement had essentially nullified the old distinctions between "high" and "low" church, at least when it came to the renewal of the public worship of the church. Professor Price was, in the mid-seventies, professor of theology at the Virginia Theological Seminary and a widely respected theologian of the evangelical tradition of Anglicanism. I was professor of liturgy at Nashotah House, with a respected pedigree as an Anglo-Catholic liturgist. Asking the two of us to write the book together was a bold idea on the part of Dean Holmes. Professor Price and I had never even met, and so the potential fruit of this undertaking was by no means clear.

Professor Price and I discussed the project by telephone in preparation for our first working session together. We decided that each of us would prepare a full outline of what such a book should include, and then compare these before we actually began to write. A few weeks later we met to sort out the work and to decide which one would do the first draft of which sections. When we compared outlines, we found that we had a virtually identical sense of what the book should include.

Our intention from the start was to offer to the Episcopal Church a basic book on the liturgy that would be useful to laity and clergy of the church with regard to the history and theology of Christian, and specifically Anglican, worship. We also wanted the book to help readers to understand more fully the pastoral and theological implications of the then proposed Book of Common Prayer. Professor Price commented to me at one point that this book would probably be read by more people than any other book either of us would ever write, and that has turned out to be true. The first edition was reprinted several times, and demand for the book, especially for use in programs of lay education and for candidates studying in seminary, has never ceased. We were therefore delighted when Morehouse approached us about the possibility of publishing a second edition.

Unfortunately, Professor Price died before our work of revision was complete. We had been in consultation by telephone about the changes that Morehouse Publishing had requested. In only a few cases were revisions or clarifications of fact made for this new edition. Otherwise, our concern was to make modest but necessary editorial changes, including references to the "new" Prayer Book. In rereading the book, I found to my delight that it is still a work of which Professor Price and I could be proud, and which might continue to be useful in the church's programs of education.

Finally, a brief word about the changes in the bibliography. Already at the time of the publication of the first edition of Liturgy for Living, the literature in the fields of liturgical and sacramental studies had mushroomed as the renewal of the liturgy in the various Christian traditions had led to a serious need for such works. That literature has continued to grow during the twenty years since the first edition was published so that it is now virtually impossible to prepare a comprehensive bibliography on all aspects of the liturgy. Such a comprehensive list, even if it were available, would probably not be needed by readers of this volume. For this edition, quite a number of classical studies have been retained in the bibliography so that readers who may want to work further on special questions will not be unaware of works which were of major importance for liturgical renewal in the mid-twentieth century. A large number of other, more occasional publications, especially articles in periodicals, have been removed, first, because much of that material has now been assimilated into more comprehensive studies, but also because most of those items are long out-of-print or available only on the shelves of theological libraries. Most of the additions to the bibliography are books which have been published in the last twenty years and which have made significant contributions to the Church's reflection on its public worship or which are particularly relevant to issues which this book addresses.

Both Charles Price and I were united in a deep commitment to theological education in the Episcopal Church, primarily of candidates preparing for ordination, but also to the education of all God's people to the end that praying and understanding might illuminate each other. The fact that Liturgy for Living is now in a second edition is a confirmation of that purpose. May this book continue to bear fruit in the lives and worship of the people of God.

Louis Weil
Berkeley, California
September 2000

Abbreviations
of the Books of
the Bible

Acts	The Acts	3 Jn.	3 John
Am.	Amos	1 Kg.	1 Kings
1 Chr.	1 Chronicles	2 Kg.	2 Kings
2 Chr.	2 Chronicles	Lev.	Leviticus
Col.	Colossians	Lk.	Luke
1 Cor.	1 Corinthians	Mal.	Malachi
2 Cor.	2 Corinthians	Mic.	Micah
Dan.	Daniel	Mk.	Mark
Dt.	Deuteronomy	Mt.	Matthew
Eph.	Ephesians	1 Pet.	1 Peter
Ex.	Exodus	2 Pet.	2 Peter
Ezek.	Ezekiel	Phil.	Philippians
Gal.	Galatians	Pr.	Proverbs
Gen.	Genesis	Ps.	Psalms
Heb.	Hebrews	Rev.	Revelation
Hos.	Hosea	Rom.	Romans
Is.	Isaiah	1 Sam.	1 Samuel
Jas.	James	2 Sam.	2 Samuel
Jer.	Jeremiah	1 Th.	1 Thessalonians
Jl.	Joel	2 Th.	2 Thessalonians
Jn.	John	1 Tim.	1 Timothy
1 Jn.	1 John	2 Tim.	2 Timothy
2 Jn.	2 John		

Contents

Part Five—Other Liturgies: Pastoral Offices and Episcopal Services

Epilogue

Note To The Reader

Unless otherwise indicated, Prayer Book references are to the Book of Common Prayer © 1979 (BCP). In referring to other editions of the Prayer Book, a following date indicates the year of publication. Thus, "BCP 1928" refers to the American Prayer Book of 1928.

All biblical references, unless otherwise indicated, are to the Revised Standard Version of the Bible, copyright © 1946, 1952, 1971, by Division of Christian Education of the National Council of the Churches of Christ in the United States of America.

1

PROLOGUE
Where We Are

This volume of the Church's Teaching Series is about worship. Why do we Episcopalians do what we do when we gather on Sundays and other special days of the year in the presence of God? What does it mean to pray, to praise, to listen? to break bread and eat it "in remembrance of me"? To initiate new members "by water and the Spirit"? What does it mean to speak at the critical moments of a person's life those words that generations of worshipers have found to be full of strength and meaning: "for better for worse, for richer for poorer, in sickness and in health, to love and to cherish . . ." "We humbly beseech thee to relieve thy sick servant . . ." "I am the resurrection and the life, saith the Lord"? What does it mean to worship God in these ways? How has the worship of the church taken shape in the course of history?

This book is not only about worship. It is also about worshipers. What does worship require of those who participate in it? What difference does it make in our attitudes and the way we live our lives? What is supposed to happen to us when we worship? What is the relationship between the activities of a congregation gathered to worship God together as a body and the prayers of individual persons morning by morning, or evening by evening, or in those unexpected times of joy, surprise, fear, and pain when all we can do is pray?

None of these questions is easy to answer. Individuals are different, with differences that God made and that the church must respect. Congregations are different. The variety of styles of worship even within the Episcopal Church is well known. Some parish churches are small, intimate, with a minimum of adornment. Others are large, formal, with considerable display of symbols and color, vestment and gesture. The gradations between are too numerous to mention.

One reason for these differences, of course, is psychological. For some people, perhaps for all of us some of the time, externals of worship interfere with prayer. For others, perhaps for all of us much of the time, images and symbols express different aspects of the inexhaustible glory of God. Their use liberates our spirits and points us in fruitful directions, where God may find us more readily and we can more easily appropriate the gift of his presence.

It would be difficult to do justice from a psychological point of view to the subtle nuances in meaning these different styles of worship involve. But psychological differences are not the whole story. Historical and cultural factors have played a role that would be difficult to overestimate. It is somewhat easier to be specific about the influence of such things.

The Episcopal Church in the United States, for example, is an offspring of the Church of England. It carries the marks of its Anglican heritage unmistakably and proudly. In worship this heritage involves clear continuity with the liturgy of the church from earliest times. For centuries each local church was the manifestation of the one, undivided body of Christ, present throughout the world. Its faith was the faith of the Catholic Church, based upon God's purposes made visible in Christ. Its liturgy was also the liturgy of the Catholic Church, with its roots in the practices of the earliest Christian community recorded in the New Testament, elaborated during the course of the Middle Ages by an ever-increasing use of physical things: stately buildings as heavy as empire, with intricately carved stonework as delicate as music; vivid stained glass windows telling the story of God's purposes for his creation, even to those who could not read; the rolling swells of plainsong, with the sound of eternity within them; elaborate ceremonial, solemn liturgical dance, whose every gesture suggested, to those who knew the key, some aspect of God's work in Christ; beautiful vestments whose changing colors registered the successive phases of the church's observances as the year made its rounds. It was a feast for the senses. A faith in God who assumed flesh and dwelt among us, who created the world and saw that it was very good, invites such a setting, even demands it. To this day, the Episcopal Church bears the marks of this epoch of worship.

Yet for all its glory, the worship of the Middle Ages had fateful shortcomings. It cut itself loose from some of the essential principles of worship established in the New Testament and in the earliest centuries of the church's life. And when it cut itself loose, it became preoccupied with itself. It developed along an autonomous route according to its own logic, rather than as subject to the free working of the Holy Spirit. Liturgy tended to become an end in itself, often fixed and rigid, little open to the particular nuances of the Christian community.

Several examples of distorted development can be identified. For one thing, the emphasis on the Word of God, so central at first, had become weak by the late Middle Ages. The language of the liturgy was Latin, the universal language of educated people. But Latin was not understood by the crowds of uneducated men and women who comprised by far the largest part of the people of God. Lessons from Scripture were often brief, and sometimes the reader read them with his face to the wall and his back to the congregation. Interest in preaching ebbed and flowed. It was not regarded as an essential element of worship.

As a consequence of the inability of congregations to understand the words of the liturgy, lay people became passive observers of the services. Clergy "took" the service; laity watched. The church in the Book of Acts is described as a group of people in which all believers worshiped in the temple together, celebrated the Eucharist together, and in every way shared a common life. Such a picture of the church had little in common with the character of the religious establishment of the later Middle Ages, when laity came to be regarded as second-class citizens.

There have been at least two major attempts within the Anglican Church to restore the quality of life that characterized the church at the beginning. One took place in the sixteenth century. One is taking place in our own time.

The sixteenth-century Protestant Reformation made a serious effort to restore to the liturgy the element of the Word, which by the end of the Middle Ages had so nearly vanished. The reading of Scripture in a language "understanded of the people" (Article xxiv of the Articles of Religion) was firmly established and is characteristic of Anglican worship to this day. Two lessons were provided for the Daily Offices and the Eucharist. To hear them is part of an Episcopalian's expectation when he goes to church. Sermons were also given a fresh emphasis and significance at the time of the Reformation, and although the place of preaching among us has not always remained as high as it was in the sixteenth century, it has remained an item of central importance in our liturgy.

Yet, in a way not intended by the reformers, this gain was balanced by a serious loss, a diminished emphasis on the sacraments. The reasons for this development are complex. It seems clear that the sixteenth-century reformers in England desired a celebration of the Lord's Supper on each Lord's Day. From the beginning, English Prayer Books provided proper collects, epistles, and gospels for every Sunday as well as for feast days and holy days. Luther and Calvin also envisioned weekly celebrations of the sacrament, but the combined force of their religious influence did not prevail against a philosophical revolution that was occurring at about the same time. This revolution of thought changed the "common sense" of Western Europeans about the nature of reality. *Nominalism*, to name this new form of thought, broke the inherent connection between individual things and larger, deeper realms of meaning and value. The reality of a thing was in itself. This point of view unquestionably made possible the rise of modern science, but it made difficult the understanding of sacraments. Gertrude Stein epitomized nominalism in the memorable line, "A rose is a rose is a rose." If a rose is a rose is a rose, then bread is bread is bread. It becomes hard to see how in any sense it could ever be the body of our Lord broken for us.

The consequences of a prevalent nominalism for Christian worship have been plain. Within decades after the Reformation, Holy Communion was celebrated in most parishes in the Church of England, with a few notable exceptions, only four or five times a year. The evangelical renewal connected with the Wesleys in the eighteenth century led to the monthly pattern that is still customary in many of our parishes; and the Catholic revival, or Oxford Movement, of the nineteenth century produced the nearly universal "eight o'clock" weekly celebrations, customary even in parishes when the main service at a later hour is Morning Prayer three Sundays out of four. Our church still labors to produce a true balance, both in thought and practice, between Word and Sacrament.

The Protestant Reformation in its English form, as in most of its embodiments, also failed to restore the role of the laity in worship. In most Protestant churches, the clericalism of the last Middle Ages, the clericalism of the priest who alone could say Mass and dispense grace, was replaced by a new clericalism, that of the preacher who alone could proclaim the Word. The preachers attracted to themselves the whole conduct of public worship. One has only to examine the early versions of the Book of Common Prayer to recognize how thoroughly the priest dominates Prayer Book worship. Only the current revision of the Prayer Book has made explicit provision for different people, both clerical and lay, to read various parts of the several services.

The Protestant Reformation had a further effect on liturgical worship: it intensified the late medieval tendency to depend on fixed forms of words to denote conformity to a fixed theological position or even loyalty to a fixed political system. Refusal to abide by the authorized liturgy could be taken to mean theological heterodoxy or even political infidelity. In the ninth century, the liturgy of the diocese of Rome became one of the cornerstones of the unity of Charlemagne's Holy Roman Empire. Its use was enforced throughout Western Europe. In a similar way, the liturgies of the Protestant churches in the emerging nations of Northern Europe came to be touchstones of both ecclesiastical and political unity. When Roman Catholics in England during the reign of Elizabeth I used the Roman rite, they were understood to have rejected both the theological position of the Church of England and allegiance to the crown. Louis XIV in the seventeenth century summed up this point in a memorable epigram: *un roi, une loi, une foi* ("one king, one law, one faith").

Thus conformity to the fixed text of an official liturgy in all its details became a matter of significance to a degree never before known in either Catholic or Protestant churches of Western Europe. Furthermore, the invention of printing in 1440 opened the way to a liturgical conformity that could never have been demanded as long as only handwritten manuscripts were available. Even in the late Middle Ages, when fixed texts were regarded as a matter of considerable importance, written manuscripts displayed a substantial amount of variation from authorized texts. The advent of printing made absolute consistency possible. The political and ecclesiastical tensions of the Reformation made it necessary. That liturgical texts should be invariable has been an unexamined assumption of Anglican liturgies, and of most Anglicans, until a fairly recent date. Revisions of the American Prayer Book in 1892 and in 1928 made cautious use of the principle of flexibility and supplied a few alternative texts. But only since new services were authorized for trial use in 1970 have Episcopalians had much opportunity to explore the question of whether a united church requires an unvarying liturgical text, and to experience the freedom and enrichment made possible by alternative services, for Morning Prayer or the Eucharist, for example.

We have been exploring some of the historical and cultural circumstances that have made the worship of the Episcopal Church what it is. There is something in our services that corresponds to the sensuous fullness of medieval liturgy. The drama of the Church Year was never lost. The use of colored vestments, candles, crosses, and the like were restored to nearly all our parishes during the nineteenth-century revival. Something in our worship matches the emphasis on the Bible and preaching that the Reformation brought, and we can still appreciate the difficulties a scientific worldview entails when it comes to sacraments. It is only in comparatively recent times that we have come to recognize that the liturgy is not the exclusive domain of the ordained ministry. For many laity this awareness requires as great an adjustment as for many clergy. There is still an inclination for both laity and clergy to think of liturgy primarily in terms of a fixed text that is performed in accordance with rubrics. These elements are among the most significant and obvious that have shaped the attitude of large numbers of Episcopalians toward worship until the recent past.

Today new forces are at work. The Protestant Reformation of the sixteenth century made one major attempt to restore worship along New Testament lines. A second such effort is going on before our eyes. The reasons such a development should be happening at the present time are as complex as the causes for the Reformation. They have to do, for one thing, with a growing dissatisfaction with the nominalistic "common sense" of reality that has been so dominant in European and American thought during the past four hundred years. Along with this restiveness goes a hunger for meaning and for that contact with the mystery of life that nominalism, in spite of its significance for modern science, seriously diminished. The reasons for the present changes in liturgy also have to do with the considerably greater knowledge of life in the early church, including its worship—knowledge gained during the intervening centuries by patient study and the discovery of priceless manuscripts from the ancient past. The reasons have something to do with impatience at the present divided and impotent state of the church, and with a new awareness that Christianity exists among many world religions that are not about to disappear from the earth in the next few decades or centuries. May not these other ways of worship even cast light upon our own?

These factors are part of our historical and cultural situation today, and they help us to understand why worship in our church is changing as it is. There seems to be a new appreciation of sacraments, for example. It has come about because of new light available to us on the sacramental worship of the early church, and because the divided churches of Christendom are once more learning to seek their unity in the risen Lord, made known to us in the breaking of the bread. It may have come about because our world is dominated by television and film as much as the sixteenth-century world was dominated by the printing press, making action and image as potent as words in shaping our ideas. It may also have come about because more and more thoughtful persons are learning to look within things like water and bread and wine for their true meanings.

There is also a new insistence in our worship on the active participation of as many people in the congregation as possible. Perhaps this development has come about because we are learning to think of the church, as in New Testament times, not as a building, not as clergy, but as the entire people of God, all with significant parts to play both in worship and in the life of the church in the world. Perhaps also, in the wake of widespread revulsion against totalitarian rule in both church and state, we are coming to an understanding of the church, not as a society where authority trickles down from the top but as an ordered body of many members where they who are greatest are servants of all—a New Testament model for the church with revolutionary implications for the state as well.

We are also at this time discovering a new freedom and variety in worship. Perhaps it is because the church has at last appropriated its separation from the state and has come to see that ecclesiastical variation is not necessarily a sign either of civil disloyalty or of theological heresy. Perhaps it is also because at this distance the spontaneity of liturgical practice in the earliest Christian community looks so very attractive.

To be sure, the present cultural and pastoral situation does not suggest a return to completely free liturgy without texts. Some basic liturgical conformity is one of the few tangible expressions of unity in the church. The creation of a common eucharistic prayer—Eucharistic Prayer D in the current Book of Common Prayer (p. 373), which with minor variations is acceptable to a number of Christian denominations—is in our day a noteworthy achievement and a foretaste of greater unity yet to be achieved, greater unity than the church has known since before the Reformation. Besides, the experience of two thousand years has taught the church that texts are important and that not all clergy have the gift of composing prayers or of uttering them spontaneously.

Yet in a world where God is worshiped in many ways and where the Anglican Church is taking root in many cultures, it is surely impoverishing to suppose that only one eucharistic prayer or only one form of the Daily Office or of any of the Pastoral Offices could be adequate for every time and place. There can be many authentic liturgical expressions of the one Gospel, and even our own American Episcopal Church may be instructed, enriched, and exhilarated by the experience of some of this variety.

In the chapters that follow, we shall explore worship in the Episcopal Church in the United States as it is taking shape through these years of growth and change. We must recognize both the psychological and historical complexity of the subject. It bears the marks of a long and varied development. It is in the process of alteration from one form adequate to the needs of a past age to a somewhat richer and more extensive form, more adequate to the religious hungers and thirsts of the age at hand. We trust it will be as adequate as the old to express the gracious act of God for us through his Son, Jesus Christ.

PART ONE

The Meaning
of Worship

2

Worship and Liturgy

At all times and in all places people worship God. The variety of Anglican worship is only a small section of a large spectrum. The austere silence of meetings of the Society of Friends is worship. The mystical splendor of the Eastern Orthodox Divine Liturgy is worship. Muslims worship when they bow their heads toward Mecca and recite the opening chapter of the Quran. Jewish Hasidim worship when they gather morning and evening wrapped in prayer shawls to study the Torah. Buddhist monks worship as they sit cross-legged, silent and immovable, contemplating the nature of the reality at the center of their being. In Egypt, Greece, and Rome; in India, China, and Japan; in Mexico and Peru, ancient temples testify that here, too, human beings have worshiped God. The earliest artifacts of human culture—amulets, primitive drawings on the walls of caves, heaps of bones piled around rough-hewn altars, circles of stones, groves of sacred trees—all speak of a human response to something beyond the human. What is worship?

Worship: A Word Study

We can learn a good deal about the activity of worship by examining what the word means. The English word *worship* is a contraction of *worth-ship*. Worship involves assigning worth to what is thought to be worthy and giving expression to that estimate of value. Worship, in fact, has to do with value.

The earliest uses of the word *worship* in English did not chiefly, or even primarily, refer to God. Worship usually referred to persons. For example, in a record of burials in a churchyard in England, dated 1598, we read:

> In this cloister were buried many persons, some of worship, and others of honor.[1]

Here, to be "of honor" indicated nobility; to be "of worship" meant to have great possessions. In medieval England, greater persons were often addressed as "Your Worship."

Today, of course, the word usually refers to the worship of God. An element of ultimacy, of absoluteness, has attached itself to the word as we normally use it. Worship involves not merely the assigning of worth to what is thought worthy, but the assigning of ultimate or absolute worth to what is believed to have ultimate value. In other words the word became religious, and its religious use has crowded out its other meanings. One of the reasons the fundamental significance of the human activity of worship has become obscure in modern times is that the religious meaning of worship has been detached from the others; and in detachment the activity of worship is found to have little connection with the perplexing, often agonizing, problems of value that we encounter day in and day out.

Worship and the Absolute

In this context of valuing it is easy enough to understand how the word *worship* might have acquired this religious or "absolute" meaning. If at the beginning, the word meant the ascribing of proper value to anything that was believed to have value, the question of relative values quickly surfaces. Why is one course of action better than another?; one goal preferable to another?; one possession more valuable than another? Which group of persons or things deserves the most worship? It is precisely in finding an answer to such ordinary, everyday questions that the worship of an ultimate or absolute, the worship of God, becomes significant. For the answer to the question of relative values depends on some commonly accepted, standard way of measuring or calculating value. Is there a fixed point of worth, some pole star from which we can take our bearings?

The fact of the matter is that there is no way to measure or compare without a standard of comparison, and when we take the problems raised by relative values seriously, we find ourselves embarked on the quest for the absolute. So difficult and elusive is this quest that in our skeptical age it has become fashionable in many quarters simply to give it up. "All things are relative," we say with a knowing sigh. Did not Einstein show twentieth-century inquirers that even such basic entities as speed, size, and weight depend on the position of the observer? Is it not even more reasonable, in view of the welter of opinions in the world about truth, beauty, and goodness, to suppose that such matters, too, depend on the stance of the person who makes judgments? If beauty is in the eye of the beholder, surely truth and goodness must be there as well. Most people accept the fact that we live in a relativistic age.

But this conclusion is not the last word on the subject, even in science. The most elementary knowledge of Einstein's theory of relativity includes the recognition of a constant factor, the speed of light. The speed of light is not relative to the position of the observer. It is invariable throughout the universe. In the famous equation that expresses the fundamental insight of relativity theory, $E = mc^2$, c, a constant, stands for the speed of light. The equation shows how indispensable the constant factor is. The fact that something is fixed makes this theory intelligible. By analogy, must there not be a moral, esthetic, and intellectual equivalent of the speed of light, constant throughout the universe? Do not we human beings need some fixed point, some place to stand, some absolute, in order to make value judgments? And are we able to live from day to day or even from minute to minute without making such judgments, judgments about what is most important, or truest, or best?

Of course, to *need* an absolute and to *have* an absolute are not the same things. If you are lost in the desert, you need water. But unless you stumble upon an oasis, you do not have it. So it is with the absolute. We may need it, but we cannot make it for ourselves. If we try, if we decide to "let something be the absolute," by some process of emotion or reason, we do so upon the basis of some criterion, either implicitly or explicitly. Many people, for example, regard themselves as this necessary point of reference. If you don't put "number one" first, no one else will, as we sometimes hear. But such a decision for the absolute is almost ludicrously self-contradictory. It is not a very convincing absolute that differs for each individual!

In fact, to decide for the absolute is a contradiction in terms. If we do the deciding, we have somehow put ourselves in the position of being more ultimate or more absolute than it. Or we appeal to a principle more ultimate or more absolute than what we decide.

If we cannot choose the fixed point of value, then either we do not have it at all, or it must be given to us in some way. One chief characteristic and function of religion is to celebrate the giving of an absolute, a fixed point of value. Through religion, human beings seek to enshrine, remember, understand, and communicate certain moments when they believe the absolute is given and received. A few such moments are well known to us. When Moses was tending his father-in-law's flock on Mount Sinai, for example, "the angel of the LORD appeared to him in a flame of fire out of the midst of a bush, and he looked, and lo, the bush was burning, yet it was not consumed" (Ex. 3:2). The bush, burning yet not consumed, is a marvelously suggestive symbol for the absolute giving itself from beyond the realm of human possibility. In this encounter with the absolute, or God, Moses dares to ask God his name. He receives the enigmatic answer "I am what I am." God, the absolute, does not depend on the position of the observer.

Muslims remember "the Night of Power and Excellence," when a strange peace pervaded creation, all nature was turned toward its Lord, and Mohammed, lying on the floor of his cave, received passively, three times, a command from God:

> Cry! Thy Lord is wondrous kind
> Who by the pen has taught mankind
> Things they knew not, being blind.[2]

This command, in other words, was not invented or thought out. It was given.

Similarly, early Christians believed that Jesus was the revelation of God, not because they reasoned to that conclusion, but because his life, his teachings, and his works changed their lives so dramatically that no other conclusion was possible. When Peter, James, and John saw Jesus in a vision, alongside Moses and Elijah representing "the law and the prophets," Peter wanted to make equal shrines to honor the three. It was a voice from the cloud beyond them, and not their instinctive reaction, that said, "This is my beloved Son; listen to him" (Mk. 9:7). And at the Last Supper, the Fourth Gospel records Jesus as saying to his disciples, "You did not choose me, but I chose you" (Jn. 15:16).

In none of these cases does the initiative come from the human side, but rather from beyond it. Religion is the response that humans make to these initiatives. Worship is the first of these responses.

Worship and the Holy

We are speaking of experiences that occur when an overpowering, overshadowing presence stands before frail, finite, human beings and elicits from them the recognition of an absolute, beyond them. The word *holy* best expresses the impossible actuality of such a presence. What we need in order to live as human beings, what we could not supply for ourselves, or figure out, or discover, has in fact, beyond any expectation, been given. Studies like Rudolf Otto's classic book *The Idea of the Holy* or Mircea Eliade's more recent *The Sacred and the Profane* show how this tense and mysterious sense of holiness has been expressed in the religions of many times and places.

Worship is our human response to the *holy* God. It is our ascribing of ultimate value to what we know to be worthy of such a response. "Love so amazing, so divine, Demands my soul, my life, my all," as Isaac Watts' hymn puts it.[3] For consider all the especially human capacities that flow from this encounter with the holy, when we learn to see the holy as the absolute, the fixed point to which we are able to refer our decisions. In the encounter with the holy, when the absolute gives itself to us, we become able to make decisions, we are free enough from our environment to compare one thing with another and to choose one thing in preference to another. In that freedom we are able to worship in the original sense of the word. We are able to assign proper values to the whole range of things that we encounter in our daily lives.

Christians worship God as he has given himself to us in his Son, Jesus Christ. We believe that he is of absolute worth for us, for he has shown us, through the church and the sacraments, through the lives of other persons, and in the many other ways in which he communicates himself, his life-changing power to forgive sins and his power over death itself. In Christian worship, we commit ourselves ultimately to Christ, for in him we perceive the ultimate meaning of existence.

At this point, we can begin to address our attention to one of the most important contentions of this book—that worship has implications for the whole of life. Worship and ethics are intimately related. After we have responded to God in Christ as the ultimate or absolute in an act of worship, we go on to ascribe or assign value to the persons and things we encounter in the ordinary course of life, using the criterion provided by our meeting with the holy. For Christians, the criterion is the love of God revealed in Jesus Christ, the love which "bears all things, believes all things, hopes all things, endures all things" (1 Cor. 13:7). The application of this criterion to the decisions that

Christians make is the content of Christian ethics, which is not the subject of this book. Here we must content ourselves with emphasizing the close relationship between worship and ethics. Worship undergirds ethical activity. In fact, ethics is a form of worship.

Worship and Ritual

The English word *worship* has led us to a study of worship as a valuing activity. In the Bible the Hebrew and Greek words for worship point in quite a different direction. The most frequent Hebrew word, for example, is *shachah*. It denotes a physical activity—falling prostrate. Like the word *genuflect*, which also denotes a physical activity, *shachah* is used only in a religious context. It is a ritual word. The connection between falling prostrate and the worship of the holy God is expressed in the line of the Venite:

> O come, let us worship and fall down,
>   and kneel before the Lord our Maker.

as well as in Psalm 99:5,

> Proclaim the greatness of the Lord our God
>   and fall down before his footstool;
>   he is the Holy One.

Similarly, one of the Greek words for worship, *proskynëö*, is used to designate the custom of prostrating oneself before another and kissing the other's foot. Persians did this in the presence of their kings, Greeks in the presence of their gods. It is obvious that prostration is not a characteristic Anglican response to the holy God. Nevertheless, these words serve to remind us that worship has physical components. When we stand in the presence of God, we not only engage in the moral and intellectual activity of assigning values. More immediately and dramatically, we do something with our bodies. Ritual action, as well as decision making, is an inalienable part of worship. Worship is an activity of human beings in their complete selfhood, flesh in inextricable unity with spirit. The holy God demands of us a total response.[4]

Individual and Corporate Worship

The discussion of worship has proceeded to this point almost as if worship were purely an individual matter. It is, after all, individuals who make decisions and who engage in ritual acts like falling prostrate, kneeling, standing, singing, or closing one's eyes. It would be misleading to leave our discussion without balancing this description with another. Worship is also a community affair, and the role of the community is at least as important as the role of the individual person.

One way of grasping the importance of the community in worship is to consider the nature of values themselves. Values, the result of worship, are almost always the property of a community. The worship of God leads to shared values, shared estimates about the worth of life, the nature of marriage, the place of the state, private property, and many other things. Worship, as we have already indicated, leads to ethics. Ethics, in turn, does not deal with a countless number of separate reactions and evaluations of an encounter with God; ethics deals with *ethos*, the spirit of a people who make a common corporate response to the holy God.

For the most part, individuals share this common life, and common worship leads to common values. It is true, of course, that the translation of a people's encounter with the holy God into a way of life and a series of decisions about worldly values may involve distortions and misunderstandings. In fact, it usually does. In this respect Jesus alone was sinless. That is, Christians believe that Jesus alone interpreted the will of God without distortion. The ethos of any church or society, even if it is based on the spirit of Christ, is certain to fall short of what holy love requires of it. Individuals may therefore be highly critical of the ethos of their church or of their society in the name of love. Such individuals are our prophets. We should honor them, though we often stone them. Even prophets, however, exercise their role for the sake of the community, that it may be more faithful to God when it draws the ethical consequences of worship. Although prophets and godly critics may seem to constitute an exception to the overarching importance of community in worship, this is more apparent than real. Christian worship is both individual and corporate. For the foregoing reasons, corporate worship has some priority.

Liturgy: A Word Study

One of the words that appears most frequently in connection with worship is *liturgy*. We speak of services of worship as liturgical if they seem to have a certain formal quality. We hear of the liturgical movement as an expression of the study of the history and theology of Christian worship, leading to a renewal of its vitality. Orthodox churches speak of their main service as the Divine Liturgy. We have used the word in the title of this book. We shall use it often as we go along. It designates the focus of our attention. What is the meaning of this word?

The word is Greek, a compound of the word for people (*laos*) and the word for work (*ergon*). Liturgy has to do with people and work. Like the word *worship* in English, the word *liturgy* in Greek was not a religious term at the beginning. It meant a public work done at private cost. Public works in ancient Greece were regularly undertaken by private citizens, apparently in place of an orderly and effective system of taxation. For example, to build a bridge for a public road across a stream on one's private property would constitute a liturgy. Military service at one's own expense would be a liturgy. Wealthy people sought popularity by lavish "liturgies," one of which was the production of dramas for the citizens of their city. Liturgy is work for the people.

This word *liturgy* was employed by the men who translated the Old Testament into Greek about 250 B.C. They used it occasionally in its original sense,[5] but for them it ordinarily meant services of worship. The word *liturgy* was more appropriate to describe the services of the Hebrew temple than the customary Greek word for religious exercises, *orgia* ("orgy"), which, though also derived from *ergon* ("work"), had nearly the same connotations then as now.

In the New Testament, the word *liturgy* continues to be used of services of worship in the temple, as in Luke 1:23; but a new use appears that is decisive for understanding Christian liturgy. The new use is found in the Letter to the Hebrews. In the course of a lengthy comparison between the death of Christ and the services of the temple, we read that Jesus is the true priest because he offers himself, not animals, as a sacrifice. It is total obedience that God desires from his people. Jesus gave the obedience, and his death on the cross is the climax and symbol of this obedient life. Consequently,

> Christ has obtained a ministry [the Greek word is *liturgy*] which is as much more excellent than the old as the covenant he mediates is better, since it is enacted on better promises. (Heb. 8:6)

Christ's life of obedience and death on the cross is the Christian liturgy, replacing the liturgy of the temple. His life and death are the ultimate work for the people, their redemption from sin and death, at the ultimate private cost, the complete obedience to the point of death of the one whom we acknowledge to be the Son of God.

The word *liturgy* is used in a few passages of St. Paul's letters in an analogous way. From prison he tells the Philippians, for example, that he is "to be poured as a libation upon the sacrificial offering of [their] faith" (Phil. 2:17). The Greek text literally translated reads, "poured on the sacrifice and *liturgy* of [their] faith." The obedient and faithful life of Philippian Christians is their sacrifice and their liturgy. Paul had urged them to form and base their lives on Christ, who

> . . . though he was in the form of God,
> did not count equality with God
>   a thing to be grasped
> but emptied himself, taking
>   the form of a servant,
> being born in the likeness of men.
> And being found in human form
> he humbled himself and became
>   obedient unto death,
> even death on a cross. (Phil. 2:6–8)

Such a life of faith and trust constituted their liturgy.

In other words, the New Testament enshrines an understanding of liturgy that has been almost lost in translation. Christ's life and death is in fact the one liturgy; and Christians whose lives are "in Christ," formed and shaped in his likeness, constitute a liturgy also. It would be even better to say that they constitute a working out and a making present "in all times and in all places" of the one liturgy. To speak in such a way is obviously not very different from saying that Jesus worshiped God truly, not only in his ritual actions but also in his ethical response to the holy. We worship God truly when we acknowledge Christ as the absolute made present and given to us. He is the Word made flesh.

Today, of course, we use the word *liturgy* in a very different sense. It has come to denote either what is done in church or the text of what is done in church (for example, the Liturgy of the Lord's Supper, which was the first alternative to the service of Holy Communion authorized by the Episcopal Church for trial use; or the Liturgy of St. John Chrysostom, the traditional eucharistic service used in Eastern Orthodox churches on most Sundays). It is not hard to see how this shift in meaning occurred. The Old Testament, as we have seen, already used the word *liturgy* to mean the services in the temple, and the influence of the Old Testament on the life of the early church was very great. Moreover, what goes on, or should go on, in a Christian service of worship is a representation or a making present of the life and death of Christ. In worship, we appropriate Christ's liturgy as our own. It makes sense, therefore, to speak of Christian gatherings for worship as liturgies.

But we should not allow ourselves to forget that in another equally important sense, liturgy is what we do with our lives. The liturgy that Christ *is* has an *extensive* form, directly related to the intensive. The extensive liturgy begins when the gathered community scatters into the world to live obediently to the Christ whose one liturgy was encountered at prayer.

To engage in either intensive or extensive liturgy drives one to seek out the other. From the extensive liturgy of a Christian's life in the world, one comes to the intensive liturgy for assurance, pardon, and renewal. From the intensive liturgy, one "goes forth into the world to love and serve the Lord."

3

The Basis of Liturgy

Liturgy is rooted and grounded in God. It arises within a community of faith and is the inevitable outward expression of an interior confidence in the loving will of God. For Christians, the basis of that confidence, the ground of faith, is the vulnerable assurance of Christ upon the cross, vindicated by his resurrection from the dead: "Father, into thy hands I commit my spirit" (Lk. 23:46). In the mysterious power of the death and resurrection of Jesus is found the basis of the Christian faith and the ground plan of the church's liturgy. In the last chapter we began to explore the relation between worship and faith in God. Now we must carry the examination further.

The Spirit and the Liturgy

"God is spirit," runs a familiar verse from St. John, "and those who worship him must worship him in spirit and in truth" (Jn. 4:24). Our understanding of the relation between worship and faith in God will be deepened by some reflection on spirit: the Holy Spirit and our human spirits.

In the discussion of worship as our human response to the holy, it was said that the word *holy* expresses the impossible actuality that the absolute, the ultimate, has been given to us. From a Christian point of view, it would be more accurate to say that the holy communicates the reality of God's self-giving. God, we say, is invisible and infinite. "No one has ever seen God" (Jn. 1:18). John does not mean to deny the reality of inward vision, but he does deny that human beings see God with the same eyes with which they behold trees, cats, or any of the physical objects that make up the visible world. How can infinite, time-conditioned, flesh-bound mortals encounter the infinite and absolute God? We do not know. Yet it has happened! We Christians believe that it has happened to us through Christ, and that is has happened for our eternal salvation.

> No one knows the Son except the Father, and no one knows the Father except the Son and any one to whom the Son chooses to reveal him. (Mt. 11:27)

"In him [Christ] all the fulness of God was pleased to dwell" (Col. 1:19), claims St. Paul in a breathtaking assertion.

An analogy from the realm of art can perhaps help us to understand what is being said in such passages. One of the qualities of a great painting is its ability

16

to communicate to us the universal through the particular. The *Mona Lisa*, with her inscrutable smile, is a painting of a young Italian woman of the fifteenth century. For many people it is also a revelation of the essence of womanhood. Similarly, Andrew Wyeth's *Boy in Blue* depicts a particular boy of a certain height, age, and appearance. Yet to many it communicates something about the universal boy.

Abstract thought creates an unbridgeable gap between the universal and the particular. It is difficult and perhaps impossible to figure out ways to find universals through particulars. The philosophical and theological discussions about the priority of one over the other have been endless and opaque. Art, on the other hand, simply shows a way in which one can have access to universals *through* a particular representation.

The reason abstract thought fails to show us how universals may be known through particulars has to do with the elusive quality of spirit. The unity of the *Mona Lisa* with all women or of the *Boy in Blue* with boy-ness, or—to take quite a different kind of example—of the Prodigal Son with the total human situation, is perceived in the first instance by the artist, and communicated to viewers by skill and the force and truth of insight. The unity is never obvious; it is what we might call a unity of spirit. If one does not discover it, no argument will be convincing. Some viewers are caught up in that same spirit and, with the artist, perceive the larger vision through the particular image that the artist painted.

The analogy is halting. Artists are human; their insight into the nature of reality, though profounder than that of most of us, has its limits; and their skill in communicating what they see, great as it may be, is finally inadequate to the task, as most artists continually complain. The *Mona Lisa* and the *Boy in Blue* do not have the power or meaning for every person that was attributed to them in the past paragraph. Nevertheless, the analogy is significant. God, the artist, gives himself to us through a particular form, through the Spirit.

Christians believe that God has always been known through particular forms. In the biblical tradition, the forms have been chiefly words and events: saving events, like the rescue of the people of Israel from Egypt at the Red Sea; biting words, like the oracles of the prophets. "In many and various ways God spoke of old to our fathers by the prophets" (Heb. 1:1). The phrase *the Word of God* came to be the common description of these particular forms in which God was manifest. The first chapter of the Fourth Gospel asserts the unity of God and his Word. "In the beginning was the Word, and the Word was with God, and the Word was God" (Jn. 1:1). The climactic verse of the same passage asserts the unity of the Word with the man Jesus of Nazareth: "And the Word became flesh and dwelt among us, full of grace and truth" (Jn. 1:14). Later Christian theology has understood that both cases of unity are the work of the Holy Spirit. God and the Word are one "in unity of the Holy Spirit." And the Word becomes incarnate in Jesus of Nazareth by power of the Spirit, as the creeds proclaim. Worshipers, caught up in that same Spirit, recognize in Jesus of Nazareth the Word of God, or the beloved Son of God. "No one can say

'Jesus is Lord' except by the Holy Spirit" (Cor. 12:3). In the same Spirit, they come to know God Himself. "He who has seen me," says Jesus in the Gospel according to St. John, "has seen the Father" (Jn. 14:9).

Thus worship, our response to our encounter with God, is an affair of the Spirit. Our human spirits are caught up in the Holy Spirit of God. Our inward eyes and ears are opened by that Spirit, and "it is the Spirit himself bearing witness with our spirit" (Rom. 8:16) that Jesus is Lord and that we are the children of God.

> "What no eye has seen, nor ear heard,
> nor the heart of man conceived,
> what God has prepared for those who love him,"

God has revealed to us through the Spirit. For the Spirit searches everything, even the depths of God. For what person knows a man's thoughts except the spirit of the man which is in him? So also no one comprehends the thoughts of God except the Spirit of God. Now we have received not the spirit of the world, but the Spirit which is from God, that we might understand the gifts bestowed on us by God. And we impart this in words not taught by human wisdom but taught by the Spirit, interpreting spiritual truths to those who possess the Spirit. (1 Cor. 2:9-13)

Faith and Conversion

The human response to the initiative of God the Spirit is faith. Worship is as unintelligible and hollow apart from faith as it is apart from the prior action of the Spirit. Christians find focus of their faith in the event of Christ, the redeeming power of Jesus of Nazareth. The life of Jesus, and especially his death and resurrection, reveal the nature of God—a love so great that he will not let us go, power so great that he forgives every sin and overcomes even death itself. Faith in such a God is first of all total trust and confidence that no matter what life brings, his last word to us is "yes." In this primary sense, faith lies beyond words. In the last analysis Christians believe and trust in God. But secondarily, faith also involves the affirmation of certain convictions that *can* be described in words. We believe that Jesus lived and taught, that he died, that God raised him on the third day. We believe that Jesus is Lord. We believe that the death and resurrection of Jesus are the great signs of the nature of God. They reveal in the concrete forms of one human life the meaning of the whole of life as grounded in and sustained by the enlivening power of God. Authentic liturgy is an expression of faith, and any liturgy that does not grow from this kind of faith is an attempt to manipulate God, a contractual arrangement in which God's gifts are assured through the completion of some prescribed pattern of ritualistic service. Such an arrangement would be more akin to magic, in which formulas and gestures guarantee the desired effect. One would have to acknowledge that during some of the darker periods of Christian history, the church's liturgy has been performed out of a mentality little distinguishable from such an understanding. Yet any Christian liturgy worthy of the name springs from quite a different basis, not so objectified nor so lacking in personal content. Authentic liturgy arises from faith.

The call of faith, in turn, requires of us a change in direction, a change of center. Without that, to speak of faith is nonsense, for it is a refusal to take sin seriously—sin in our world, sin in our own individual lives. Conversion involves the recognition that the world is God's and that the responsibility that God has entrusted to us has been used in destructive ways, contrary to God's purposes. It is a terrible thing to recognize this self-centered destructiveness in each one of us. We look into the depths of our own sin, and in pride we try to close off the abyss. It is quite possible to do so even while appearing to maintain a religious commitment. But the gift of faith, in response to God's gracious initiative, calls us to a reality greater than superficial religiosity. External religious routines can be performed with little engagement of the self. By any faith worthy of the name, we give ourselves to God. Then the often painful process can begin by which we ourselves become outward and visible signs of God's work in us, bringing us to wholeness of life.

Faith requires conversion.

Liturgy and Community

This response of faith to the actions of God on our behalf must not, and indeed for Christians *cannot*, be conceived in narrowly individualistic terms. The response of faith is a personal response within the community of faith, the church. At the very beginning of the Christian life, at baptism itself, our relation to God through Christ is set in the context of the Christian community. The faith we profess at baptism and reaffirm at every Eucharist is the faith of the church, the faith of the one people of God gathered in the unity of the Spirit.

The unity of the church is thus not an organizational option; it is a divine imperative. The faith proclaimed and made manifest in the Eucharist is the basis for our unity in Christ, a unity forged by his presence through the Spirit: "Christ has died, Christ is risen, Christ will come again." This is no mere social unity, as in a club of like-minded members. It is a unity of identity in the Spirit. "We are one in the Spirit, we are one in the Lord," as a familiar hymn runs. Baptism has made us one with Christ. Our common memory is the source of our common identity and at the same time the imperative for our unity, locally within the congregation and universally as a worldwide fellowship of love. This spiritual unity in Christ will be a sign to the world, for the goal of the incarnation is not merely the unity of the congregation or even of the whole church. It is the unity of humanity itself.

From all this it is manifest that the liturgical celebration of the church is no narrowly religious activity. It finds its meaning in the total extent of Christian life and witness in the world. Our parochial liturgies are often lifeless because their rooting in this wider framework has not been perceived, and thus the authentic sources of liturgical vitality become dry and withered. True liturgy, on the other hand, is the expression of an authentic Christian community. It springs from the common life of the church and becomes a sign of the existence of that common life and a source of nourishment for it.

The scandal of our present liturgical situation is not its diversity of style. Most of us, often to our surprise, discover that we can adjust to new styles of worship rather easily, if they are celebrated with integrity and express a true community of faith. Diversity is not the problem. The problem is the separation of liturgy from the life of the Christian person and from the life of the Christian community. Liturgy then becomes objectified and depersonalized, a printed text, rather than the expression in action of a community of faith.

Is the church a static reality? Its worship, doctrine, and organization fixed once for all time? Or is it an unfolding life, a community confident of the abiding presence of Christ with his people in the Spirit, leading us into all truth? We make no claim to infallibility, but we insist that God is with the church today, through the Spirit, and always has been. Authentic liturgy is the expression of that presence.

Mystery and Liturgy

In discussing faith as the basis for liturgy, we pointed out that faith has the primary meaning of trust and confidence in God, and also the secondary meaning of the conviction that certain things are true. The particular affirmations of faith are described as *mystery*.

> Great indeed, we confess, is the mystery of our religion:
>> He was manifested in the flesh,
>> vindicated in the Spirit,
>>> seen by angels,
>> preached among the nations,
>> believed on in the world,
>>> taken up in glory. (1 Tim. 3:16)

When we speak of a mystery in contemporary language, we usually mean an obscure situation whose causes are not clear. A mystery is something we do not understand. A mystery story is usually a novel about a puzzling crime that a detective unravels. Our confusion is artfully dispelled by the detective in the story. We learn how the crime was committed and who did it. A mystery in the religious sense is also something we do not understand, but there the similarity ends. A mystery in this original sense of the word denotes the secret thoughts and plans of God for the redemption of the world. They are hidden from reason but are revealed to those whom God wishes to redeem.

A story in the second chapter of the Book of Daniel illustrates this characteristic of a mystery in the biblical sense of the word. Nebuchadnezzar, as the story is told, had a dream that disturbed him. Since he wanted to understand the dream, he called his magicians to ask what it meant. "Tell us the dream," they said, "and we will tell you the interpretation." "No," replied the king. "You must tell me the dream and the interpretation. Otherwise you will die." Since they could not comply with this command, they were destroyed. But Daniel, a Jew in exile in Babylon, who offered to interpret the dream for the king, prayed to God "concerning this mystery," and "the mystery was revealed to Daniel in a vision of the night." Daniel went to Nebuchadnezzar and told him:

> To you, O king, as you lay in bed came thoughts of what would be hereafter, and he who reveals mysteries made known to you what is to be. But as for me, not because of any wisdom that I have more than all the living has this mystery been revealed to me, but in order that the interpretation may be made known to the king, and that you may know the thoughts of your mind. (Dan. 2:29–30)

For Christians the mind of God has not been revealed in a dream but in a person. Instead of Daniel's mystery or any other, the New Testament speaks of the life, death, and resurrection of Jesus as the mystery of God. The significance of these events could not possibly have been figured out ahead of time. It was hidden from reason in that sense. But God has revealed the mystery of Christ to the church through the Spirit.

> For he has made known to us in all wisdom and insight the mystery of his will, according to his purpose which he set forth in Christ as a plan for the fulness of time, to unite all things in him, things in heaven and things on earth. (Eph. 1:9–10)

As Jesus was teaching the parable of the seed, sown partly along the path, partly on rocky ground, partly among thorns and weeds, and partly on good soil, he said to his disciples,

> To you has been given the secret [the Greek word is *mysterion*, "mystery"] of the kingdom of God, but for those outside everything is in parables, so that they may indeed see but not perceive, and may indeed hear but not understand. (Mk. 4:11–12)

The facts about the teachings of Jesus and his life and death could be known to everyone. Only those to whom the mystery was revealed, however, could understand those facts as God's plan for delivering the world from sin and death. Thus the "Christ-event" is a mystery—not a mystery in the modern sense that its unknown causes could be figured out by someone with enough patience and ingenuity, but a mystery in the ancient sense of something that human reason could never figure out, but that God has declared.

Later in this book, we shall speak of the "paschal mystery," or the "Easter mystery." This phrase means essentially the death and the resurrection of Christ, but since Christ died for us at Passover time, in the spring, we have come to see the Christ-event as the climax of God's deliverance of his people, a deliverance that encompasses the new life of spring overcoming the death of winter, as well as the deliverance of Israel at the Red Sea. The paschal mystery is the fulfilment of all that God has done to deliver us from bondage to all our enemies—natural enemies like the death of winter, historical enemies like tyrants, and spiritual enemies like sin and death.

The sacraments of baptism and Eucharist are often called "holy mysteries." They are mysteries, to be sure, in the sense that we do not fully understand them. But, more specifically and accurately, they are mysteries because through them we participate in the one Christian mystery, the death and resurrection of Christ. In baptism we are buried in water, participating by faith in the death of Christ; when we come out of the water, we participate by faith in his new life.

"We thank you Father, for the water of baptism," runs the prayer of Thanksgiving over the Water in the baptismal rite of the current Book of Common Prayer. "In it we are buried with Christ in his death. By it we share in his resurrection. Through it we are reborn by the Holy Spirit" (p. 306).

And in the Eucharist, we proclaim the mystery of faith:

> Christ has died.
> Christ is risen.
> Christ will come again. (p. 363)

Faith involves not only understanding the Christian mystery but living in its power.

Liturgy and Symbol

Liturgy, as we have said, involves not only words but ritual action. Ritual is symbolic action. Objects, movements, gestures, words, even the participants themselves, all point to the holy. When we take part in worship, we use our capacity to make, understand, appreciate, and enjoy symbols. This capacity is one of the bases of liturgy.

A symbol is one thing "thrown with" another. *Syn* is the Greek word for "with," *bolein* means "to throw." A symbol is something that, having been "thrown with" something else, stands for that other thing. It "means" something else. It is obvious that language and action used to describe the realm of the holy God, whom no one has ever seen, must be highly symbolic. God is infinite, ultimate. The inadequacy of language and art to portray the divine is well known to anyone who has tried. Any attempt to communicate or mediate the truth about God involves symbols.

Not all symbols, of course, are religious. There are different kinds of symbols. Some are able to communicate religious reality. Some are not. It is useful to distinguish *arbitrary* symbols from *participating* symbols. The clearest examples of arbitrary symbols come from mathematics. Let x equal the number of apples in the first basket and y equal the number of apples in the second basket. X and y are symbols. They stand for something else. But there is no inner connection between x and y on the one hand and apples on the other. X and y might equally well stand for the number of miles John and Bill row in an hour. Mathematical and scientific symbols are for the most part arbitrary.

Words also, on the whole, are arbitrary symbols. The word *table* is not a table. It is a sound uttered, and then a mark on a piece of paper. But the word *table* stands for a table, and has the significant additional property of being able to be spoken and thought about. Words summarize experience. The word *table* means the totality of a person's experience with objects to write on, eat on, pile things on. When a community shares those experiences, the word *table* is a common possession. When it is written or spoken, that experience is transmitted. These symbols make verbal communication possible.

Human beings have experiences that cannot readily be summarized and symbolized in a word. Then other symbols are used, and we come to rely not on precise representation but on a larger and less tangible realm of connotation. Poetry and art are extended means of communication, made possible by means of symbols. Symbols not only stand for objects but can evoke feelings, call forth memories long buried, and combine references in a way that makes the world new. Poets are creators. The very word *poet* means "one who makes."

In this area, we become aware of the second kind of symbol, the participating symbol. Participating symbols do have a connection with what is symbolized. A country's flag stands for the country. It could not equally well stand for another country. When the flag of a nation is changed, there has usually been a profound alteration in the government or in the temper of the people. To dishonor the flag is to dishonor the country itself. Leaders of a nation have something of this representative, participating, symbolizing quality. When John Kennedy died, the people of the United States were mortally affected. Something in them died too. In the Christian community, the cross is a participating symbol. It represents to us the reality of God's self-giving love, which spends itself to death. Its full meaning can never be exhausted by verbal paraphrases, and it is in no sense exchangeable. In a unique and powerful way it stands for the revelation of God in Jesus Christ.

In a good deal of recent writing on this subject, arbitrary symbols have been called "signs." It is inconvenient and in the end confusing to do so, however, since in the New Testament, for example, and especially in the Fourth Gospel, the word *sign* does not mean arbitrary symbol but participating symbol. In the present volume, the words *sign* and *symbol* are used interchangeably.

There is also a third kind of symbol, a participating symbol put to special use. It can conveniently be called a *communicating* symbol. A communicating symbol not only stands for the reality it represents, but transmits that reality, and indeed *is* that reality. A dollar bill is such a symbol. It is the symbol of a dollar; but unlike $, which is also the symbol of a dollar, a dollar bill transfers a dollar's worth of value within the community that honors it. We do not hesitate to say that a dollar bill is a dollar.

The profoundest religious symbols are communicating symbols. Bread and wine at the Eucharist *are* the body and blood of Christ, and they communicate that reality within the community of faith. So deep is the identity between thing and symbol that some theologians have been unwilling to speak of sacraments as symbols at all, lest they be confused with arbitrary symbols. Yet is has always been recognized that to outward sense perception, bread and wine remain unchanged. The change in the sacramental elements is inward, effected by the Spirit. "Sanctify them by your Holy Spirit to be for your people the Body and Blood of your Son," as Eucharistic Prayer A in the current Prayer Book puts it (p. 363).

The role of the Holy Spirit in establishing the identity between the infinite God and the realm of finite reality has already been noted. It came to our attention first in the case of Christ himself. Jesus, we say, is the incarnation, enfleshment, of God. In the broad sense of the word *symbol* that we are using in this chapter, we might say that Jesus is the symbol of God, but he is the *communicating* symbol of God, brought into identity with God by the work of the Spirit.

The New Testament, it is true, does not use the word *symbol* in this connection. It uses the word *image*. "He is the image of the invisible God" (Col. 1:15). And in a familiar and important passage, Jesus is identified with the Word.

> In the beginning was the Word, and the Word was with God, and the Word was God . . . And the Word became flesh and dwelt among us, full of grace and truth. (Jn. 1:1, 14)

To say that Christ is the image of God, or that Jesus is the incarnation of the Word of God that is God, is symbolic language. Yet we are not dealing with arbitrary symbols, but with communicating symbols, which by virtue of the work of the Holy Spirit, *are* the reality they represent.

The capacity to deal with symbols is almost as unique to human beings as the relation to the holy expressed in worship. There is some indication that other living creatures have this capacity to communicate by symbols. Bees who discover a source of honey, for example, are said to communicate this information at the hive by a dance that indicates direction and distance. Human beings have developed this ability to a point where it is virtually different in kind as well as in degree from other possessors of it. Humans, made in the image of God, are inveterate symbol makers; they grasp and communicate by means of symbols the deepest mystery of their existence. Symbols are at the heart of liturgy.

4

Features of Liturgy

In this chapter, we shall consider certain aspects of liturgy: sacrifice, priest-hood, prayer, myth, and ritual. These features appear in most of the world's religions as well as in Christianity. In Christian liturgy, however, each of these features undergoes a decisive shift of meaning.

Sacrifice

The word *sacrifice* in contemporary usage is becoming a secular word; it means "giving up something," usually with regret. An investor in the stock market sells "at a sacrifice." He loses money in the sale, but realizes enough to meet some obligation that is required of him. In connection with liturgy, however, sacrifice is altogether a religious word. The Latin word *sacer* means "sacred" and *facere* means "to make." Sacrifice denotes the process of making something holy by giving it to God.

When we think of sacrifice in this connection, we often think of the ritual killing of animals. In primitive belief, an animal became God's possession by being destroyed. The worshiper gives up ownership of the animal by the sacrificial act. He hopes and prays to get something better from God in return. Many sacrifices can be understood as having this meaning. One gives in order to get. It is because of these considerations that the word *sacrifice* has the secular meaning we have noticed: giving up something to get something better.

But we must not let the matter rest at this point, for it misses the characteristic Christian contribution to our understanding of sacrifice. In the earlier discussion of liturgy in chapter 2, it was pointed out that when liturgy is considered in its basic sense as "work for the people," there is one fundamental Christian liturgy: Christ himself. An analogous point must now be made about sacrifice. In Christian belief, Christ is the one sacrifice. "When Christ had offered for all time a single sacrifice for sins, he sat down at the right hand of God" (Heb. 10:12).

What is at issue in a discussion of sacrifice in Christian terms is similar to the point we tried to establish in the case of liturgy. Liturgy in Christian terms is what one does with one's life, before it means what one does in church. By the same token, the sacrifice God desires, in Christian understanding, is a life of joyful obedience. "To obey is better than sacrifice, and to hearken [is better] than the fat of rams" (1 Sam. 15:22). In the following discussion of sacrifice, we shall see facets of what we might call the great covenant of trust and obedience that did not appear in our consideration of liturgy itself.

We cannot examine in great detail ancient sacrificial practices. In his article "The History of Israel's Religion" in *The Interpreter's Bible*, James Muilenburg has this to say:

> To the fundamental question of the cultic community, "How shall I come before God?" Israel, like other ancient people, had a ready reply. "Through sacrificial gifts." By the offering of sacrifice, the cleavage between the holy and the unholy was overcome. From the world of the profane, man entered the area of the holy. Sacrifice is *the* holy act.[1]

Yet it must be plain to anyone who reads the Old Testament with care that if the theory of the sacrificial gifts was of this nature, the practice did not achieve the desired results. Although we read how sacrifices were multiplied endlessly, the sense of alienation and separation from God mounted. Some of the Old Testament prophets understood the root of the problem and expressed it eloquently. Sacrificial gifts could achieve the end of communion with God only if they were a *symbolic* offering—of the part for the whole. To sacrifice the first-born of the cattle ought to be a symbolic way of saying that the whole flock, the entire wealth of the offerer, would be devoted to the service of God. To offer the first fruits of the crop in an obvious ritual act ought to mean that the whole crop was being given to God by intention. Sacrifice was meant to be an expression of the worshipers' obedience, a giving of themselves to be "a living sacrifice, holy and acceptable to God" (Rom. 12:1). The prophets consistently complained, however, that sacrificial gifts were offered *instead* of obedience. It is with this understanding that one of the most familiar passages about sacrifice in the Old Testament ought to be read:

> Will the LORD be pleased with thousands of rams,
>   With ten thousands of rivers of oil?
> Shall I give my first-born for my transgression?
>   the fruit of my body for the sin of my soul?
> He has showed you, O man, what is good;
>   and what does the LORD require of you
>   but to do justice, and to love kindness,
>   and to walk humbly with your God? (Mic. 6:7)

In Christian experience and belief, the death of Christ has accomplished what the ancient sacrificial system did not achieve. By this obedient living and dying, Jesus closed the gap between the holy God and the sinful world. Therefore, his life, culminating in his death, was interpreted as a sacrifice—in fact, the one, true sacrifice.

Nothing inherent in the crucifixion of a man on a hilltop outside Jerusalem would have suggested this interpretation to pious Jews. No other crucifixion was so interpreted. The brigands crucified with Jesus were not understood by anyone to have died as sacrifices. Even in Jesus' case, the victim was wrong, the place wrong, the time wrong, the officiants wrong. For a valid Jewish sacrifice, all the rubrics were wrong. Nevertheless, his death has made possible the communion between God and God's people that prior generations had hoped for. The life and death of Jesus is therefore a sacrifice. And the sacrifice has never had to be repeated. Jesus is "the full, perfect, and sufficient sacrifice for the sins of the whole world." The reason for this claim does not lie in the external circumstances of his life and death but in the experience of joy and release that comes when the cleavage between the holy and the unholy has been overcome once and for all.

This last statement, of course, is a confession of faith. "Until he comes in glorious majesty" there will be no closing of that gap which can be known apart from faith. In the meantime, believers know that the cleavage has been overcome at the cost of Christ's death, even while they experience a disjunction between the sacred and the profane. In this meantime, both Christian worship and the lives of Christian people can be understood as sacrificial. Both Christian liturgies and Christian lives *are* what they symbolize: the sacrificial life and death of the Lord. Sacrifice applies both to our life in Christ and to our worship of him.

Priesthood

Priesthood and sacrifice are closely related. A discussion of priesthood in the Christian community will be found to run along familiar lines.

In the ancient world, whether of Greece and Rome on the one hand or of Israel on the other, a priest was one who discerned and communicated the will of God. Although it happened in the course of time that priests came to be associated almost exclusively with the offering of sacrifices in the temple, the more basic association in the Old Testament was between priest and Torah, the Law, which was believed to be the revelation of God's will. Thus in the Book of Jeremiah we read, "the law shall not perish from the priest, nor counsel from the wise, nor the word from the prophet" (Jer. 18:18). In Malachi we read, "For the lips of a priest should guard knowledge, and men should see instruction from his mouth, for he is the messenger of the LORD of hosts" (Mal. 2:7). The priest was the custodian of the Law, charged with instructing the people about God's will by means of it.

In the New Testament, the only individual in the Christian community recognized as a priest is Christ himself. "Christ appeared as a priest of the good things that have come," says the Letter to the Hebrews (9:11), and the author makes it very clear that the reason Christ is the priest has nothing to do with either sacrifice or the Law (in any narrow sense), but with his radical devotion to doing the will of God. Once again we meet the great covenant of faith and obedience.

> Sacrifices and offerings thou has not desired,
> but a body hast thou prepared for me;
> in burnt offerings and sin offerings
>   thou hast taken no pleasure.

> Then I said, "Lo, I have come to do thy will, O God,"
> as it is written of me in the roll of the book." (Heb. 10:5–7)

Christ's life of service in obedience to the will of God makes him the priest, as it makes him the sacrifice and the liturgy. He is the one and only priest, because he uniquely embodies the will of God in his own person and communicates it to us through his love. "Lo, I have come to do thy will, O God."

In Catholic tradition, the celebrant at the Eucharist is called a priest. This usage almost certainly does not appear in Christian sources before the late second century. Tertullian and his younger contemporary Cyprian, both North African theologians of the late second and early third centuries, are usually credited with having introduced it.[2] For them the bishop, who at this time was the customary celebrant of the Eucharist, was the priest. The Eucharist was the Christian sacrifice in the sense described in the last section. Since those who offered sacrifices were usually priests, the celebrant of the Christian sacrifice could be called a priest in the same derivative sense that the Eucharist is a sacrifice. The development was probably inevitable and seems perfectly logical. This usage of the word *priest* has been accepted in Eastern Orthodox, Roman Catholic, and Anglican churches.

Protestant churches, however, rejected this designation, along with sacrificial terminology for the Eucharist itself. This rejection should serve to remind us that sacrifice and priesthood are not the same thing in Christian liturgy as in pagan or Jewish ritual. In the most important sense, sacrifice and priesthood come to their completion and fulfillment in Christ. Christian sacrifice and Christian priesthood are completely dependent upon and derivative from his. They have no independent status.

Protestant theology, on the other hand, has made a great deal of the "priesthood of all believers" as an alternative to the priesthood of the ordained ministry, and Anglicans have incorporated this understanding into their teaching about priesthood. The idea that the church, the "blessed company of all faithful people," is priestly also has roots deep in the Old Testament and comes to clear expression in several New Testament passages. It is connected with Israel's understanding of its role and mission as God's agent in world history. Almost from the beginning, Israel was taught to think of itself as a "kingdom of priests." When Moses was summoned to Mount Sinai to receive the Ten Commandments, we read in Exodus that God told him to say to the people,

> . . . if you will obey my voice and keep my covenant, you shall be my own possession among all peoples; for all the earth is mine, and you shall be to me a kingdom of priests and a holy nation. (Ex. 19:5–6)

The conception is breathtaking in scope, particularly in view of what we have called the great covenant of faith and obedience. What a priest was to a congregation—the mediator of the will of God—Israel was to be for the nations of the world. By obedience to the will of God revealed in the Law, Israel was to "show forth [God's] praise among the nations of the earth" (BCP, p. 820). The world would be called into a single history by the priestly mission of Israel. In fact, this understanding of Israel's role in the world is probably foreshadowed already in God's call to Abraham in Genesis:

> Behold, my covenant is with you, and you shall be the father of a multitude of nations. No longer shall your name be Abram [the exalted father], but your name shall be Abraham [here taken to mean "the father of a multitude"]; for I have made you the father of a multitude of nations. (Gen. 17:4–5)

This prophecy about Israel's role on the stage of history was not fulfilled in an obvious or literal sense. God works out his purposes in surprising and unexpected ways. Israel did not become a "great nation," preeminent among the world powers of antiquity. "God's people" were disobedient to God's will. Enemies destroyed Israel and scattered it among the shifting populations of the empires of the ancient world.

The remarkable prophecies in the second half of the Book of Isaiah suggest that this fate, however, was in fact the instrument by which Israel was to make God's will known among the nations. At the climax of this work, in a passage known to Christians through its use on Good Friday, the prophet declares that Israel fulfilled her role as priest to the world by being sacrifice for the world's sin:

> He was despised and rejected by men;
> > a man of sorrows, and acquainted with grief . . .
> Yet is was the will of the LORD to bruise him;
> > he was put him to grief;
> *when he makes himself an offering for sin,*
> > he shall see his offspring, he shall prolong his days;
> the will of the LORD shall prosper in his hand;
> he shall see the fruit of the travail of his soul and shall be satisfied;
> by his knowledge shall the righteous one, my servant,
> > make many to be accounted righteous;
> and he shall bear their iniquities.
> > (Is. 53:3, 10–11; emphasis added)

Christians believe that this vision of the communication to the world of God's will by the sacrificial love of the "man of sorrows" was fulfilled by Jesus of Nazareth. Those who believe that his obedience constituted the perfect revelation of God's will become a "priestly nation," mediating by their life of trust and obedience this new comprehension of God's innermost reality.

> But you are a chosen race, a royal priesthood, a holy nation, God's own people, that you may declare the wonderful deeds of him who called you out of darkness into his marvelous light. Once you were no people but now you are God's people; once you had not received mercy but now you have received mercy. (1 Pet. 2:9–10)

The Christian people are a priestly folk, commissioned to mediate God's will revealed in Christ, the one true priest. As we in company with the rest of the catholic church continue to pray that God will make our ordinands priests, we keep in mind that we are a priestly church. Faithful to our Reformation heritage, we believe in the priesthood of all believers. Just as liturgy and sacrifice pertain to the lives of Christians in the world, as well as to the worship of the church, when we are true to the great covenant of faith and obedience, so priesthood is a quality of our lives in this world as much as it is an aspect of liturgical worship. These two aspects of priesthood are inseparable in a true Christian understanding of the term.

Prayer

Another aspect of worship closely associated with sacrifice is prayer. In pre-Christian liturgy, prayer accompanied sacrifices and expressed their intentions.[3] One recalls the prayer of Hannah for the gift of a son after she had eaten and drunk the sacrificial gifts of Shiloh, and the eloquent prayer of Solomon at the dedication of the temple, when he sacrificed "so many sheep and oxen that they could not be counted" (1 Kg. 8:5).

Prayer is the utterance of a person who stands in the presence of the holy. The sacrifice that the prayer accompanies attempts to bridge the gap between the sacred and the profane. Thus prayer is not a casual matter. Those who truly pray, in the power of the Spirit, are driven beyond their normal selves. In the account of Hannah's prayer, we read that Eli mistook her for drunk (1 Sam. 1:13), and the apostles on whom the Spirit fell on the first Pentecost were similarly accused of being "filled with new wine" (Acts 2:13). There is an element of ecstasy in true prayer. In fact, Paul Tillich, writing in our own time about prayer, says:

> Speaking to God and receiving an answer is an ecstatic and miraculous experience;
> it transcends all ordinary structures of subjective and objective reason.[4]

What distinguishes the Christian in prayer is the basic conviction that Christ is the one true sacrifice and that through his obedient life and innocent death, the gap between the holy God and finite, sinful humanity has been bridged once and for all. Confidence in prayer is therefore a Christian hallmark. "Therefore I tell you, whatever you ask in prayer, believe that you have received it, and it will be yours" (Mk. 11:24).

In fact, one does not even have to articulate prayer. "We do not know how to pray as we ought, but the Spirit himself intercedes for us with sighs too deep for words" (Rom. 8:26). The Letter to the Hebrews says that Christ himself mediates our prayers to God. "He is able for all time to save those who draw near God through him, since he always lives to make intercession for them" (Heb. 7:25). One might say that when we pray, Christ prays in us—or even that Christ is our prayer.

Christ does not pray *instead* of us. We are never told that prayer is unnecessary. Quite to the contrary, we are told to be persistent in prayer, and to pray continually for all things. "Pray constantly" is St. Paul's advice to the Thessalonians (1 Th. 5:17). There is an Orthodox discipline of prayer that aims to establish such a constant prayer in the heart.[5] Even if such a discipline should seem out of reach to most of us, there is a prayer that we make continually with our lives, as there is a liturgy and a sacrifice. That imperfect prayer is purified and rectified when it is joined to the continual prayer that Christ makes to the Father. That prayer goes on in us without ceasing, and when it is offered "through Jesus Christ our Lord," as most liturgical prayers formally conclude, prayer expresses our relationship with God in Christ. Special prayers articulate that relationship at special times under special circumstances.

Myth and Ritual

What is a myth? The term is widely and variously used, not only in theology but in anthropology and sociology as well. It would be difficult to find one definition to embrace all its uses, but a simple one is adequate for our purposes. A myth can be understood as any narrative in which God or the gods appear as chief actors. The word is Greek. Greek myths are stories of Greek gods. Since in contemporary Western culture no one seriously believes in the Greek gods, the word has come to be associated with a story that is not true. Nevertheless, Greek worshipers believed their myths.

A number of contemporary Christian theologians have adopted a similar use of the word *myth*. Using it to apply to biblical narratives runs the risk of seeming to deny their truth, yet the careful use of the word has two advantages. In the first place, it allows Christianity to be understood as a religion, comparable in some respects to the Greek religion and others. More important, the use of the word *myth* makes clear that the biblical narratives of the acts of God do not have the same quality as narratives involving only human actors. The reason for this difference in quality is one we have already encountered several times. No one has ever seen God. One has encountered specific revelations of God, to be sure. And we know about forms of God that are God. Jesus Christ himself is such a form. But God is, as the hymn runs, "in light inaccessible hid from our eyes."[6]

Narratives about God, therefore, point to a dimension of reality that ordinary history does not include. Narratives about God are a special form of discourse. They use language in a special way. Many theologians, though by no means all, call this special form of discourse *myth*. We shall adopt this usage because it illuminates Christian worship.

It would not be possible to survey all ancient myths at this point. But, at least in the Near East, where Israel developed and the Christian Church was born, myths originally had a religious setting. That is, they were used in worship. The stories expressed a certain relationship between the divine and human realms, and when used in worship to assist the worshipers to participate in that relationship, they would be accompanied by some liturgical action. The ritual accompanied the myth; the myth commented on and elucidated the ritual.

In popular belief these myths and rituals were "realistic." That is, they not only symbolized and expressed the action of the gods in an arbitrary way; they were participating and communicating symbols of the divine acts. They participated in the reality of God's activity and in a certain sense, "made" it happen. The temple was believed to be the model of God's celestial home, and the liturgy of the temple was the mirror image of God's action.

There is something of this quality about Old Testament worship. The temple was built as a model whose description was written by God's own hand, as the Book of Chronicles tell us. After a passage describing the plan of the temple and its furnishings, the following verse appears:

> All this he [David] made clear by the writing from the hand of the LORD concerning it, all the work to be done according to the plan. (1 Chr. 28:19).

A similar note is added to the instructions for making the golden lamps and snuffers for the wilderness tabernacle, as they appear in the Book of Exodus: "See that you make them after the pattern for them, which is being shown you [Moses] on the mountain" (Ex. 25:40). One might say that the liturgy of the temple itself is the image and revelation of God's will, the bearer and intermediary of heavenly strength.[7]

One of the themes of myth and ritual in the Old Testament is the creation of the world, as it was in most other Near Eastern religions. The stories of creation in the early chapters of Genesis are myths in the sense we have tried to establish, narratives in which God appears as the chief actor. Another cluster of narratives in which God appears as the chief actor, however, represents a sharp difference from Israel's neighbors. Many Near Eastern myths have to do with the death and rebirth of vegetation year by year, as winter is overcome and spring returns. They describe a ritual struggle between death and life in the annual cycle of nature. In Israel, the chief concern is not the overcoming of winter, not a struggle with the forces of *nature*, but the conquest of Israel's *historical* enemies. The exodus from Egypt is the focal point of this other cluster of Old Testament narratives—the defeat of Pharaoh and the triumphant crossing of the Red Sea to safety and freedom. "This is the LORD's doing; it is marvelous in our eyes" (Ps. 118:23). This story, too, is a myth in the technical sense of our definition. God is the chief actor in the story. Human powers alone could not account for it. But in this case, the ritual action of the myth does not occur in the temple, mirroring the heavenly courts. The action of this myth occurs in history, once and for all, at a particular time and place. And the power of that deliverance is made accessible to worshipers again and again by a proclamation or recital of what God did at that time. Myth has become history. Ritual is the recital of those historical events, recalling them to the present.

We are now in a position to see the bearing of Christian "myth and ritual" on Christian worship. Christ is our liturgy, our sacrifice, our priest, and our prayer. His story is our myth, and our ritual is the reciting of it. The ritual action, the Christian liturgy, is embodied in Christ's overcoming of temptation and death, which he did once and for all by his life of trust and obedience, by his faithfulness to the great covenant. Our myth is the narrative that recounts this action. It is the story of his life as the action of God through him. It is particularly important that we emphasize, in the case of Jesus of Nazareth, that we are using the word *myth* in its technical sense. Our myth is not an untrue story. In the case of Jesus, even more plainly than in the case of Old Testament narratives, the myth is embodied in historical events. When the Word becomes flesh and dwells among us, myth becomes history. The action of this myth occurred at a particular place and time, in Judea "under Pontius Pilate." The earthly model of the divine plan was the historical life of Jesus, not a temple ritual; and the power of his life and death is made accessible for us, humanly speaking, not by temple sacrifices, but by services of Word and Sacrament that rehearse and represent again and again that one sacrificial liturgy enacted by the one true priest. As the Scottish preacher Sir George McLeod used to say, "Jesus was crucified for us on a hill outside Jerusalem between two thieves, not on an altar between two candlesticks."

In the view of St. Paul, the Christian person, not the church building, replaces the temple in Christian worship. There were no church buildings for generations. "Do you not know that your body is a temple of the Holy Spirit within you, which you have from God?" (1 Cor. 6:19). Our lives lived in trust and obedience are Christian liturgy, sacrifice, priesthood, and prayer. Similarly, the one place where Christian myth and ritual is continually reenacted is within us. This place is at least as important as the church building for the conduct of Christian liturgy. In fact, these two aspects of Christian myth and ritual—self and sanctuary—are inseparable.

5

Implications and Consequences of Liturgy

The fact that Christian liturgy is related so closely to Christ himself on the one hand and to the daily lives of Christians on the other bears further examination. It is the purpose of this chapter to trace some of the implications and consequences of liturgy.

Christian Worship as the Transformation of Time

In the last chapter we found ourselves saying three rather different things. On the one hand we found that Christ fulfills and preempts each of the aspects of worship we discussed. He is the sacrifice, the priest, the prayer, the myth, and the ritual. In short, *he* is our liturgy. At the same time our lives as Christians, lived obediently to the covenant of trust and obedience, also constitute sacrifice, priesthood, prayer, myth, and ritual. *We* are the Christian liturgy. Furthermore, the gatherings of the Christian community to worship the God revealed in Christ are characterized by liturgy, sacrifice, prayer, and ritual, led by officiants called priests. How can Christian worship mean all of these things simultaneously?

A clue to this complicated situation is to be found in what we have already said in chapter 3 about the role of the Holy Spirit in worship. We said that the Spirit constitutes the unity between the holy God and the finite, particular manifestations of the divine. Jesus Christ and the Father are one "in the unity of the Holy Spirit" as numerous Prayer Book collects express it. The Spirit is the bond of unity—not only between these two ways God has of being God, but also between Christ Jesus, who lived and died in Palestine two thousand years ago, and our lives and our worship "at all times and in all places" and especially here and now. We are one with him in the Spirit, our liturgy one with his, our sacrifice one with his, our prayer one with his. This unity is accomplished by a transformation of time.

In the act of worship, we come into the presence of God. In the ecstasy of prayer, our spirits are caught up in God's Spirit. Since God is equally present at all times and in all places in the Spirit, our time in particular is contemporary with that time in which the decisive revelation of God appeared.

Were you there when they crucified my Lord?
Were you there when they nailed him to the tree?
Were you there when they laid him in the tomb?[1]

The answer implied is yes! And we were there also when God raised him from the dead, and when he sat at God's right hand.

When myth becomes history, that history, whether of the Exodus or of the cross and resurrection, has the possibility of entering subsequent moments of history, to transform them. "Not with our fathers did the LORD make this covenant, but with us, who are all of us here alive this day" (Dt. 5:3). Those words were said to the people of the Old Covenant, gathered to renew the covenant many generations after that covenant was first made on Mount Sinai. The Book of Deuteronomy, in which the verse appears, has been dated as early as the eighth century B.C. and as late as the fifth, but in any case centuries after the Exodus and the initiating of the covenant under Moses in the thirteenth century B.C. The context of these words in worship is a renewal of the Old Covenant, very much as our eucharistic worship is a renewal of the New Covenant. In worship, the new generation becomes contemporaneous with the first generation. Such an event is not an ordinary occurrence. *It is a religious possibility*, an implication of liturgy, made possible by the Spirit, in worship.

Like the Old Covenant, the New is made "not with our fathers but with us, who are all of us alive here this day." This continual renewal of the New Covenant, established by the liturgy and sacrifice of Christ our priest, is a possibility of worship in the Holy Spirit. When we worship, we "celebrate the memorial of our redemption . . . Recalling his death, resurrection, and ascension, we offer you these gifts" (BCP, p. 363). Our time has been transformed into his time.

It is not simply that the moment of past revelation becomes present by the Spirit in worship. The time of future consummation also becomes present. Christian life is lived between the time when our Lord Jesus Christ "came to visit us in great humility" and "the last day" when he shall come again in glorious majesty to judge both the living and the dead" (BCP, p. 211). Christian worship occurs in a time that, regarded from an ordinary point of view, is between those times. But by the power of the Spirit, worship occurs in the presence of God, in a time when the Lord, crucified and risen, is present and when we share the coming victory of God, also known as present.

The presence of both past and future in the time of worship is expressed most clearly in Eucharist Prayer D of the current Book of Common Prayer, although this transformation of time is implied at every Eucharist and indeed at every meeting of the Christian community to worship God:

Father, we now celebrate this memorial of our redemption. Recalling Christ's death and his descent among the dead, *proclaiming* his resurrection and ascension to your right hand, *awaiting* his coming in glory; and offering to you, from the gifts you have given us, this bread and this cup, we praise you and we bless you. (BCP, p. 376; emphasis added)

Christ is known as our liturgy, sacrifice, priest, prayer, myth, and ritual, because he is present to us in worship, by the power of the Spirit through the transformation of time. It is God the Spirit who makes real the mystery of Christian worship.

Worship and Reconciliation

Liturgy not only implies the transformation of time, but the transformation of worshipers, and finally the transformation of the world. The liturgy, of course, does not do such things by itself. It is not magic. As God the Spirit works through the liturgy to become present and accessible to us, so God the Spirit works through the liturgy to lead us to reconciliation with our neighbors and with the world.

The ways by which God calls us to reconciliation are infinitely varied. Sometimes it is not through the liturgy at all. For some it has been initiated through a casual, even indifferent, attendance at church services. Whatever the means, the depth of Christian life is not achieved, even through the liturgy, unless it is internalized and takes root in a true change of heart.

On the other hand, this interior change, which moves us from preoccupation with ourselves to a life centered on God, must externalize itself in concrete ways. If I am not the center of the world, if all things are not for the enhancement of my life, if I am a child of God—and if all these things are similarly true of those who acknowledge the same God—then the texture and quality of relations between us who share this common Father is a matter of utmost importance. The life of those who truly worship is community in Christ. Common worship, especially the Eucharist, is the sign of the unity that exists among us. More than this, it is the sign of judgment upon our sinful violations of unity; and even more than this, it is a source of nourishment as we press toward our common goal, which is Christ. We are fed by what we become. To borrow a phrase, "You are what you eat."

Worship in the Christian community, therefore, leads to acknowledgment of our guilt for breaking the community and to reconciliation with our brothers and sisters in Christ. Estranged neighbors always confront us with the need to set aside our pride for their good, and for the good of the community as a whole. Penitence is one of the first implications of the Christian liturgy. Penitence leads to reconciliation. Reconciliation with neighbors is a sign of our mutually being drawn away from our self-centeredness into a centering on Christ. Luther spoke of sin as a state of being "turned in on one's self" (*incurvatus in se*). Christ enables us to escape the tyranny of our egos and turn toward the world. Apart from Christ, such a denial of the self is a type of madness. In him it becomes the deepest fulfillment of the self, realized in communion (common union) with our neighbors. This insight lies at the heart of the New Testament image of the church as the Body of Christ.

Where this sign of reconciliation is present, it is the distinctive sign of Christian discipleship and the hallmark of life in Christ: "By this shall all men know that you are my disciples, if you have love for one another" (Jn. 13:35). A true Christian liturgy implies a reconciled community of faith. An individualistic approach to the sacraments can altogether avoid this implication. In such an approach, the relation of individuals to their neighbors has nothing to do with liturgy. The fundamental action takes place between the individual and God. When this is the case, worship has no bearing on the quality of life in the community. One worships wearing spiritual blinders, so that one does not have to see the people on either side. Yet if through the Christian liturgy one is not enabled to see Christ in one's neighbor, one has missed the whole point. One of the most familiar passages of the New Testament, the parable of the Last Judgment, indicates that the very basis of God's judgment of us is our treatment of others. "LORD, when did we see thee hungry and feed thee, or thirsty and give thee drink? . . . And the King will answer them, Truly, I say to you, as you did it to one of the least of these my brethren you did it to me" (Mt. 25:37, 40).

The imperative of the liturgy is a commitment to reconciliation. Reception of the sacrament with such an intention is no mere act of personal piety. It is the sign of our dependence on him who is our unity and our peace. An indifferent reception of the Eucharist, when we are not "in love and charity with [our] neighbors" and don't even see the need to be, is a blatant refusal to discern the Lord's body (cf. 1 Cor. 11:29). Indifference to reconciliation as an implication of the liturgy is itself a judgment. It is no small thing to approach the altar of God.

Worship and Mission

As the liturgy leads to reconciliation with our neighbors already within the Christian community, it also leads to the evangelization of those not yet members of the Body of Christ. Mission is another consequence of worship. A popular name for Eucharist among Roman Catholics and some Anglicans is *Mass*. The name establishes this connection. For it is taken from the short sentence which once stood at the end of the Latin liturgy, addressed by priest to people, *Ite, missa est.* "Go, it is dismissal." *Mass* is the English form of the Latin *missa*. Mass is dismissal, sending into the world. Mass implies mission.

To speak in this way expresses a truth about Christian worship that we have encountered a number of times in these pages. Worship always has two phases: in one phase, the community gathers to celebrate its liturgy in the usual sense of the word, its praise and thanksgiving, its penitence and adoration in the presence of the crucified and risen Lord; in the other phase, the community lives in the world according to the love and power that come from him, in obedience and trust.

From our risen Lord, the church has received its apostolic commission: "Go therefore and make disciples of all nations, baptizing them in the name of the Father and of the Son and of the Holy Spirit, teaching them to observe all that I have commanded you; and lo, I am with you always, to the close of the age" (Mt. 28:19–20). The church exists to announce "to all nations" that the rule of God is at hand. This outreach of the Christian community to the whole world in the name of Jesus Christ has been characteristic of the church's life from the beginning. Without it, the church would not be the church. Liturgy that does not lead to evangelism is not authentic and does not communicate the power of the Spirit.

During the past hundred years or so the mission of the church has often been confused with the dissemination of Western culture and distorted by the dominance of American and European power. Under these circumstances the true quality of Christ made possible by Word and Sacrament has been communicated only with the greatest difficulty. Moreover Asian and African churches are themselves becoming missionary churches to an extraordinary degree. Consequently, the nature of missionary activity in our own church is going through a process of radical criticism and reformulation. We have learned that the mission of the church is directed at least as much to those who are near as to the those who live in some distant place. It involves the self-giving of Christian worshipers expressed in many more ways than in the gift of money alone. It involves a concern for men and women with various hungers and needs who live on our own streets and in our own towns. There can be no thought of giving up the missionary activity of the church, for the church in every time and place is essentially and irreducibly missionary. When we hear the word of Christ proclaimed in the liturgy and receive his life given for us, we accept a commission to give every person in every place accessible to us an opportunity to hear the same word and receive the same life. Authentic liturgy makes missionaries of us all.

Worship and Ministry

Such a deepened understanding of the implications of the liturgy makes us rethink many of our provisions for the external ordering of our common life. One of the most obvious areas in which such rethinking is necessary is ministry.

For most people, the word *ministry* calls to mind ordained persons—bishops, priests, deacons. In fact, the word *ministry* has far broader reference than merely to the ordained. Its essential meaning originates in baptism. It pertains to every Christian person. Unfortunately in the course of the Christian centuries we have lost that association. The idea that every Christian is a minister comes to the ears of many as something strange and new.

We are heirs to a long tradition of clericalism, as we said in an earlier connection. We often picture the church as a group of active clerical suppliers to passive lay consumers, with the laity not as the basic category of church membership but as quite a secondary one. Actually the church *is* the laity—the *laos* ("people"). The church is the people of God. Within the *laos* there is an extraordinary diversity of ministries, each of which expresses some particular way in which a member of the body of Christ actualizes the Christian liturgy in the world.

Clergy, of course, have their distinctive roles to perform, and the focal role that clergy play in a church service inevitably tends to emphasize the significance of clerical ministries. The prominence of the clerical office has developed to such a point, however, that the chief function of ordained persons, to *serve* the body, has become grossly obscured. At the worst periods of Christian history, the perversion has been complete. Laity have been seen as the servants of the clergy.

Today we are a long way from such an extreme. Yet clericalism lingers, for it appeals not only to clergy but to some lay persons as well. It is a tempting attitude for laity who want to be passive, either because they find security in having an omnicompetent oracle or because they do not want to accept the responsibilities of Christian life implied in their baptism. A living body requires the living participation of all members. So too does the body of Christ.

Ministry is the activity of the entire body of Christ. Each person has a special ministry, shaped to fit the given reality of that person's life. Ministry is not enactment of a predetermined pattern of action. An individual or a parish or a diocese may be called upon to minister in unexpected ways, since ministry is always a response to a unique situation. Ministry is the way in which individuals or communities respond to the persons or situations in which they find themselves, in obedience to the command proclaimed in the liturgy: to love others as Christ loved them. Ministry is not to another person at another time. It is here and now. It is not what we would do if we had greater resources or if the situation were somehow different. Ministry is what is done with existing resources in existing circumstances in obedience to Christ the Lord. If the person who crosses our path is hungry and our response is "I would feed you *if* I had more bread," then we have failed to minister in the name of Christ.

These remarks about ministry may seem obvious, yet the clericalization of ministry has beclouded its essential character. When ministry is viewed primarily as the work of ordained persons, it comes to be understood almost exclusively as actions within the church, often as those ceremonial actions that ordained persons do. Thus the whole implication of liturgy for service to the world is lost.

It is of little value to aim criticism at the highly clericalized concept of the liturgy that dominated the Middle Ages and the Reformation. The Protestant preacher, as we have seen, was as highly clericalized a figure as the Roman priest. The problem was not with the liturgy in either case. The problem was more deep-rooted, a basic distortion in the idea of the church. The primitive community was genuinely an organic, priestly body, and its worship manifested this corporate character because its self-image was corporate.

This is not to question a legitimate role for ordained persons both in leading the liturgy and in enabling the priestly ministry of the whole people of God both to the church and to the world. When the particular ministries of clergy are seen in the context of the ministry of the whole church, as a service to the whole church for its life in the world, then the ordained priesthood emerges with its own integrity. It reminds the whole church, through Word and Sacrament, of the sources of its common life in Christ, so that all the members can be nourished and strengthened to fulfill their particular vocations and ministries.

These comments suggest that the active participation of the laity in the liturgy, which has been one of the principal tenets of the liturgical movement, is not merely whim or fad on the part of liturgists. It expresses the nature of the church as portrayed in the New Testament. St. Paul compared the church to a body made up of interdependent members. It is a society "from whom the whole body, joined and knit together by every joint with which it is supplied, when each part is working properly, makes bodily growth and upbuilds itself in love" (Eph. 4:16). This proper working of each part has to do primarily with the way each person does ministry in the world. But it has to do also with the way each person fulfills a liturgy in worship. When life is conceived in terms of the mutuality of all vocations within the church, and not in terms of the primacy of the clerical vocation, this mutuality within the common life must and will demand expression in the liturgical assembly. Liturgy leads to the ministry of the entire people of God in the world. Liturgy also expresses this mutual ministry.

It remains to be said that all ministry is related to Christ's own ministry of service. The very word *ministry* is derived from the Latin *minus*, lesser. The word calls to mind what Jesus said to his disciples:

> . . . whoever would be great among you must be your servant, and whoever would be first among you must be slave of all. For the Son of man came not to be served but to serve ["not to be ministered unto but to minister" as the King James Version runs], and to give his life as a ransom for many. (Mk. 10:43–45)

Like nearly everything else we have considered in our survey of Christian worship, ministry depends on Christ. He thought of his role as being that of a servant. Consequently, the church that he founded is a servant church. His body in the world, filled with his Spirit, moves from the service of God in the liturgy to the service of God in the world. The whole church was founded to minister and to exercise its ministry in the spirit of Christ. Each member of the body has a special ministry that belongs to that person alone.

We have seen now how participation in liturgy has consequences for a person's life. It should lead to reconciliation with one's neighbors and to the unity of the church. It should lead to involvement in mission, and so to reconciliation with the world. It should lead each Christian to regard life in the world as a ministry. Ministry is the means to reconciliation. It is also true that reconciliation, evangelism, and ministry deepen and intensify the liturgy. The reconciliation of church members to one another strengthens the bonds of love that bind Christians together. The corporate nature of the community, which we have already seen to play a decisive part as a ground of the liturgy, is enhanced. The mission of the church brings a larger and more varied chorus to join the praise of God. The implications of the expanded sense of ministry for the active participation of the laity in the liturgy are evident.

Thus liturgy not only has consequences for life. Life has consequences for the liturgy. Christians move away from prayer and praise in the church to life and work in the world. The two activities, properly understood, flow into each other, and reinforce each other to the greater glory of God. When the connection is broken, both worship and witness suffer.

PART TWO

Liturgy and the
Book of Common Prayer

6

The Background
of the Prayer Book

The first part of this study of worship has attempted to examine Christian liturgy in the broadest possible setting. We have tried to understand the fundamental features and meaning of liturgy against the background of worship in Israel and in the ancient Near East in general, and to trace the implications of worship for Christian life. We have not been interested as yet in particularly Anglican aspects of the liturgy. Yet the purpose of this volume is to help its readers to a clearer appreciation of the liturgical worship of our own church, the Episcopal Church. In our worship, we use a prayer book. Subsequent parts of this volume will examine the contents of that book. In this part, we shall ask how our Prayer Book came to be. First we will take a bird's-eye view of the development of Christian liturgies prior to the appearance of the first English Book of Common Prayer in 1549. Then, in the next chapter, we shall briefly trace the development of English and American editions of the Prayer Book through their subsequent revisions.

Christian Worship in the Earliest Church

The liturgical records from the earliest days of Christianity are scant. There are a number of references, a few descriptions, but very few actual texts. Christianity began as an heretical Jewish sect. Its customs of worship were Jewish.

From the New Testament itself one learns that the first Christians in Jerusalem, "day by day, attending the temple together and breaking bread in their homes, . . . partook of food with glad and generous hearts" (Acts 2:46). "They devoted themselves to the apostles' teaching and fellowship, to the breaking of bread and the prayers" (Acts 2:42). Like all Jews, they went to the temple. Although it is not explicitly stated, they presumably organized themselves as a synagogue for daily prayers, morning and evening. The reference to "the prayers" may refer to these synagogue prayers. They kept the times of individual prayer at the third, sixth, and ninth hours of the day, according to Jewish custom (Acts 2:15, 10:9, and 3:1, respectively). This is a reasonable conclusion from passing references.

The "breaking of the bread" is surely a reference to the bread and wine eaten and drunk in remembrance of the Lord. As we shall see in chapter 14, this was a reference to a meal, accompanied by prayers of thanksgiving, as all Jewish meals were. The New Testament does not provide us with any text for such prayers, although the accounts of what Jesus himself did and said at the last meal he took with his disciples are well known. These words and actions obviously became an important part of the Christian version of such meals. We know that these celebrations often occurred at night (Acts 20:7ff; 1 Cor. 11:23), sometimes daily (Acts 2:46) and sometimes weekly (Acts 20:7; Rev. 1:10).

A number of baptisms are described in the New Testament. The formula for baptizing is stated occasionally, sometimes in the Trinitarian form that has endured to this day: "in the name of the Father, and of the Son and of the Holy Spirit" (Mt. 28:19); sometimes merely "in the name of Jesus Christ" (Acts 2:38). The detailed account of the baptism of the Ethiopian eunuch in Acts 8 possibly contains the nucleus of an early baptismal text:

> "Here is water! What is to prevent my being baptized?"
> "If you believe with all your heart, you may."
> "I believe that Jesus Christ is the Son of God." (8:36–37)

The text of the Lord's Prayer is given twice, in Matthew 6:9–13 and in Luke 11:2–4. The ancient Christian prayer expressing the hope and expectation of the return of Christ in glory to judge the world, the *Maranatha* ("Our Lord, come"), appears in two places (1 Cor. 16:22; Rev. 22:20). St. Paul describes services of worship that were free, spontaneous, even charismatic (1 Cor. 14:26–33).

We learn that the elders of the church anointed the sick and prayed over them (Jas. 5:14), that Christians confessed sins to one another, and that they prayed for forgiveness for others (Jas. 5:16). Timothy was ordained by the laying on of elders' hands accompanied by prophetic utterance (1 Tim. 4:14). In the entire New Testament, no mention is made of a Christian liturgy for marriage or for the burial of the dead.

In 1875 a manuscript was discovered in the patriarchal library of Jerusalem at Constantinople. It is called the *Didache* or, in English, *The Teaching of the Twelve Apostles*. Currently, scholars believe it to be very old, older, in fact, than some of the New Testament documents. Like the New Testament, it contains a number of references to worship and some descriptions. It also contains the text of a prayer said over a cup and bread at the Eucharist.[1] The prayer is remarkable, for it makes no mention of Jesus' command "Do this in remembrance of me." In fact, it makes no explicit mention of Jesus' death and resurrection, giving thanks rather "for the life and knowledge which thou didst make known to us through Jesus thy child,"[2] or "for the knowledge and faith and immorality which thou didst make known to us through Jesus thy child."[3] It mentions the cup before the bread. This text is the basis for the well-loved communion hymn:

> Father, we thank thee who hast planted
> Thy Holy Name within our hearts.
> *Knowledge* and faith and life immortal
> Jesus thy Son to us imparts.[4]

The text concludes with the prayer *Maranatha*.

In the year 112, a date also prior to parts of the New Testament, Pliny the Younger, when he was governor of Bithynia, reported to the Emperor Trajan on the rise of the Christians, who were troublesome because they refused to take part in the worship of the emperor as God. In the course of one of his letters he gave a curiously out-of-focus description of a Christian service of worship as reported to him by a Christian defector.

> . . . on an appointed day they had been accustomed to meet before daybreak, and to recite a hymn antiphonally to Christ as a god, and to bind themselves by an oath [the Latin word is *sacramentum*], not for the commission of any crime but to abstain from theft, robbery, adultery, and breach of faith, and not to deny a deposit when it was claimed. After the conclusion of this ceremony it was their custom to depart and meet again to take food; but it was ordinary and harmless food.[5]

Since the services were "on an appointed day," they were presumably weekly; and the time has moved from night to early morning. The use of the word *sacrament* to describe the Christian mystery is interesting since it does mean "oath" or "pledge" in Latin. The emphasis on morality is almost certainly accurate, as we shall see. The mention of food is what we should expect.

A generation later, about A.D. 150, we have an even more detailed description of a Christian Eucharist in the *First Apology* of Justin Martyr, a Samaritan-born convert to Christianity who taught in Rome. We shall consider his evidence in detail when we discuss the Eucharist itself. Here it is sufficient to observe that the service is on Sunday morning. It is conducted by someone described as "the president of the brethren." For the first time we learn that readings from the "memoirs of the apostles and writings of the prophets" are prefixed to the meal. The president preaches a sermon, exhorting to virtue, and offers a prayer of thanksgiving to God "through the name of the Son and Holy Spirit," spontaneously "according to his ability." The people assent by saying, "Amen."

The evidence that we have presented in this section covers a little more than the first century of the church's life. Obviously nothing like a prayer book has appeared. There were probably no written texts. Even the eucharistic prayer was free. We find a number of familiar practices, although we can never be sure, in the New Testament or early documents, how widespread any given practice may have been. The documents themselves pertain to one specific locality. There was obviously a great deal of variation and much freedom in the Spirit-filled body of early Christians.

The Emergence of Liturgical Texts

During the next two centuries or so written texts of liturgical prayers appeared. Three documents are of particular importance for understanding the development of liturgies: (1) the *Apostolic Tradition* of Hippolytus, presumed to be a Roman document from the early years of the third century; (2) the sacramentary of Serapion, an Egyptian document from the middle of the fourth century; and (3) the *Apostolic Constitutions*, an extended tract probably from the church in Syria toward the end of the fourth century. Each of these documents contains one or more liturgical texts. In no case, however, have those texts been in continuous use. They are not the present-day liturgies of the Roman, Egyptian, or Syrian churches.

The *Apostolic Tradition* and the *Apostolic Constitutions* are typical examples of a larger class of documents that appeared in the church as time progressed and the interval between the present age and the age of the apostles grew longer and longer. The *Didache* is also such a document. These so-called Church Orders are collections of teaching and liturgical material that express the thought and practice of a church in a given place. This material is represented as having been handed down from the apostolic age. *Apostolic Tradition* represents what was received at Rome, and *Apostolic Constitutions* is said at the beginning of the document to have been written by "the apostles and elders to all those who from among the Gentiles have believed in the Lord Jesus Christ." *Apostolic Constitutions* include the *Didache* as its seventh book.

This family of documents includes ethical exhortation as well as liturgical provisions. One thinks of the stress laid in Pliny's letter and in the description of the sermon in Justin Martyr's *Apology* on moral uprightness. Quality of life mattered as much as liturgical detail at this period of the church's life; even if one misses the theological profundity of the New Testament itself in these writings, one must recognize how important it must have been, in a period of moral license somewhat like our own, to maintain an ethical life that conformed to the Gospel. In any case, the association between life and liturgy, represented in these Church Orders and emphasized also in this volume of the Church's Teaching Series, is not some new idea. It has been a concern of thoughtful Christians from the outset.

There is no sense in which the Church Orders could be called "prayer books." The kind of material they contain is, on one side, too diverse. And, on the other hand, they do not make provision for all the situations covered by Anglican Books of Common Prayer. There is still no form for marriage or burial, for example. At the same time, these Church Orders recognize the desirability of some kind of common liturgy. The liturgical forms in these documents are probably to be regarded as models for liturgical prayers, and not as standards from which no deviation was permitted. Nevertheless, even by providing a model on which the "president of the assembly" could base his freely composed prayers, a step toward uniformity had been taken.

The sacramentary of Serapion introduces us to a somewhat different kind of liturgical collection. A *sacramentary* is a collection of liturgical prayers used by the celebrant of a liturgy. Serapion was a contemporary and correspondent of Athanasius, the famous upholder of the equality of the Father and the Son at the Council of Nicaea in 325. Some of Athanasius' letters to Serapion are still extant. Serapion was bishop of Thmuis, a town in the region around Alexandria, and under its influence. Bishop Serapion's sacramentary includes some thirty prayers, including the text of a eucharistic prayer.

Before the invention of printing, it would have been unthinkable to put into each worshiper's hands the text of the whole liturgy. Only those who had speaking parts would have had a text at all. A sacramentary included all the material a celebrant of sacraments would need. It is still obviously not a prayer book, but as a collection of prayers that the celebrant would have used regularly, it is a step closer.

It is not the purpose of this chapter to consider the contents of these documents. Specific aspects of them will be considered in connection with various services. Here we simply record one stage in the fixing of liturgical texts and their collection into even more inclusive books. *Apostolic Tradition* contains a eucharistic prayer in the course of the service for the ordination of a bishop, a full text for a baptismal liturgy, and a detailed description of prayers to be made at stated hours of prayer. There are also formulas for various blessings. The whole document has been quite influential on liturgical forms that we still use, as we shall see in subsequent chapters.

The material in Serapion and *Apostolic Constitutions* is not so familiar. When we compare these documents with what we find in Hippolytus, we see a few similarities. The eucharistic prayers in these documents have the same parts, the same sequence, and in the case of crucial sections like the institution of the Supper, nearly the same words. On the other hand, we encounter the beginning of a recognizably different liturgical and cultural style. Byzantine, not Roman. Eloquent, with a sense of mystery achieved by a cloud of words, rather than terse, with a sense of mystery achieved by utter economy of language. East and West begin to separate.

Official Liturgies for an Official Church

At some time between the sixth and the ninth centuries the church in both the East and the West developed the liturgical forms that have continued in use, with minor revisions, to this day: in the East the Liturgy of St. John Chrysostom, with the older Liturgy of St. Basil used instead on certain days each year; and in the West the Roman rite.

The details of the process need not concern us. The forces at work and the significance of the result were the same in each case. Christianity became the official religion of the Roman Empire. The unity of the empire required a common faith; in the course of passing centuries, after the great theological debates of Nicaea, Constantinople, Ephesus, and Chalcedon produced common creeds, it became the practice of the emperors to enforce spiritual unity through liturgical conformity. The use of one liturgy throughout the Eastern empire and the other throughout the West became a test of political allegiance.

These official liturgies, of course, were not the only ones to emerge after the period of the Church Orders. In fact, at the beginning of the process, each bishop, like Serapion, probably had his own particular customs. Nevertheless, the number of significantly different liturgies was probably not as great as this bare statement might suggest, for the great cities, the centers of culture and of Christian vitality, produced certain styles of worship. Small local dioceses would conform more or less to the influential patriarchal centers of Jerusalem, Antioch, Alexandria, Constantinople, and Rome. In France and Spain, where there was no such center, the picture did remain confusing. The so-called Gallican rite in France and Mozarabic rite in Spain consisted of a large number of entirely different liturgies, which apparently could vary week by week.

All these local variations, of so many different kinds, did not completely disappear under the political pressure for uniformity. Occasions during the year were found to use older liturgies, or places were set aside where the older liturgy would be perpetuated throughout the year. The cathedrals in Milan and in Toledo, for example, down to our own time, have preserved very ancient customs and rites, quite different from the standard Roman liturgy.

We shall not concern ourselves further with this host of variations.[6] Nor shall we pursue the history of liturgy in the East. The story of the various editions of the Anglican Prayer Book belongs to the West. Although we must bear in mind this larger picture of great complexity and richness when we try to evaluate the Anglican liturgical achievement, the development of the Roman rite is of most immediate and direct concern.

In the sixth century the Roman rite underwent considerable elaboration and enrichment as well as standardization. From the beginning of this period we have a sacramentary, the so-called Leonine Sacramentary, from which many collects in Anglican prayer books, including the current Prayer Book, are drawn. The one copy we have, however, is incomplete; it does not even contain a eucharistic prayer, for example. Later sacramentaries do present eucharistic prayers, collects for a well-developed and familiar church year, and prayers for marriages, burials, and other pastoral offices. The earliest text, the source for much of the pre-Vatican II Roman rite, *Ordo I*, can be dated in the seventh century, in about the year 650 A.D.

But a sacramentary is only one of the books needed to celebrate Mass. There had to be a book of epistles and a book of gospels. There also had to be a book of chants for the choir, and a book of rules and directions for putting it all together. It was an important step on the way to a prayer book when all of this material, necessary to say Mass, was gathered together under one cover—the *Missal*. Missals originated about the ninth century and had finally replaced sacramentaries by the thirteenth.

The Eucharist, of course, was by no means the only liturgical service of the medieval church. Clergy, at least, were expected to say the Office, the daily hours of prayer that are rooted in Jewish custom. To say the Hours also required a number of books: one containing the musical parts of the service; another containing readings from the lives of the saints; another containing psalms and canticles; another containing the "chapters," or short readings from the Bible provided for the offices, and the collects. It was another step on the way to a prayer book when all of this material was collected into a four-volume seasonal, *Breviary*, or in a one-volume Book of Hours.

A parish priest needed a book for the several pastoral offices: baptism, marriage, visitation of the sick, penance, and burial of the dead. Liturgies for these occasions developed during the Middle Ages. Pastoral offices were collected into what was called a *Manual*. A bishop needed a book for the special services performed by him alone: confirmation, ordinations, dedication of churches. Episcopal offices were gathered into the *Pontifical*. The book of directions for those who performed the various rites was called the *Pie*.

These various books, which gathered the necessary liturgical material for these different purposes, had all appeared by the end of the Middle Ages. They represent a rich, imposing, all-encompassing liturgical life. We are almost ready for the appearance of the Prayer Book, which provides in one book all that is necessary for all the participants in all these services—including the congregation.

The "Deformation" of the Liturgy

The sixteenth-century reformation of worship cannot be understood apart from a steady "deformation" of the liturgy, to use a phrase from Dom Gregory Dix. It began when Christianity became the official religion of the Roman Empire. It accelerated when tribes of northern barbarians were baptized, having little preparation for taking part in the liturgy. It reached its climax in the development of Low Mass, said by a priest alone, and in the practice of clergy reading the Daily Office by themselves rather than in community.

These developments touched every aspect of the liturgy. At the beginning, the whole community gathered week by week to meet with joy the risen Lord in the breaking of bread. By the late Middle Ages, however, services had acquired predominately penitential overtones. A continual emphasis on moral purity coupled with a loss of confidence in justification (the adequacy of Christ's one sacrifice for all sin) resulted in imperfectly accepted forgiveness and unrelieved guilt. The customary symbol behind the altars of Western medieval churches came to be the crucifix, the figure of a suffering Christ, rather than the *Christus Victor*, a triumphant Christ reigning from his cross, which is characteristic of the Eastern church.

Laity gradually withdrew from receiving the cup altogether, and from receiving the eucharistic bread except for once each year at Easter. They refused to take the cup out of fear of spilling the consecrated wine and so defiling the Lord's blood. The fear is connected with a too literal understanding of the connection between Christ's presence and the wine, fostered by the doctrine of transubstantiation, taught and learned without the philosophical subtleties that made it intelligible to scholars at the universities. Theologians, obligingly and doubtless correctly, decided that Christ was fully present in the bread alone (as in the wine alone); but the fact that the church had to make such a decision at all pointed to a serious change in the character of participation in the Eucharist.

Laity withdrew from frequent and regular communion for another reason. It came to be believed that one should not receive communion at all unless one had confessed sins and received absolution from a priest. This development in itself is intelligible. One certainly should not receive communion thoughtlessly. Nevertheless, since confession was private and required a special liturgical act of its own, the Eucharist lost its own power to mediate forgiveness to penitent sinners through the presence of Christ; and in the practice, the number of worshipers who received communion regularly drastically declined. Christians went to church and said their own private prayers while the priest celebrated Mass in virtual silence. The French idiom for going to Mass is still *assiter á la messe*, "to be present at Mass." Since most lay persons could not have understood Latin in any case, the participation of intelligent listening was impossible.

For these reasons, and probably for others as well, the performance of the liturgy came to be thought of as the duty of the priest alone. Liturgy was what clergy did. This process of clericalization became complete when priests began to "say Mass" whether any other person was in attendance or not. The walls of large churches where several priests were assigned came to be lined with small altars for these private celebrations.

A similar deformation took place in baptism. In the early church, baptisms were administered at great public liturgies on Easter Eve and perhaps on one or two other occasions each year. Many were baptized, both adults and children. The bishop officiated. It was a great occasion for all Christians in the area.

Notice what happened. After the conversion of barbarian invaders, virtually every adult in Europe was Christian. The only candidates were children. Because of the high rate of infant mortality and the fear of a child's dying unbaptized, baptism came to be required within eight days of a child's birth. The ceremony had to be in a local parish and not at a central place where the whole diocese could gather. The bishop authorized presbyters to baptize, as he authorized them to celebrate the Eucharist. Because of the eight-day custom, candidates were not baptized in large numbers on one or two public occasions. Private baptism became the rule.

Baptism had once been an occasion of great rejoicing, when the people of God received new members and welcomed them to their new destiny in eternal life. It came to be a service that the church performed for parents, delivering them from the fear that their children would die unbaptized and the accompanying anxiety of their spending eternity separated from God.

Deformation also took place in the Daily Office. The Hours were developed and elaborated by monks in community. They gathered together several times a day, to chant the psalms, to hear the Bible, and to praise God. Such a communal discipline was impossible outside a monastery, however. Outside the monastery, only ordained people said the Office, another mark of the widening chasm between clergy and laity. As time went on, the elaboration of festivals and the increasing number of saints' days caused frequent interruptions in the regular reading of the Scripture. Lessons tended to grow very short, in some of the offices reduced to one verse, called a *chapter*. To find out what was supposed to be done on a certain day was difficult, time-consuming, and often unedifying.

Despite the richness and profundity of many of the liturgical developments in the Middle Ages, these considerations make it clear that reformation was necessary.

7

Anglican Prayer Books

On June 9, 1549, Whitsunday, the first Book of Common Prayer was introduced into the parishes of the Church of England by an act of Parliament. It was one of the most characteristic and permanently influential products of the English Reformation. It is the focal point of Anglican liturgical study. To it the discussions of the last chapter have led, and from it the discussions of subsequent editions of the Prayer Book must proceed. Later books can best be understood in relation to this one. It has become a monument of English prose, and, as the Anglican communion has spread around the world, the liturgical style that it originated has been translated into many other languages and has influenced the customs of worship of many peoples. In this chapter we shall examine what a prayer book is, at least what the Prayer Book in the Anglican fashion is, and glance briefly at the various revisions of the English and American editions of the Book of Common Prayer that have appeared since 1549.

What Is the Book of Common Prayer?

Anyone familiar with an American Prayer Book, whether of 1928 or 1979, would feel at home in the first English book. Like its American successors, it begins with a preface and a calendar of holy days. There are services of prayer for morning and evening, though called Mattins and Evensong. There is a service of Holy Communion, together with collects, epistles, and holy gospels for all the Sundays of the Church Year and a number of other days. Provisions for the critical moments in a Christian's life follow: baptism, confirmation, matrimony, visitation of the sick, burial of the dead. The Psalter and the forms for ordaining deacons, priests, and bishops were not bound with the Prayer Book at first, although they were published shortly thereafter.

In view of the trend noticed in the last chapter, it is plain what this Prayer Book aimed to do. It gathered together, in a drastically simplified way to be sure, the material that in the Roman rite at the end of the Middle Ages was found in the *Missal*, the *Breviary*, the *Manual*, and the *Pie*. What is more, the current book was in English, with the whole available in print to clergy and laity alike. Formerly this material had been used mainly by clergy. It had been in a language and form that only clergy could use and was of a complexity that required professional training to handle. Now it was in a language "understanded of the people." Soon even the psalms and ordination services were in the volume. Because the book was printed, there was at least the possibility that the liturgical text would become the familiar possession of God's people in England.

The simplification of rites and ceremonies constituted a large part of the reformation of the liturgy and was perhaps the chief factor in making liturgy again accessible to the people. In the preface to the 1549 Prayer Book, Archbishop Cranmer, its chief Architect wrote:

> . . . the number and hardness of the Rules called the Pie, and the manifold changings of the service, was the cause, that to turn the Book only, was so hard and intricate a matter, that many times, there was more business to find out what should be read, than to read it when it was found out. (BCP, p. 866)

The calendar was simplified, and only New Testament saints were recognized. The complicated scheme of the Daily Office, with its eight Hours, became Mattins and Evensong, or Morning and Evening Prayer. The use of holy things—ashes, palms, holy water—was eliminated in the face of widespread superstitions regarding unusual powers transferred by blessing to the things themselves. Individual services were stripped of the liturgical accretions of centuries, making them shorter, simpler, and more direct.

One of the striking features of this book was its provision for the reading of the Bible. At the Daily Offices, a full chapter of the Old Testament and a chapter of the New were read morning and evening, and individual books of the Bible would be read continuously from beginning to the end. All one hundred and fifty psalms were to be read in order each month, according to the divisions for morning and evening still marked in our American Prayer Books. Little effort was made to insure that the readings of psalms and Scripture were appropriate to a given season of the year. Every effort was made to let the Word of God contained in the Bible sound loud and clear in the church.

The book of 1549 attempted to deal directly with a number of the other problems mentioned in the last chapter, as well as the short and fragmentary readings from the Scripture. Laity were instructed to receive both cup and bread, and the priest was directed always to have someone to communicate with him. Baptisms were to be administered publicly only on Sundays and holy days, "when the most number of people may come together." Private baptism was an emergency procedure.

In all these respects, the book of 1549 was a tremendous achievement and has earned for Thomas Cranmer, who as far as we know produced it almost single-handed, a place in the first rank of the liturgists of Christendom. In view of its excellence, it is astonishing that it was used in English churches for only three years. Yet when one considers what a moderate and irenic production it was, intended to reconcile opposing points of view so that all England could worship as a united body of Christians, it is not so surprising that it should finally have pleased no one—as so often happens with compromises. In any case it was withdrawn under pressure in 1552 and another book substituted for it. The book of 1552 and the succession of revisions that followed it will be dealt with in a later section of this chapter.

What we need to observe now is the fact that no liturgical production is perfect, nor will it satisfy the needs of the church forever. Not only did the book of 1549 not go as far in a Protestant direction as the ruling powers desired, but it also had other liabilities that later generations have discovered. Some of these it passed on to its successors.

In some cases its work of removing the accretions of generations did not go far enough. The service of baptism is a good example, as we shall see in chapter 8. In some cases, the book went too far and eliminated valuable liturgical material that has only gradually been recovered. The special services for Holy Week are an example. Moreover, the prevailing penitential mood of medieval worship was not shaken in 1549. As a mater of fact, subsequent Prayer Books retained or even intensified it. Only recently has there been a serious effort to make the liturgy express the joy and thanksgiving that crown the New Testament and some of the most ancient liturgies.

Perhaps the most serious lack in the liturgy of the Prayer Book was already evident in 1549. The book failed to correct the clerical domination of worship that prevailed in the Middle Ages. Because of the inability of many people in the sixteenth century to read, the possibility inherent in the availability of printed prayer books was never completely actualized. When every worshiper has a copy of the text, worship can become a corporate action in which many persons, lay or ordained, take part. Yet, in practice, Prayer Book worship from the beginning tended to be almost as much the domain of clergy as the forms it replaced. One of the salient features of the current Prayer Book is its attempt to break this pattern.

Proclamation

Even with these faults, the English Book of Common Prayer and its counterparts in many countries around the world have been an unusually effective means for proclaiming the Gospel. Gospel is good news, and news can be spread only by telling other people about it. It cannot be figured out like a puzzle or dredged out of our subconscious minds by meditation or analysis. The news of what God has done for us must be proclaimed.

Authentic liturgy is one of the chief means for proclamation. Liturgy is the ritual celebration of the acts of God for us, and when God's acts for us are in and through historical events, liturgy rehearses the story of those deeds. By telling the old, old story when the congregations of God's people gather to worship in the power of God's Spirit, the same saving power is communicated again and again.

The effectiveness of the Book of Common Prayer in proclaiming what God has done for us in Christ is connected in the first place to its intelligibility. When the acts of God are told in a strange tongue, they can hardly be appropriated. In the Middle Ages, those who did not know Latin had to rely on the stories told by pictures or the marvelous stained-glass windows, or on the preaching and teaching that did occur—in some periods more effectively than others. To most people, the liturgy was a closed book.

The Word of God burst forth with new energy at the time of the Reformation. There was a revival of preaching. The 1549 Prayer Book required a homily at the Eucharist. But even more significant was the steady, systematic reading of Scripture in the vernacular tongue, both at the Eucharist and in the Daily Office. Worshipers could hear in their own tongue the marvelous works of God.

Not only did the lessons from the Scripture proclaim the Gospel, the texts of the various services themselves were now able to communicate the significance of Christ's death and resurrection, the Christian or paschal mystery. In the Eucharist, the exhortation to be read at every service, in 1549 and long afterwards, contained these words:

> And to the end that we should always remember the exceeding love of our master and only savior Jesus Christ, thus dying for us, and the innumerable benefits (which by his precious blood-shedding) he hath obtained to us, he hath left in those holy Mysteries, as a pledge of his love; and a continual remembrance of the same his own body, and precious blood, for us to feed upon spiritually to our endless comfort and consolation.[1]

Not only is the Eucharist proclamation; so is Baptism:

> . . . remembering always that Baptism doth represent unto us our profession, which is to follow the example of our Savior Christ, and to be made like unto him, that as he died and rose for us, so should we (which are Baptized) die from sin, and rise again unto righteousness . . .[2]

So is Matrimony:

> . . . which is an honorable estate instituted of God in paradise, in the time of man's innocency, signifying unto us the mystical union that is betwixt Christ and his Church. . .[3]

So is the Burial of the Dead:

> I am the resurrection and the life (saith the Lord): he that believeth in me, yea though he were dead, yet shall he live. And whosoever liveth and believeth in me shall not die forever.[4]

From one end of the Prayer Book to the other, in Daily Office, Eucharist, Pastoral Offices, and Ordinal, the English liturgy has vividly proclaimed the great deliverance God has brought to us through his people Israel, and most of all, through his Son, Jesus Christ.

English Revisions of the Prayer Book

The Prayer Book of 1549 was never popular. Conservatives disliked it because it changed too much. Radicals disliked it because it changed too little. In the conservative counties of western England riots broke out on June 10, the day following the introduction of the current Prayer Book. "We will not receive the new service," the rioters said, "because it is but like a Christmas game; but we will have our old service of Mattins, Mass, Evensong and precession in Latin, not English."[5] On the other hand, the cities, centers of Protestant influence, particularly London, rioted because statues and ornaments remained in the churches. Mobs tore out images and altars from a number of London churches in 1550 and 1551.

Finally, in 1552, the government withdrew the Prayer Book of 1549 and, by the Second Act of Uniformity of 1552, Parliament required the use of the Second Prayer Book of Edward VI beginning on All Saints' Day.

The book of 1552 would seem even more familiar to a contemporary Anglican worshiper than the book of 1549. It contains the Psalter and Ordinal as well as the other services. What is more, the Daily Office in this book, called Morning and Evening Prayer, begins with opening sentences and an exhortation, confession of sin, and declaration of absolution, as subsequent English and American editions of the Prayer Book have all done. The communion service drops "Mass" as a subtitle, and is called by the name it has had in every English and American book until the current Book of 1979: "The Order for the Administration of the Lord's Supper, or Holy Communion." As in all these later books, the service of Holy Communion begins with the Ten Commandments, arranged as an examination of conscience for the worshipers. Each commandment is followed by the expanded version of the Kyrie, "Lord, have mercy upon us, and incline our hearts to keep this law." Communion takes place at "the Table." There is no mention of an altar. Even in the American Prayer Book of 1928, an altar is mentioned only in the Office of Institution of Ministers.[6] In 1552 the service of Holy Baptism was further shortened.

In all these respects, the book of 1552 more closely resembles later books than does the book of 1549. The book of 1552 specified also that at communion services, a priest should wear only a surplice, a bishop only a rochet—his long white vestment with gathered sleeves. Albs, vestments (presumably chasubles) and copes were forbidden. The 1549 instruction had run ". . . the Priest that shall execute the holy ministry shall put upon him the vesture appointed for that ministration, that is to say: a white Alb plain, with a vestment or cope," thus keeping the old custom.[7]

A more serious change in the 1552 Book is its treatment of the offering. The sixteenth-century reformers objected strenuously to the idea that the Mass was something that human beings offered to God. This idea lay behind the late medieval practice of offering private Masses for the shortening of the stay of a dead person's soul in purgatory. It was believed that the offering of Mass to God would be pleasing and would cause God to have mercy on the soul for whom it was offered.

The reformers understood how far this notion departed from the eucharistic devotion of the early church. Mass, they knew, could be offered by us. Its benefits are offered by God to us. Therefore they carefully removed from the communion service any mention of offering. Bread and wine were prepared and put upon the table *before* the service. The offertory sentences all have to do with giving alms, and money received for the poor is put not upon the table, as our custom has come to be, but "into the poorman's box."[8] In the eucharistic prayer the familiar phrase in the American Prayer books, "We . . . do celebrate and make here before thy Divine Majesty, with these thy holy gifts, *which we now offer unto thee*,"[9] was not to be found, and the offering "of our selves, our souls and bodies, to be a reasonable, holy, and lively sacrifice unto thee"[10] was placed after the people received communion. In this service God acts; worshipers only receive and respond.

Later versions of the Prayer Book have tried to express a view of the eucharistic offering that lies between the two extremes encountered in the sixteenth century: the late medieval view, according to which the Mass was offered as a gift pleasing to God, and the extreme Reformation position, according to which God offers himself to a purely passive and receptive congregation. It is certainly true that God's grace and forgiveness are free gifts and that God's love is not dependent on anything that we do. It is also true that the congregation at the Eucharist consists of men and women who through baptism have already received and benefited from the unmerited love that God has shown us in Christ. The Eucharist represents our thankful offering to God of what we have to offer—all we have, as represented in bread and wine. We do not think that we earn God's favor by doing so, but we do think that such an offering both expresses our thanksgiving and makes intelligible the rest of the eucharistic action. We do not offer Christ. We do offer, in thanksgiving and praise, bread and wine for the eucharistic action. We offer ourselves to be filled with the presence of Christ in the Spirit.

The other numerous liturgical changes introduced by the 1552 Book of Common Prayer were of minor significance and will not concern us.

There have been three later revisions of the English Book of Common Prayer, each connected with the accession of a new monarch: the book of 1559, when Elizabeth I came to the throne; the book of 1604, when James I succeeded her; and the book of 1662, when Charles II restored the monarchy after the Protectorate of Oliver Cromwell. These books are all so close to that of 1552 that they can be described very quickly.

The Elizabeth Prayer Book (1559) was a peacemaking book. A rubric in it secures the use of vestments "as in the second year of Edward VI." This provision would permit the use of albs, chasubles, and copes. It was not widely obeyed, but it has appeared in all the later books. A few churches did take advantage of it. This book also removed a clause from the Litany, offensive to many: "From the Bishop of Rome and all his detestable enormities, Good Lord, deliver us." In 1549, the sentences of administration for the bread and wine at Holy Communion were objective: "The Body of our Lord Jesus Christ which was given for thee, preserve thy body and soul unto everlasting life." In 1552, the sentences were made subjective: "Take and eat this in remembrance that Christ died for thee, and feed on him in thy heart, by faith with thanksgiving." In 1559, the two sentences were combined, suggesting the mutual and equal importance of these two understandings of Christ's presence. This compromise continued until recent prayer book revisions.

The Jacobean Prayer Book (1604) added to the catechism the section on the sacraments and, as evidence that the sixteenth-century Reformation left its own peculiar legacy of clericalism, added a rubric requiring that baptisms should be performed by a "lawful minister." Early practice had always provided for lay baptisms in emergencies. This rubric, of course, has not persisted.

The revision of 1662 made a great number of small changes, modernizing language extensively and making clear directions for the conduct of services. In view of the themes being traced in this chapter, perhaps its most significant change was the introduction of a rubric cautiously allowing the offering of bread and wine: "And when there is a communion, the Priest shall *then* place upon the Table so much Bread and Wine as he shall think sufficient" (emphasis added). Henceforth this action would no longer be done before the service.

The book of 1662 is the first revision of the Prayer Book to appear after the publication of the King James Version of the Bible. Earlier versions of the Prayer Book used the Great Bible for epistles, gospels, and the psalter. In the book of 1662 epistles and gospels appear in the King James translation. The psalter of the Great Bible, the work of Miles Coverdale, was retained in the 1662 book, however, and has been kept in subsequent revisions. It is the basis of the version in the current Prayer Book. Anglican worship has clung to the Coverdale translation of the psalms because of its rhythmic cadences and vivid imagery.

A commission was appointed to review the 1662 Book of Common Prayer when William and Mary became king and queen of England in 1689. In view of the previous history of the Prayer Book, such a review would have been quite natural in connection with a new political settlement. This attempt miscarried, however, and since then, the book of 1662 has been simply reprinted at the beginning of each subsequent reign without any change except for the name of the new monarch.

In the 1920s the Church of England made a further attempt to revise its Prayer Book, at the same time that other churches of the Anglican communion, including the American church, were revising theirs. The English Proposed Book of 1928, which needed parliamentary approval, was defeated in the House of Commons by a narrow margin. The *Prayer Book as Proposed in 1928* was published, nevertheless, and has been widely used despite the fact that Parliament never authorized it.

The stake of a national government in the liturgical provisions of an established church was considered obvious both in the Middle Ages and in the Reformation. The religious settlement in the emerging nations of northern Europe was regarded as an important factor in the spiritual welfare of a people, and therefore in their political unity and stability. The failure of the book of 1689 might be taken as a turning point in this attitude toward the church. In the eighteenth century, the role of the state in the regulation of church affairs, particularly of worship, began to be questioned. The refusal of Parliament to accept the book of 1928 evoked radical criticism of the establishment of the English church.

During the 1960s, Parliament passed several Prayer Book measures that made the process of Prayer Book revision considerably easier. The General Synod, the legislative body of the Church of England, can now legally authorize alternative forms of worship. During the 1970s, the English church, like the other churches of the Anglican communion, was involved in extensive liturgical study, the drafting of revised services, and a program of trial use.

In 1980, *The Alternative Service Book* was authorized for use in conjunction with the Book of Common Prayer (1662). In practice, in a great many parishes in England, this rather recently authorized book has completely replaced the traditional book. A new revision is authorized for use from Advent 2000.

American Revisions of the Common Prayer Book

The Church of England was at work in all thirteen of the American colonies at the time of the American Revolution. American victory left these colonial churches in disarray, without bishops and with a liturgy that included prayers for the English king.

When the hostilities ended, this offspring of the Church of England in the thirteen American colonies slowly and painfully gathered itself together for life under the new regime, which was committed to the separation of church and state. In the United States the church was to be free to make provisions for its own life without regard to the dictates of the national government.

Representatives of seven of these colonial churches met in the first General Convention, held in Philadelphia in September, 1785. This convention authorized William White, later bishop of Pennsylvania, and William Smith of Maryland, possibly together with Charles H. Warton of Delaware, to work on a revised liturgy for the American church. They produced a book later in the same year, the Proposed Book of 1785.

Samuel Seabury had already been consecrated bishop of Connecticut by Scottish bishops on Aberdeen. The English Parliament at first refused to let English bishops consecrate bishops for the American church without including an oath of allegiance to the king. Since the Scottish Episcopal Church was not established and bound by Parliament, its bishops did not fall under this prohibition. In the course of negotiating for his consecration, Seabury promised to try to secure the use of the Scottish communion service in the new American church. But he refused to go to the convention of 1785 at all, because the proposed organization for the convention did not in his view make a proper place for bishops in the structure of the church. As a consequence of his refusal, none of the New England churches sent representatives to this convention. Neither did North Carolina and Georgia, where the church was apparently too weak to respond.

The convention adjourned later in 1785, but reconvened in the fall of 1786. By this time, English bishops had secured Parliament's permission to consecrate American bishops, and three had been elected: White for Pennsylvania, Provoost for New York, and Griffith for Virginia. By this time the English bishops had had an opportunity to study the Proposed Book of 1785. They objected strongly to certain features of it.

The 1785 Proposed Book was the book of 1662 in most respects. Prayers for the king, of course, were removed, and prayers for the president of the United State substituted. Such changes occasioned no difficulty. Neither did minor changes like the substitution of two verses of Psalm 96 for the end of Psalm 95 in the Venite. (This change, effecting a positive instead of a threatening beginning for Morning Prayer, has been characteristic of subsequent American revisions until the present.) The English bishops, however, refused to accept the elimination from the 1785 Proposed Book of both the Nicene Creed in the communion service and the Athanasian Creed, which appears in the English Book as an alternative to the Apostles' Creed in Morning Prayer on certain feast days.

Consequently when the convention reconvened in the fall of 1786, with these facts before it, it did restore the Nicene Creed to the communion service (although the Apostles' Creed was retained as an alternative). It continued to reject the Athanasian Creed, although it compensated for this refusal by printing the Nicene Creed as an alternative to the Apostles' Creed at both Morning and Evening Prayer. These changes and a few others satisfied the English bishops that the current Prayer Book would be adequate. The archbishop of Canterbury, assisted by the bishop of Bath and Wells and the bishop of Peterborough, ordained White and Provoost in February, 1787. Griffith did not make the journey and was never consecrated.

A new General Convention met in 1789. One of its chief accomplishments was to authorize the first American Book of Common Prayer, based on the English book of 1662 and the Proposed Book of 1785, as revised in 1786. The convention also succeeded in unifying the New England churches with the others, and in bringing Bishop Seabury into union with White and Provoost. Among its conciliatory actions, this convention incorporated the chief features of the Scottish communion service into the American book, enabling Seabury to keep his promise to the Scottish bishops. The two most obvious contributions of the Scottish liturgy to the American rite are the introduction of Jesus' summary of the Law after the Ten Commandments and the addition to the Prayer of Consecration of the Oblation and of an explicit invocation of the Holy Spirit. Those two paragraphs are marked Oblation and Invocation in the 1928 Book, and are retained though not titled in Rite I (p. 335) of the current book:

... we, ... do celebrate and make here before thy divine Majesty, with these thy holy gifts, which we now offer unto thee, ...

... vouchsafe to bless and sanctify, with thy Word and Holy Spirit, these thy gifts and creatures of bread and wine; ...

The reappearance of the Oblation marks a significant step in recovering an explicit statement in the liturgy of what the eucharistic action is: the congregation's offering of bread and wine in thankful remembrance of all God has done for us through Christ. The Invocation of the Spirit simply brings into sharper focus material that has always been in the eucharistic prayer in English books, before the account of the Supper.

Other changes are worth noting: The Ornaments Rubric, which had been regularly included in English books after 1559 and regularly ignored, was dropped in 1789. American editions of the Prayer Book have never specified anything about vestments or the ornaments on altars, except for a bare minimum in ordination services. Among us such matters have been governed by custom and taste. For a brief period in the 1870s there were canons governing such matters, but they proved to be both unenforceable and divisive.

The book of 1789 made a number of other changes, including some modernization of language. By all odds the most significant aspect of the 1789 book was the discovery that revision did not have to be connected with political alterations in the state. The words of the Preface to the 1789 book are worth quoting:

The attention of the Church was in the first place drawn to those alterations in the Liturgy which became necessary in the prayers for our Civil Rulers, in consequence of the Revolution. ...

But while these alterations were in review before the Convention, they could not but, with gratitude to God, embrace the happy occasion which was offered to them (uninfluenced and unrestrained by any worldly authority whatsoever) to take a further review of the Public Service and to establish such other alterations and amendments therein as might be deemed expedient. (BCP, pp. 10–11)

By doing so, the American church asserted the freedom of liturgical revision from political control, as had the Episcopal Church of Scotland before it. Subsequent revisions have explored this liberty with increasing confidence.

The nineteenth century produced one revision of the American Book of Common Prayer in 1892. In the twentieth century a further revision was authorized in 1928.

Two different sets of pressures acted upon the church in the latter half of the nineteenth century to create a climate for liturgical change. One was the influence of the Catholic revival, led by Newman, Pusey, Keble, and their successors. A new appreciation of the richness of medieval liturgy developed, and with it the desire to incorporate some of its features into the Anglican worship.

The other influence was that of the changing style of life in our society. Industrialization and technical change speeded up the tempo of life. Two lengthy Sunday services, morning and evening, proved impossible to sustain. At the same time, the prevailing tolerant pluralism of American religious life encouraged a group of Episcopalians led by William Mulenberg to urge the bishops to ordain priests who would not be bound to the discipline of the Episcopal Church, and who would be free to use the Prayer Book with more flexibility than its rubrics and the canons of the church then permitted. Episcopal clergy themselves desired greater freedom in the use of the book. The greater literacy of congregations made variety more desirable and attainable since variations would not so easily exclude congregational participation and would heighten interest.

Two words, *enrichment* and *flexibility*, summarize the aims of the revision of the Prayer Book undertaken in response to these influences. The chief figure in the nineteenth-century revision, William Reed Huntington, chaired a committee that made proposals for alterations in the Prayer Book in 1883 and again in 1886. The controversial character of both the Catholic revival and the liberal proposals, however, generated a tension that made action impossible. A compromise book was finally passed in 1892. It authorized some desirable but scarcely earth-shaking changes. It added seasonal and general opening sentences at Morning and Evening Prayer to the largely penitential opening sentences provided in earlier books. It permitted the omission of the long exhortation "Dearly beloved brethren, the Scripture moveth us in sundry places . . ." at Morning Prayer on weekdays and at Evening Prayer, at any time. The traditional canticles at Evening Prayer, the Magnificat and the Nunc Dimittis, unaccountably left out in 1789, made their American debut. The Feast of the Transfiguration was added to the calendar on August 6. Many new occasional prayers enriched the book. The communion service changed only in minor ways.

Such modest changes obviously could not turn aside the forces at work. Pressure for further revision along the same lines continued until a new revision was accepted in 1928. Of its many alterations, the ones that have made the most obvious difference in our worship are the dropping of all penitential opening sentences from Daily Offices, with a compensation emphasis on the seasons of the Church Year, and a number of changes in the communion service. Except for once a month, the reading of the Ten Commandments became optional. Rubrics direct an offering of the bread and wine: "And the Priest shall then offer, and shall place upon the Holy Table the Bread and the Wine." The money offering is also placed on the table. The lengthy exhortations, one of which was required at every celebration of the Eucharist by earlier English and American books, were removed to the end of the service and required only on the First Sunday in Advent, the First Sunday in Lent, and Trinity Sunday—a rubric often honored in the breach. Several new Proper Prefaces appeared, consistent with the emphasis on the Church Year in the rest of the book, and many more occasional prayers were added.

The Convention of 1928, which authorized this book, realized that further change was inevitable. It established "a continuing Liturgical Commission" to make an ongoing study of the Prayer Book and to recommend revisions to meet the changing needs of the church. In 1940 this commission was reconstituted as the Standing Liturgical Commission. The 1979 revision is the product of its labors during the intervening years.

We must postpone a discussion of many of the specific features of this current book for subsequent chapters. Three general features, however, can be mentioned, for they bring this survey of English and American Prayer Books to a logical conclusion: its ecumenical features, the new stress on lay participation in worship, and the increased adequacy of the liturgical provisions of the book to proclaim the Gospel.

The ecumenical dimensions of the current Prayer Book are many and plain. Liturgical texts used by a number of English-speaking denominations are given in the translation prepared by an international and interdenominational group, the International Consultation on English Texts: the Lord's Prayer, the creeds, the hymns of the Eucharist (Kyrie, Gloria in excelsis, Sanctus, Benedictus, and Agnus Dei), and several canticles. Thus the fact that liturgical revision and renewal go on in most of the churches of Western Christendom does not have to result in a new Tower of Babel. The main service lectionary, the schedule of lessons to be read on Sundays and holy days, is also an ecumenical production, shared in large measure by the major Christian families: Roman Catholic, Lutheran, Reformed, and Methodist, as well as Anglican. One of the alternate eucharistic prayers in the current book, Prayer D (pp. 372–376), is the product of an American interdenominational committee, including Roman Catholic, Lutheran, Presbyterian, Methodist, and United Church of Christ scholars. Baptism has been treated along Eastern Orthodox lines, as we shall see; one of the Prayers of the People is virtually a translation of the intercessions of the Eastern Orthodox Liturgy of St. John Chrysostom; and some of the new prayers and anthems in the burial service are based on Orthodox models.

As far as lay participation goes, each service is now prefaced by a page of suggestions ("Concerning the Service"), which specifies the parts of the liturgy appropriately done by bishop, priest, deacon, and lay person. Thus the full liturgy of the church in all its orders has been made as explicit as possible, to correspond to the ministry of the church in the world in all its orders. At the Eucharist, for example, the pertinent paragraphs begin:

> At all celebrations of the liturgy, it is fitting that the principal celebrant, whether bishop or priest, be assisted by other priests, and by deacons and lay persons. (p. 322)

The following paragraphs describe the appropriate roles of other priests, deacons, and laity. These provisions represent a new note in Anglican liturgical practice. They make it possible, however, to actualize dimensions of Prayer Book worship already present at the first.

The increased adequacy of the services to proclaim the Gospel is achieved by the amplitude of Scripture that is read: at the Eucharist, three lessons on a three-year cycle, and at the Daily Offices a two-year cycle, cover the Scripture more thoroughly than earlier lectionaries. Sermons have become a main part of the eucharistic celebration, and the Proper Liturgies for Special Days—Ash Wednesday, Palm Sunday, Maundy Thursday, Good Friday, and the Great Vigil of Easter—provide a dramatic and eloquent presentation of the Paschal mystery, the death and resurrection of Christ, which is new to Anglican books.

PART THREE

Christian Initiation: Baptism and Confirmation

8

Holy Baptism

Christian life begins with baptism, a ritual immersion in water "in the Name of the Father, and of the Son, and of the Holy Spirit." This chapter is an attempt to understand Christian baptism and its relationship to our life in Christ. Our account starts in the New Testament, at "the beginning of the gospel of Jesus Christ, the Son of God" (Mk. 1:1).

A large crowd had gathered on the banks of the Jordan. John the Baptizer, a strange man wearing only the skin of a camel, stood before the people and called them to repent of their sins. The sign of repentance was to be baptism, a washing in the waters of the river as they confessed their transgressions. Moreover, another baptizer was coming, he promised, who would baptize in a different way: "I have baptized you with water; but he will baptize you with the Holy Spirit" (Mk. 1:8).

The Baptism of John

What led John to this extraordinary proclamation? What are the origins of baptism? Nothing in the Old Testament corresponds to this rite. Yet baptism became the way in which a Gentile convert entered the Jewish community. Orthodox Jews still practice it. St. Paul must have known about this Jewish baptism when he wrote to the Corinthians,

> I want you to know, brethren, that our fathers were all under the cloud, and all passed through the sea, and all were baptized into Moses in the cloud and in the sea. (1 Cor. 10:1–2)

There is nothing Christian in this reference.

The beginning of Jewish baptism is shrouded in obscurity. Two threads of meaning seem to be woven together in it. One has to do with baths for ritual purity. Israelites were held to be unclean, for example, if they touched a dead body, or if they had menstrual or seminal discharges. In order to cleanse themselves and make themselves fit for society, they had to bathe. This was entirely a ritual concern. There was no ethical dimension to it. In the Old Testament there was no baptism "for the remission of sins." The earliest references to baptism in Jewish literature emphasize ceremonial purity.

The other strand of meaning woven into Jewish baptism has to do with an expectation that was expressed by some of the later prophets, a hope they held out to discouraged Israelites in the bleak days of exile and poverty. The day would come, "the day of the Lord," when God would act decisively to establish his rule of justice and peace over the whole world. As part of this action, God would lead the people to Israel out of the lands where they lived in exile, back to the land of Canaan. There would be a new exodus, a new Passover, a new journey through the wilderness beyond Jordan, a new crossing of the Jordan, a new entrance into the Promised Land. Israel, having crossed her deep waters, would be home at last! Some of the most familiar Old Testament passages—the prophecies of Second Isaiah, for example—refer to this hope. The familiar Advent lesson—

> In the wilderness prepare the way of the LORD,
>   make straight in the desert a highway for our God . . .
> And the glory of the LORD shall be revealed,
>   and all flesh shall see it together . . .
> He will feed his flock like a shepherd,
>   he will gather the lambs in his arms,
> he will carry them in his bosom,
>   and gently lead those that are with young. (Is. 40:3,5,11)

—describes this procession of the people of Israel through the wilderness at the coming of God's kingdom.

One prophecy of Ezekiel brings the two threads together—a washing away of uncleanness on the one hand, and on the other a gathering together of the people of Israel as a prelude to the final establishment of God's rule. This passage is appointed as the Old Testament lesson for services of baptism according to the current Prayer Book.

> For I will take you from the nations, and gather you from all countries, and bring you to your own land. I will sprinkle clean water upon you and you shall be clean . . . A new heart I will give you, and a new spirit I will put within you . . . . (Ezek. 36:24–26)

When we move beyond the Old Testament into the practices of Jesus' time, we notice the emergence of baptism for converts. If Gentiles wanted to join the people of Israel and become Jews, they had to be circumcised (if male) and baptized. All the Jewish evidence indicates that the significance of baptism for converts was the washing away of the defilements of the Gentile world. It was a special case of washing to achieve ritual purity. An early rabbi is reported to have said, "If you were not baptized, you remain as unclean as if you had come away from a dead body."

But the verse of St. Paul from First Corinthians cited earlier associates baptism with the crossing of the Red Sea, with the central Jewish mystery of deliverance. It seems reasonable to think that Jewish baptism combined both meanings. If this were true, it could be said that every Jew had to participate in the Jewish mystery—the exodus from Egypt, the crossing of the Red Sea, the wandering in the wilderness, the crossing of the Jordan. Participation in that story makes one a Jew. This participation might be experienced in two ways. One could be born into it or be baptized into it. One could be part of it through the loins of one's ancestors or through a ritual washing.

The discovery of the ruins at Qumran and the Dead Sea Scrolls shed new light on our understanding of baptism. We know from excavations that life in that community was centered around a great pool, and we know from their documents that they bathed frequently for ritual purity. Even more to the point, we know that this community had settled along the banks of the Dead Sea quite explicitly to wait for the fulfillment of the prophecies of Isaiah regarding the last days. In the *Manual of Discipline*, their purpose is stated in these words:

> to go to the wilderness to prepare the way of the Lord; as it is written, "In the wilderness prepare the way of the Lord, make straight in the desert a highway for our God."[1]

The monks of Qumran lived on the banks of the Dead Sea waiting for God to appear at the head of the people to bring them one final time to the Promised Land.

Against this background, the baptism of John comes into sharper focus. We notice that John baptizes "for the remission of sins." Ethical wrongdoing is washed away by his baptism. John exhorted tax collectors who were baptized to stop their wealth. John's baptism has to do with sin, understood as moral unrighteousness.

John's baptism, moreover, was not in a pool. He made a point of baptizing in the river Jordan. It was not a baptism of Gentile converts, nor a baptism of Jews returning to Palestine; rather, it was a baptism of Jews who lived in Jerusalem and Judea. With the same expectation of the coming glory of God that the Qumran community had, quoting the same prophecy, John announced that the Jewish community *at home* had been so disobedient to God's laws that they had lost their Jewishness. They too had to come back into the land again through the waters of the Jordan, confessing their sins, in order to be cleansed of their unrighteousness. The time was short. The axe was laid to the root of the tree. Repent and be baptized. Go to the Jordan and enter the land again, renewed. Reaffirm the covenant with its demands. The Messiah would come soon. God's kingdom was at hand.

Jesus' Baptism and Ours

In the gospels Jesus' baptism is obviously understood as the fulfillment of the promise of John the Baptizer. Jesus is the one who will come to baptize with Spirit. Through him the power of God's Spirit will be revealed. He is the bringer of God's kingdom.

Even more is contained in this event. Gospel passages describe not merely the experience of Jesus, but also give the model of the experience of everyone who is related to Jesus in faith as Lord and the God who is his father and theirs.

We must ask how the development of the Christian understanding of baptism occurred. What happened to the two strands that taken together comprised Jewish baptism? First, the Red Sea-Jordan River motif: briefly, it was replaced by the cross of Christ. Baptism became a kind of death. Jesus himself spoke of his death in terms of baptism. When the disciples James and John looked to share his glory by sitting at his side, Jesus warned them that prior to that time of glory, there would be a time of suffering and death. He referred to that time as "the baptism with which I am baptized" (Mk. 10:39).

In the early church, baptism was understood as a sharing of this baptism-death that Jesus had himself foreseen as the lot of his disciples. Baptism was nothing less than a dying with Jesus. Through that death, members of the church were brought to a new life, empowered by the Spirit that God had promised.

Second, the cleansing from ritual impurity became washing for the forgiveness of sins. To enter the new life in Christ requires not ceremonial purity but ethical righteousness. The Christian believer repents and, through the water of baptism, dies to an old way of life and enters a new life of moral uprightness.

The original significance of baptism was Jewish—a participation in the Jewish mystery. The Christian church has preserved the form of that rite—washing with water—but bestowed upon it a new meaning, participation in the Christian mystery, the death and resurrection of Christ. Participation in that mystery includes the forgiveness of sins and membership in the people of God.

The baptism of Jesus is one of the few incidents in his life mentioned in all four gospels. The practice of baptizing Christians is mentioned, directly or indirectly, in most of the other New Testament books. These two facts are mutually dependent. The meaning of baptism was experienced not merely as a pattern of general religious initiation, but rather as the explicit way in which each believer was related to Christ, and through Christ to God. The significant place of the baptism of Jesus in the gospels points to it as the basis upon which the early Christian community formed its theological understanding of the meaning of Christian initiation and of Christian living. To be baptized was to be "in Christ," to be members of his body, the church, and thus to share a common way of life.

As we said, Jesus came to associate his baptism with his death. Even more inclusively we may say that his baptism signified his entire mission, which came to its culmination in his death, resurrection, and ascension. Similarly, our baptism signifies our union by faith with the mission and work of Jesus. Our baptism involves dying to a self-centered understanding of reality and being reborn to a life of self-giving grounded in Christ. Baptism is no insurance policy for salvation, but rather a commitment to a lifestyle radically different from that of the world. In the new life we are "dead to sin," as St. Paul put it. A dead person no longer sins, no longer asserts a dominant self will. What is more, the baptism-death of Christians carries the promise of new life. "For if we have been united with him in a death like his, we shall certainly be united with him in a resurrection like his . . . If we have died with Christ, we believe that we shall also live with him" (Rom. 6:5,8). The new life promised in Christ

Jesus is not merely a future reward. The baptized members of his body have already seen, embraced, and proclaimed it. Faith in God is the basis of this new life in the Spirit, and baptism is the sign of our participation in it.

In this perspective, the church is nothing less than the community of those who have received the Spirit sent by God upon those who share the Son's life. The baptism of Jesus in the gospels is thus the event that underlies the meaning of the Christian practice. For baptism *makes* a person a member of Christ and a child of God. Baptism is the radical sign of a new framework for human life, a life sustained by the power of the Spirit that is Christ's. Baptism is always a question of the relation to Christ, in and through the church. It is the most "churchly" of all liturgical activities, because it is the action that makes explicit the union of Christians with their Lord in the context of their relation to each other. For this reason, baptism has been traditionally understood as the door to all other sacramental activity. Eucharist, marriage, the anointing of the sick, penance, ordination—*all* presume the essential act of baptism, participation in the Christian mystery through membership in the church. All these other acts are the living out of the basic reality that baptism is.

Early Liturgical Patterns of Baptism

JUSTIN MARTYR

One of the earliest descriptions of the pattern by which a person was made a member of the church appears in Justin Martyr's *First Apology* (ca. A.D. 150). The pattern is at once simple and rich in its implications. The moral significance of baptism is emphasized, through reference to the candidate's intention to live according to the truth of Christianity that he has learned and now professed to believe. While fasting, the candidates pray for the forgiveness of sins, supported by the prayer and fasting of the whole community. The passage suggests that the rite of initiation implies a transformed life.

The ceremony was apparently quite simple. Justin writes:

> . . . they are reborn after the manner of rebirth by which we also were reborn: for they are washed in the water in the Name of the Father and Lord God of all things, and of our Savior Jesus Christ, and of the Holy Spirit.[2]

Essentially, that is all Justin tells us of the rite itself, except that following the baptism, the newly baptized Christians are led to the assembly, which they join in prayer and in the celebration of the Eucharist.

Despite the simplicity of this pattern nothing essential to Christian initiation is missing. Quite the contrary. The implications of this embryonic act are far-reaching and reveal an enviable balance between the sacrament itself and the preparations for it. Baptism does not stand alone. It follows upon instruction in Christian truth and a period of testing. Teaching of the Christian faith by the community and profession of it by the candidates in word and deed are prerequisites to the celebration of the baptismal liturgy.

Justin speaks of no auxiliary gestures or actions, no laying on of hands, no anointing with oil. His focus is on the central act: the pouring of water in the name of the Father, of the Son, and of the Holy Spirit. For two thousand years, this act and this formula have remained the essential parts of Christian initiation. These acts often occur within a larger and more complex liturgical framework. The meaning of the water rite has been amplified by anointings introduced from the secular customs of the ancient world and by the laying on of hands, the church's act of blessing. Water baptism is the constant, the essential rite known as Holy Baptism in the church.

HIPPOLYTUS

A more elaborate service of baptism together with the manner of preparation for it is described in the *Apostolic Tradition* of Hippolytus, written some fifty years or so later. According to this document, the normal candidates for Christian initiation were adults. Children were accepted and mentioned in such a way as to indicate that their presence raised no problems: "And first baptized the little ones . . . ."[3] Newcomers were brought before the community's teachers, who would question them concerning their reasons for coming to the faith. Members of the Christian community would accompany the inquirers and testify to their receptivity toward the word of God. Of special interest is the fact that new candidates had to state their occupations. Those who plied certain trades—for example, sculptors or painters of idols for pagan worship—had to give up their work in order to be accepted for instruction. A soldier had to promise not to kill. Prostitutes, magicians, and astrologers had to change their occupations. One recalls the ethical requirements that John the Baptist laid upon his hearers. Commitment to Christ through baptism had profound implications for one's moral life. The list of occupations is open-ended. Hippolytus was confident that the church would recognize any occupations irreconcilable with faith in Christ, "for we all have the Spirit of God."[4]

Those who passed this initial "scrutiny" were called "catechumens." Candidates remained catechumens for a three-year period of preparation for baptism. During this time, they received regular instruction, and they prayed together with their teacher. The teacher would lay hands upon them with prayer, from time to time, and dismiss them with a blessing. Since they were not baptized, they could not attend the Eucharist.

This period of preparation seems long, especially since, during a time of persecution, there was danger of arrest and death. Yet even in such situations the preparation was not shortened, since it was the time for a gradual shifting of one's center of life from the world to Christ. It involved continual testing. Those who died for their faith prior to baptism, Hippolytus tells us, were baptized in their own blood. The candidate's participation in the death of Christ through dying for Christ's sake was a more than adequate substitute for ritual participation in the death of Christ through baptism.

This rite of initiation represents a great enrichment of the pattern described by Justin. The rite of Hippolytus seems to presuppose that baptism is celebrated during the all-night vigil before the dawn of Easter. The candidates removed their clothing, as in Jewish baptism. One carried nothing of the old life over into the new. Children were baptized first, then the men, and last the women. Before they entered the water, the candidates made a final, dramatic renunciation:

> I renounce thee, Satan, and all thy servants, and all thy works.[5]

A presbyter then anointed each candidate with the "oil of exorcism," which the bishop had blessed earlier, and said, "Let every evil spirit depart from you." Each candidate then descended into the water accompanied by a deacon, who submerged the person three times, once after each section of the baptismal creed (virtually the creed we know as the Apostles' Creed in an interrogative form): "Do you believe in God the Father Almighty. . . ? Do you believe in Jesus Christ, His only Son our Lord. . . ? Do you believe in the Holy Spirit. . . ?" Each time the candidate responded "I believe." There is no other formula of baptism. The trinitarian form of the creed itself is obvious. As the candidates came out of the water, the presbyter anointed them a second time with the "oil of thanksgiving": "I anoint you with the holy oil in the name of Jesus Christ."

Then the candidates dried themselves, put on their clothes, and were next taken before the bishop, who laid his hands on them with a prayer whose translation runs,

> Lord God, who hast made them worthy to obtain remission of sins through the laver of regeneration of the Holy Spirit: send into them grace, that they may serve thee according to thy will; for thine is glory, to the Father and the Son with the Holy Spirit in the holy Church, both now and world without end. Amen.[6]

The implication of the prayer is that the coming of the Spirit is connected with the water. The petition is a prayer for grace. After the prayer the bishop took the "oil of thanksgiving" and anointed the newly baptized persons a third time saying:

> I anoint thee with holy oil in the Lord, the Father Almighty and Christ Jesus and the Holy Ghost.[7]

After all this was done the candidates could join the congregation in prayer. The kiss of peace was exchanged by the entire assembly. The liturgy continued with the Great Thanksgiving over the gifts of bread and wine, and the new members of the church received the Eucharist for the first time.

What impresses one about this rite, in spite of the complexity of details, is its basic unity. The entire liturgy is one experience without a break, the entire pattern forming the liturgy of Christian initiation. It is the enactment of the mystery of Christ, and the incorporation of new members into the common life that flowed from faith.

What do these ancient rites have to do with us? Should we not be concerned with the meaning of membership in the Body of Christ today? Of course. Yet the study and reflection of liturgical scholars, pastors, and many lay persons during the past several decades have revealed how much the medieval development of the baptismal liturgy distorted our perception of the meaning of some of the most basic aspects of the Christian faith. These ancient documents enable us to look at the practice of the church in its early development. Our purpose in such study is not merely to copy the liturgy of the early centuries. That procedure would be as artificial as to take the baptismal rite of the Middle Ages or the Reformation as normative. These early documents serve as a corrective, however, to the constant tendency to suppose that the liturgical customs we have inherited from the fairly recent past somehow have apostolic origin.

Development of the Baptismal Liturgy

It will be instructive to examine briefly the liturgical pattern of baptism as it was practiced in the Middle Ages, and then to consider the successive attempts of English and American Prayer Books to simplify the rite. We have already noticed, in chapter 6, some of the factors at work to produce the change. The rite of Hippolytus presupposed that most of the candidates would be the mature persons who had gone through extensive preparation. The medieval rite presupposed that most of the candidates would be infants, baptized within eight days of birth. This major change had an unexpected effect on the liturgy. At the beginning, preparatory sessions, with prayers, laying on of hands, exorcisms, signing with the cross, and later the giving of salt, stretched over the whole three-year period of preparation and study. These sessions came to a climax during Holy Week, when the actual baptism was performed. All of this material was eventually compressed into a disjointed series of liturgical actions, disconnected from any instruction, done immediately preceding the baptism itself. In this way, the simple service of baptism outlined by Justin Martyr acquired a complex introduction, far longer than the profession of faith and the rite of water baptism that constitute the heart of the sacrament.

Additions were made at the end of the service also. The baptized child was clothed in a white robe, for is it not written that the saints in heaven who surround the throne of God are "clad in robes of white"? A lighted candle was also given. Christians are to be "lights of the world." Both acts are useful teaching devices, but they can obscure the simple clarity of water baptism as a participating symbol of the death and resurrection of Christ.

The rite of initiation underwent an additional piece of surgery that was even more drastic. In the church at Rome, and finally in all the churches of Western Christendom, the final appearance of the candidate before the bishop was separated from the water rite and became a distinct ceremony called *confirmation*. The rite of initiation lost the splendid unity that for centuries had characterized the great public act of incorporation into the church. Such a violation of the basic integrity of the rite was possible because the understanding of initiation had become obscured by the variety of elements that now made up the rite. The accretions concealed the essential action of initiation. This division into two parts (in the West, though not in the East) betrayed a similar fragmentation of meaning.

The Anglican Rite of Initiation

Anglican Prayer Books from 1549 to the present have aimed at simplifying the liturgy of baptism. One of the basic principles of Archbishop Cranmer's work in preparing the first Book of Common Prayer was the simplification of the rites. By the time of the Reformation, all the church's liturgical rites had become highly complex as each generation added elements of one kind or another to the basic structures. Recent accretions were often held to be as important as the fundamental substance of a rite. There was little if any awareness even among the clergy that the later developments of a rite often obscured its primary meaning.

In the first Book of Common Prayer (1549) Cranmer reduced the introductory ceremonies at baptism to a single signing with the cross and a single exorcism. He moved the naming ceremony to the place that has become familiar to us, at the baptism itself. He retained three dramatic questions of renunciation and, also, the three creedal questions for professing faith. His language recognized the importance of the Red Sea crossing, the Jordan River, and John's baptism. He provided for anointing and the giving of a white baptismal garment after water baptism, but no candle.

In 1552 there were no acts at all before baptism in water, only long prayers, exhortations, and the reading of the Scripture. The three questions of renunciation were reduced to one long question, and similarly the creed was recited as one long question: "Dost thou believe in God, the Father Almighty . . . ?" As we have noted, there was a laying on of hands after water baptism, presumably in place of the anointing with oil retained in 1549. The use of oil in the 1549 baptismal rite seems strange, since even in the book of 1549 all other uses were eliminated. In 1552 no white garment was given at the end. Mention of Israel's crossing of the Red Sea and Jesus' baptism in the Jordan remain.

American Prayer Books from 1789 to 1928 unfortunately eliminate any mention of the Old Testament background of baptism, and they reduce the question about believing from the whole Apostles' Creed to simply "Dost thou believe all the articles of the Christian faith as contained in the Apostles' Creed?" (BCP 1928, p. 278). Although at the end, the officiant prays that the newly baptized ". . . Being buried with Christ in His death, may also be partaker of His resurrection," this is the sole mention of baptism as participation in the Christian mystery of Christ's death and new life. The emphasis falls almost entirely on the forgiveness of sins, just one of the two original basic threads of the meaning that were found in early Christian baptism.

As far as the integrity of the rite of baptism was concerned, Archbishop Cranmer was opposed to any suggestion that Christian baptism was incomplete and needed a supplementary rite added to it. He apparently wished to cut through the ambiguity implicit in the medieval practice of confirmation and to give the Church of England a rite of initiation that would express its full meaning in one simple rite. In the 1552 rite, after the pouring of water in the name of the Hole Trinity, Cranmer required the priest to sign the newly baptized person with the cross, saying:

> We receive this child into the congregation of Christ's flock; and do sign him with the sign of the cross, in token that hereafter he shall not be ashamed to confess the faith of Christ crucified, and manfully to fight under His banner against sin, the world, and the devil, and to continue Christ's faithful soldier and servant until his life's end. (BCP 1552, p. 129)

Although it is difficult to know with certainty what Cranmer intended by this change, the added text is, in fact, a rather typical expression of the concept of confirmation prevalent at Cranmer's time. By inserting this material into the rite of baptism, Cranmer seems to have restored the integrity of the baptismal liturgy, which had been fragmented for so long. It is true that the priest rather than the bishop performs this signing, but in Eastern Orthodox churches, priests had been designated to perform this action for centuries. At the very least, one would have to conclude that Cranmer's new service of baptism in 1552, perhaps in ways that he did not realize, reestablished the unity of the baptismal liturgy. One might even come to the conclusion that Cranmer himself was tacitly affirming that if it is appropriate to delegate part of the rite, then it is more fitting to delegate it in its integrity.

Perhaps as an expression of caution or compromise, Cranmer retained the title "confirmation" for a separate rite of mature profession of faith consequent to at least a minimum of instruction. In fact, he attached the catechism to the new rite of confirmation. Cranmer, like all the sixteenth-century reformers, was concerned about the need for some kind of basic Christian teaching for persons coming to an age of mature responsibility. Cranmer's rite of confirmation was built upon this pastoral need. This service has been retained throughout the history of Anglicanism as a separate rite, but the retention of the name "confirmation" opened the door to a division of opinion about its meaning from the beginning, as we shall see in the next chapter.

Baptism in the Current Prayer Book

When we turn, therefore, to the latest revision, we can readily see the influence of recent study of Scripture and history. The dramatic threefold questions for renunciation and profession of faith have been reintroduced. There is a new stress on the presence of the community. The whole congregation recites the creed in response to the questions; the whole congregation reviews its baptismal pledge; the whole congregation promises to support the candidates in their life in Christ. The significance of the Old Testament background of baptism is stated in the Thanksgiving over Water, and at the climax of this prayer, at the central place in the service, the meaning of baptism as dying and living with Christ is proclaimed:

> We thank you Father, for the water of Baptism. In it we are buried with Christ in his death. By it we share in his resurrection. Through it we are reborn by the Holy Spirit. (p. 306)

Provision is made for anointing with oil if desired.

The prayer of the celebrant after the baptism itself (which is similar to the prayer from the former English and American confirmation service for the sevenfold gifts of the Spirit) makes plain that, as in Hippolytus, the action of the Spirit is associated with water:

> Heavenly Father, we thank you that by water and the Holy Spirit you have bestowed upon these servants the forgiveness of sin. (p. 308)

The new rite of Holy Baptism attempts to take our entire history into account and to recognize that Anglican teaching about the nature of baptism depends on the whole development of Christian initiation in the life of the church. This long-range perspective faces us with ambiguities. There is no single, golden norm on which to model a new rite or baptism today. Around the simple act of pouring water, the church has clustered a variety of actions with a diversity of meanings. The fundamental principle underlying the rite of baptism in the current Prayer Book, however, is that "Holy Baptism is full initiation by water and the Holy Spirit into Christ's body the Church."

From New Testament times on, baptism has meant repentance, renunciation of an old way of life ("the world, the flesh, and the devil"), confession of faith in God, and a ritual participation in the death and resurrection of Christ. These meanings appear with greater or lesser clarity in every baptismal liturgy. The current Book of Common Prayer makes these elements stand in particularly bold and clear relief for our time.

A Note about Infant Baptism

Between the appearance of the *Apostolic Tradition* of Hippolytus in the third century and the development of the standardized Latin rite for Charlemagne's empire in the eighth, infant baptism replaced adult baptism as a norm. How and why this process took place is not altogether clear, but a few remarks are in order.

The New Testament neither forbids nor explicitly commends infant baptism. When Jewish converts were baptized, children were accepted with their parents. When we read in Acts that Paul baptized his jailer in Philippi "with all his family" (16:33), it seems natural to suppose that children were included. Nevertheless, the text does not say so explicitly, either here or elsewhere in the New Testament.

In any case, it probably was not New Testament precedent that influenced the baptism of infants in the early Gentile church. It was rather the high rate of infant mortality and the fear of infants dying unbaptized, as already mentioned.

In those early centuries, serious Christians put off baptism until late in life, *for it was held that sins committed after baptism could not be forgiven.* One was baptized at an early age only if death threatened. It took the church several centuries to understand that the gospel really meant that God freely pardoned sinners who repented, even after they were baptized. This realization finally undercut the tendency to put baptism off as long as possible; it also removed scruples that parents might have had about early baptism without due preparation. Bishops first encouraged infant baptism if there was any danger to life. Finally, as a protective measure, baptism was required within the first eight days after birth. This decision to require baptism at such an early age, however, was reached only after many centuries. Baptism had long been associated with the celebration of Easter, and the custom of placing the rites of initiation at the Easter Vigil was so firmly rooted in ancient Christian tradition that it could not be easily destroyed. Eventually the meaning of baptism came to be narrowly associated with cleansing from sin. The relation of baptism to the Christian mystery, to dying and rising with Christ, was obscured and virtually lost. At that point, the pressures created by high infant mortality became the dominant concern.

In view of this history, should the church continue to baptize infants? The argument for infant baptism today, of course, has nothing to do with infant mortality. It does have a great deal to do with membership in the Christian community. Citizenship in a nation offers a suggestive analogy. Americans are in no doubt that children born to citizens of this country, or born in this country to parents who are not themselves citizens, are in fact United States citizens. They are eligible for whatever benefits citizenship involves (protection in a foreign country, for example) and are responsible for whatever obligations they are able to undertake, more and more as they mature. Children *grow* into the meaning of citizenship, but they belong to the community all along.

The situation is similar with baptism into the church. Baptized children are eligible for all the benefits of belonging to the kingdom of God—love, joy, peace, forgiveness. They are responsible for whatever Christian obligations they are able to undertake, more and more as they mature. Children *grow* into the meaning of their membership in the people of God, but they belong to the community all along.

This principle has implications beyond itself. Once baptized, children belong to the church, not only in a general way, but in a particular way to the local church at worship. And when children are present at the liturgy, they must be allowed to take part in it as much as they are able. Liturgy should be designed and conducted with sensitivity to their needs and awareness of their limitations. To be sure, adults should not be ignored either, but the one Body has many members, all first-class citizens. The Spirit moves in them all. Worship must include them all. All should be able to participate in worship as they are able to participate in life.

9

Confirmation

Opinion about confirmation in the Anglican communion is divided. This division has existed from the time of the Reformation. The purpose of this chapter is to trace the development of confirmation, to set down the differences of opinion about it as objectively as possible, and to assess the provisions of the current Book of Common Prayer as a significant breakthrough in a four-hundred-year stalemate. The story begins in the New Testament.

Baptism and the Spirit in the New Testament

John baptized with water. His baptism was an enacted parable of the coming of God's kingdom. He promised that one would come in the future who would baptize with the Spirit. When Jesus was baptized by John, as he came up from the water, "immediately he saw the heavens opened and the Spirit descending upon him like a dove" (Mk. 1:10). In the case of Jesus himself, John's prediction was fulfilled. His baptism in water and the Spirit became the model for Christian baptism, which was regularly coupled with the gift of the Holy Spirit as Jesus' own baptism was. "Repent," Peter preached to the crowd on the first Pentecost, "and be baptized every one of you in the name of Jesus Christ for the forgiveness of your sins; and you shall receive the gift of the Holy Spirit" (Acts 2:38).

In the Book of Acts, one customary sign of that gift was speaking in tongues. The apostles spoke in tongues in the upper room on Pentecost; the household of Cornelius spoke in tongues (*before they were baptized!*) in Caesarea (10:46); and the disciples in Ephesus spoke in tongues after Paul laid hands on them (19:6).

To be sure there were other signs. After Saul, the persecutor of the church, had been blinded on the Damascus road by his vision of Christ, he was baptized by Ananias and given his new name, Paul, for his new life. At his baptism, he regained his sight. When Peter and John laid hands on the Samaritan disciples, great wonders took place. Simon the Magician even tried to buy the power that could produce such miracles. Paul wrote to the Corinthians that each Christian had a specific gift of the Spirit "for the common good." He knew that there were many gifts of the one Spirit, not all of them so dramatic: "to one . . . the utterance of wisdom . . . to another the utterance of knowledge . . . to another faith . . . to another gifts of healing . . . to another the working of miracles, to another prophecy" (1 Cor. 12:7–10). In these many ways, the Spirit was poured out without measure on the early church.

How did the Spirit come? The evidence is confusing. Sometimes the Spirit came after baptism, sometimes before. Sometimes we read of the laying on of hands, sometimes we do not. It would be very difficult to prove from the available descriptions of baptism in the New Testament that dipping in water was regularly followed by a laying on of hands when the Spirit was conferred. In the case of Jesus' baptism we are probably not meant to think of the outpouring of the Spirit in any way separated from his entrance into the water. These two aspects of that event may be distinguished but not separated. New Testament evidence cannot be used to justify the laying on of hands after baptism as the distinct act by which the Spirit is conveyed.

If the giving of the Spirit cannot be limited to a laying on of hands, can it be identified with an anointing, as some later traditions hold? The evidence for anointing with oil after baptism as the liturgical sign of the coming of the Spirit is also ambiguous. A case can be made, to be sure. The coming of the Spirit is described as "anointing" in an Old Testament passage used by Jesus himself to describe his ministry:

> The Spirit of the Lord is upon me, because he has anointed me to preach good news to the poor. . . . (Lk. 4:18 citing Is. 61:1)

The church acknowledged Jesus as Messiah, or Christ, which means "the Anointed One." Kings and priests of Israel were anointed with oil; Christians, "anointed ones," are described in the New Testament as "kings and priests unto God" (Rev. 1:6, KJV). It would seem reasonable, particularly in view of later developments in the baptismal rite where anointings are a prominent feature, to suppose that even in New Testament times, the baptismal liturgy included an anointing to symbolize the gift of the Spirit. There are, in fact, several possible allusions to such an anointing, as in St. Paul's word to the Corinthians.

> But it is God who establishes us with you in Christ, and has *commissioned* us. (2 Cor. 1:21; emphasis added)

The Greek word translated as *commissioned* in this verse means literally *anointed*. The King James Version so translates it. But in spite of a number of learned arguments to amplify this chain of evidence, it must be said that they constitute less that proof. It remains equally possible (in view of the Old Testament background) that this language is simply a figurative way to describe the coming of the Spirit

We can say that both the laying on of hands and the anointing with oil are naturally associated with the coming of the Spirit in the New Testament and would be available for appropriate use in baptismal liturgies. But the notion that the Spirit was conveyed only through such subsidiary rites, rather than through water, is far from the thought of the New Testament.

Additions to the Baptismal Liturgy

We have already commented on Justin Martyr's description of baptism, which mentions nothing but washing in water, and on the considerably more extensive rite in the *Apostolic Tradition* of Hippolytus. In the latter, the presbyter anoints twice, once before and once after baptism. The bishop lays his hands on each candidate also and anoints him or her with the "oil of thanksgiving."

One can only speculate about the origin of these additional ceremonies. In the Hellenistic world, bathers customarily anointed themselves with oil, much as we anoint babies. The use of oil in baptism would not have been thought extraordinary. Once it was used, of course, it invited interpretation. In Hippolytus, the oil was the "oil of exorcism" and the "oil of thanksgiving." In neither case was there any explicit connection with the Spirit. Hippolytus' contemporary, Tertullian, understood oil to be for the anointing of the Christian priesthood, following the example of Christ, the great high priest.[1] In the liturgy of the Eastern Orthodox Church, the formula for the final anointing is "The Seal of the Gift of the Holy Spirit."

Similarly the act of the laying on of hands was quite a usual gesture of blessing. It was done on numerous occasions in the New Testament and in the church thereafter. In the Hippolytus, the laying on of hands receives no interpretation at all. But in Tertullian's description of baptism, he says:

> Next follows the imposition of the hand in benediction, inviting and welcoming the Holy Spirit. . . .[2]

Neither in Tertullian nor in other liturgical texts is the action of the Spirit confined to the laying on of hands. The Spirit is understood as present and active throughout the entire rite. In fact, it is impossible to understand any Christian liturgical action as effective or powerful unless the Spirit acts through it and is apprehended as acting by faith of the church.

The Separation of Confirmation from Baptism

It is important to emphasize that the action of the Spirit pervades the entire baptismal rite, especially in view of the difficulties that arose when the presentation of the candidates to the bishop was separated from the rest. Why did this separation occur? What happened to disrupt the original unity of the initiatory rite? The chief factor at work in this case was the growth of the church during the centuries after Constantine.

In Hippolytus' time, the entire Christian population of Rome constituted a single congregation that could meet in one place. The president and chief officiant at all liturgies was the bishop. Presbyters and deacons would attend him and assist in liturgical functions. At first they had no independent liturgical role. They did not preside at the assembly.

Expansion of the church led to the division of the congregation in a city into a number of congregations, which met in separate places for the weekly liturgy.

The bishop would simply delegate one of his presbyters to act for him in the local setting. During the fourth and fifth centuries, presbyters came to be regular celebrants of the Eucharist; they also came to be celebrants of baptism, although this development proceeded more slowly because of the association of baptism with the Easter Vigil, at which the bishop presided. In most localities the bishop authorized presbyters not only to baptize with water, but also to perform the additions to the water rite, including the anointings and the laying on of hands. In the case of both Eucharist and baptism, no theological judgment was involved, simply organizational wisdom.

In the city of Rome, however, for reasons now lost, the bishop continued to reserve for himself the last part of the baptismal liturgy, the final anointing and laying on of hands. Presbyters officiated at the first part of the service, but they were instructed to bring newly baptized persons to the bishop for the completion of the rite *as soon as possible*. It was understood, however, that the sacrament of baptism was complete when the water ceremony was done. Those who were baptized in an emergency could receive the Eucharist. If they died without the bishop's blessing, they died nevertheless in the communion of the church.

In a diocese the size of Rome this condition did not impose any particular hardship. Travel to meet the bishop was not difficult. Consequently, the time between baptism by the presbyters of the city and the completion of the rite by the bishop was probably short, and the separation of the initiatory rite in to these two parts occasioned no difficulty. The practice would be regarded as a device to allow the bishop some personal contact with the individual members of his now extensive congregation.

The situation became very different, however, when this local Roman custom became the practice of the Holy Roman Empire under Charlemagne. In northern Europe, dioceses were large and travel difficult. Many bishops were officials of the empire and had little time for liturgical functions in their dioceses. Moreover, the mass conversion of barbarian tribes resulted in generations of Christian people who did not enjoy the careful preparation that Hippolytus' baptism enjoined. There was not much understanding of the need to present one's self or one's child to the bishop to be "completed" or "confirmed." The length of time between the two parts of initiation grew longer and longer.

Decisions of English diocesan church councils in the thirteenth century help us to see the futile rear-guard action fought by the church to keep the time between baptism and confirmation as short as possible. A child was to be confirmed by the age of one (Council of Worcester, 1240), by the age of three (Councils of Winchester, 1262; Exeter, 1287), by the age of five (Richard Poore of Salisbury, c. 1217), by the age of seven (Council of Durham, 1249).[3] In 1281 Archbishop Peckham complained about the "damnable negligence" which allowed large numbers of people to grow old in evil ways without seeking the grace of confirmation, and he employed the ultimate weapon to deal with the problem. A person should not be admitted to communion until confirmed.[4]

His ruling became a rubric at the end of the service of baptism according to the Sarum (Salisbury) rite; and from there it was picked up by English and American Prayer Books after 1549. It has been dropped from the current Prayer Book. One can see how the force of this provision has changed with changing circumstances. It was originally intended to encourage early confirmation. As a matter of fact, infant confirmation was practiced in England, at least occasionally, until the eve of the Reformation. Elizabeth I was baptized and confirmed at the age of three days. From the late Middle Ages on, the custom grew of delaying confirmation until a child was seven, twelve, or older. In that case, the force of the "confirmation rubric" is to exclude people from communion if they have not reached a certain age. And in a religiously pluralistic society, it has the added effect of excluding from communion those who are not Episcopalians, or members of churches where episcopal confirmation is practiced. Confirmation has become the mark of an adult Episcopalian. Many thoughtful members of our church have come to feel that both of these unintended effects are undesirable. What should be a source of strength and joy has become a barrier to fellowship.

The Divided Anglican Tradition about Confirmation

When confirmation became isolated from baptism, it could not readily be grasped as part of the baptismal liturgy. As part of the baptismal liturgy, it required no particular interpretation; it was part of the one unified action of baptism. But as a rite in itself, how was it to be understood?

The relation to baptism was not forgotten. It could even be reasonably claimed to complete baptism. It surely brought new grace to the recipient. Confirmation came to be numbered as one of the sacraments during the Middle Ages. Jesus, the argument ran, breathed on the apostles in the upper room in Jerusalem after his resurrection and filled them with the Spirit (Jn. 20:22). The apostles in turn, in some of the incidents in the Book of Acts already cited, laid hands on new disciples and communicated Spirit. Bishops, as successors to the apostles, were the designated celebrants of confirmation. Confirmation bestowed on those who received it was a special grace for the strengthening of life. "The Holy Ghost bestows at the font of the fullness of innocence; but in Confirmation, He confers an increase in grace," St. Thomas Aquinas wrote. "Man is spiritually advanced by this sacrament to a perfect age."[5] It was a sacrament of maturity. Some have even argued that confirmation is *more* important than baptism because of its association with adulthood and because bishops are its ministers.

The sixteenth-century reformers, however, cast doubt on the biblical basis of confirmation. It does indeed have tenuous roots, as we have seen. Cranmer himself, early in his episcopate, answered a questionnaire about confirmation. He argued that there was no biblical basis for the institution of confirmation by Christ, that the ability of the apostles to give the Spirit by the laying on of hands was given to them for the confirmation of God's word *at that time,* and that this power did not remain with the bishops as successors of the apostles. Therefore he concludes that "the efficacy of this sacrament is of such value, as is the prayer of the bishop made in the name of the church."[6] The Thirty-Nine Articles (1572) include confirmation as among those five "commonly called Sacraments . . . [which] are not to be counted as Sacraments of the Gospel, being such as have grown partly out of a corrupt following of the Apostles, partly are states of life allowed in the Scriptures . . ." (Article xxv). Professor Marion Hatchett has argued persuasively that in the 1552 Prayer Book *rite* of baptism, Cranmer intended to make the signing of the cross after water baptism the theological equivalent of medieval confirmation and so to restore the unity of the baptismal liturgy.[7]

In view of this negative sentiment about confirmation, it is somewhat surprising to find that even in the 1552 Book of Common Prayer, the confirmation service consists of a prayer for the sevenfold gifts of the Spirit, laying on of hands by the bishop with a prayer for special grace (Defend, O Lord, this Thy child with Thy heavenly grace . . ."), and a concluding prayer that cites apostolic precedent (". . . we make our humble supplications unto thee for these children upon whom [after the example of Thy Apostles] we have laid our hands . . ."). The service is still recognizably the end of the baptismal liturgy from the *Apostolic Tradition*, although the anointing with oil has been dropped.

In fact, the liturgy for confirmation in the book of 1549 did not substantially alter the medieval pattern. The Latin rite of confirmation is very short, and will instantly be recognized as only a slightly changed version of the end of the baptismal liturgy as recorded in the *Apostolic Tradition* of Hippolytus. The confirmands come before the bishop. He invokes the Holy Spirit, naming the "sevenfold gifts" mentioned in the Book of Isaiah (11:2–3) as he extends his hands over all of them collectively. He then anoints each one with oil on the forehead and dismisses them with a prayer that mentions the bishop as the successor of the apostles in regard to their ability to communicate the Holy Spirit. Unlike Hippolytus, the Roman prayer calls upon the Spirit to be active in this laying on of hands; but like Hippolytus, this service recognizes that the Spirit has also been operative in baptism. The Spirit moves through the whole action.

Thus the English confirmation service *could* carry the same interpretation that was laid on the medieval service. The reunification of the initiatory rite, which Cranmer may have intended to accomplish, could be and often was overlooked. By the end of the seventeenth century, Jeremy Taylor wrote that "the holy rite of confirmation is a divine ordinance, and it produces divine effects, and is ministered by divine persons that is, by those whom God both sanctified and separated to this ministration."[8] Here the late Latin theory reappears in Anglican dress.

This whole argument between those who maintain a biblical basis for confirmation as a separate sacrament and those who regard it as an addition to the baptismal liturgy has engaged Anglican theologians almost continuously for the past century. Both sides have produced works of great learning and scholarship, beginning with E. B. Pusey's *Scriptural Views of Holy Baptism* (Tract 67), which asserts the unity of baptism and confirmation, though not as a major point. In later years of the nineteenth century, A. J. Mason argued that confirmation was a separate sacrament and A. T. Wirgman opposed him; in the present generation, Geoffrey Lampe's *Seal of the Spirit* has been influential in establishing the dependent character of confirmation; Gregory Dix and Lionel Thornton oppose him.[9] It seems fair to say that this divergence of viewpoint lies deep within Anglican thought. No definitive resolution has appeared, and no easy answers are available.

Confirmation and Catechism

One feature of the initiation process in the *Apostolic Tradition* of Hippolytus has dropped out of sight in our discussion: the lengthy period of instruction which preceded admission to the Christian community. At the beginning, converts were carefully prepared to do their liturgies, both in the gathered church and in their work in the world.

This careful preparation, or *catechesis*, did not long survive after Christianity became the official religion of the empire. The mass of converts, the lack of culture among the barbarian tribes who soon thronged the church, and especially the shift to infant baptism, all worked against any period of instruction before a baptism. There were ways of teaching the rudiments of faith to the untutored men and women of Western Europe, but any connection between this process and the rite in initiation was lost.

This situation prevailed, and it lasted until the thirteenth century. In the thirteenth century, in connection with the difficulty encountered in securing early confirmation, the church began in some places to change its mind about its value. Instead of saying that confirmation should be administered *before* the child reached the age of seven, the church began to insist that confirmation should not be administered until the child is at least seven. During those seven years, the child should learn the rudiments of faith: the Creed, the Lord's Prayer, and the Ave Maria.

By the time of the Reformation, this shift had proceeded a long way; in the sixteenth century, it became complete among both Protestants and Catholics. The Council of Trent established seven as the age for confirmation among the Roman Catholics. Among Protestants the age was not determined so precisely, but was commonly set at "years of discretion." Even Calvin, who completely rejected confirmation as a rite, claimed that bishops in the early church used to examine young persons in the catechism to insure that they learned what was necessary for baptism. After this examination, Calvin claimed, bishops would lay hands on the young people in blessing.[10]

There seems to be no historical foundation for Calvin's claim. Nevertheless it was influential. Most Protestant churches have come to provide a ceremony like the one Calvin described to celebrate a person's mature affirmation of baptismal vows after a more or less extensive period of instruction in the elements of Christianity. In the first part of the confirmation service, the first rubric runs,

> . . . it is thought good that none hereafter shall be confirmed, but such as can say in their mother tongue the articles of faith, the Lord's Prayer, and the x commandments. And can also answer to such questions of this short catechism as the Bishop (or such as he shall appoint) shall by his discretion appose them in.[11]

The catechism, of course, had nothing to do with confirmation at the beginning. But catechesis once had a great deal to do with baptism, and it is plainly useful and profitable that young people should receive instruction. When they are baptized as infants, they should at some point make their own and publicly acknowledge the faith of the community in which they were raised. The connection between confirmation and catechizes, in other words, did not begin in the ancient church. Yet there are good things about that connection that ought to be preserved.

Baptism and Confirmation in the Current Prayer Book

BACKGROUND

To all the confusion and complexity sketched in the previous paragraphs, the twentieth century has added more. In the first place, the theological issue has become acute. Somehow it has become an Episcopal commonplace that confirmation is the rite that "bestows the Spirit." By baptism one joins the church. By confirmation one receives the Spirit. The thrust of much popular opinion seems to be in this direction. As we have seen, the church's teaching gives little support to this point of view. Baptism apart from the Spirit is unintelligible, as is every liturgical action. According to the rites themselves, the Spirit works in both baptism and confirmation, in appropriate ways. Yet if confirmation does not represent the gift of the Spirit once and for all, but rather represents a strengthening power to bring a person to fuller humanity, why should it be administered only once? Those who have received confirmation are not perfect in any obvious sense. If we may receive a further gift of the Spirit *once* after baptism why not on a number of occasions when we especially need God's grace?

Should not confirmation be rethought, perhaps as the rite of penance was rethought early in the life of the church? In the third century, forgiveness of sins could be received only once after baptism. As the church experienced the pastoral implications of that decision and opened itself more fully to the gospel of Christ, according to which a penitent sinner can always receive God's forgiveness, the church came to understand that forgiveness must be offered without stint, even after baptism. Similarly, if we try to say that the strengthening gifts of God's grace are available only once after baptism, and then hear the Gospel, perhaps we can learn that we must not limit the strengthening gifts of God's Spirit at all. They are available, even after confirmation, without stint.

Our liturgy should express that availability. The Reconciliation of a Penitent (p. 447) expresses the continued accessibility of forgiveness. Do we not need a rite to express the continued accessibility of God's grace and power?

In addition to this *theological* development, *practical* considerations have begun to force a reconsideration of confirmation. The way in which Episcopalians are being prepared for their life in the church apparently does not produce committed members. It has been estimated that at least 50 percent of those confirmed drop out of active church membership. Practices vary widely. Confusion abounds: about the age when confirmation is advisable, about what preparation is desirable, about what confirmation means.[12] Although the causes that lie behind this situation are deep-seated and complex, part of the solution may be greater clarity and consistency about confirmation. Can a more effective procedure be devised?

Moreover, the ecumenical implications of the present practice of confirmation seem undesirable to some. When confirmation is presented to a person baptized in another denomination as "the completion of baptism," and is required for membership in the Episcopal Church, doubt is cast on the adequacy of initiatory rites in other churches, even if they practice baptism with water in the name of the Trinity.

For all these reasons, many thoughtful Episcopalians were dissatisfied with baptism and confirmation previously practiced in our church. The current rite may represent a means to change our ways and clarify our thoughts. On the other hand, it may simply represent the perpetuation in a slightly different form of the ambiguity about confirmation that has existed in Anglicanism from the beginning. Only time will tell.

TWO INTERPRETATIONS

The fact is that the rites of baptism and confirmation in the current book can be understood in two quite different ways.

1. According to the first, one notices that the prayer for the sevenfold gifts of the Spirit, a formula for laying on of hands by the celebrant, and a welcome into the church have been added at the end of the baptismal rite, after the water rite. This material is a slightly modified form of the old confirmation service, which earlier Anglican Prayer Books reserve to the bishop. One might conclude that baptism has been restored to the full form that it had in Hippolytus, and that it still has in Eastern Orthodox liturgies. The celebrant of this fuller rite may be a priest or a bishop, as in Eastern Orthodoxy, although the bishop is expected to preside if present. On this showing, our rite of initiation has been reunited at last, after its millennium-long fragmentation. The authors of this book hold this view of the current baptismal rite.

The rubric that required confirmation for admission to communion no longer appears. It is no longer necessary. The service of baptism is not only complete, but as ample as it has ever been in history. There is no need to insist on early confirmations.

There is, to be sure, a service called "Confirmation." Baptized persons are expected to present themselves for it "when they are ready and duly prepared, to make a mature public affirmation of their faith and commitment to the responsibilities of their Baptism" (p. 412). Confirmation preserves the connection with catechizes that we found to be desirable. It has sacramental power, being an outward and visible sign of an inward and spiritual grace. The laying on of hands symbolizes and communicates the strengthening power of God's Spirit on the occasion when persons assume for themselves the vows made in their name by their sponsors at baptism, after a period of instruction and study about the meaning of those vows.

Significant additions appear in the new confirmation rite. Forms have been added "For Reception" of new members and "For the Reaffirmation of Baptismal Vows." These are coordinate elements of the new service of confirmation. Thus, the strengthening gifts of God's grace are available also when a person joins the Episcopal family or when baptized and confirmed Episcopalians especially need the power of the Spirit at a time of particular significance in their lives.

The action of the bishop in performing these added rites is not specified. It may be the laying on of hands in blessing. In the opinion of the authors of this book, such a gesture is highly appropriate. New members would come to the bishop and receive recognition of their new membership by the laying on of hands, not because their former baptism was incomplete, nor because this church is unable to recognize the mature profession of faith that they made when they belonged to a different denomination, but as a matter of discipline. One joins the Episcopal Church by reaffirming baptismal vows and receiving episcopal laying on of hands. Reception into our tradition represents an important turning point in life and should be marked by a new accession of the grace of God and direct personal contact with one's bishop.

By the same token, an already confirmed Episcopalian might come to the bishop and receive the laying on of hands, not because a prior confirmation had not been effective, but because prayer by the bishop and the laying on of hands for a new accession of the strengthening power of the Spirit is appropriate at every important turning point in life.

2. The foregoing interpretation constitutes one way of understanding the confirmation service in the current Prayer Book. But the rite is capable of a second, quite different reading. According to this second view, the initiatory rite of the current book is not significantly different from that of prior Anglican Prayer Books.

There is a service of baptism with water; in the current book this service concludes with the laying on of hands and possible anointing by a presbyter, or even by a bishop if present. But from the earliest times there has been a concluding ceremony after the water baptism *and before the candidate comes to the bishop for the conclusion of the service.* One may interpret the end of the baptismal rite in the current book as corresponding to the anointing with the oil of thanksgiving by the presbyter in Hippolytus.

The rite of confirmation appears in the current book, according to this second view, as it has for a thousand years in the Catholic churches of Western Christendom, as the act of the bishop. He administers it in the words that have been associated with confirmation in Anglican Prayer Books since 1552: "Defend, O Lord, this thy child with thy heavenly grace . . ." Thus this rite is, as before, the proper and necessary completion of the initiatory rite. It does not "give the Spirit" as if baptism did not; but it does represent the decisive gift of the Spirit for a person's maturity, enabling further growth into the full stature of one's humanity in Christ.

The added features of the confirmation service—Reception of new members and Reaffirmation of Baptismal Vows—are indeed useful liturgical expressions of the continued availability of the Spirit, but they are not coordinate with confirmation. New Episcopalians would be confirmed unless they come from the Roman Catholic or Orthodox churches in which case they should be *received*. Episcopalians may *reaffirm their baptismal vows*. Confirmation is always signified by the laying on of hands. In the other two cases, other gestures could be used.

These two understandings of confirmation are both reasonable. They represent a new version of the age-old division in Anglicanism. They diverge no more widely than the earlier set of opinions and perhaps not so far. These two different practices among us will not result in any more uncertainty that we face at present. In both cases every person who grows to an age of discretion within the Episcopal Church will be confirmed, and every person who joins our fellowship from another denomination will receive episcopal laying on of hands, either in confirmation, according to the second view, or in the reception of new members according to the first.

INFANT COMMUNION

The elimination of the "confirmation rubric" is a great gain. Baptism is now the one sufficient condition for admission to the Eucharist. One must be admitted to the Christian mystery through the participating symbol of baptism before one can be nourished by the Christian mystery through the participating symbol of the Eucharist. No other considerations regarding admission to communion are as decisive.

This situation will require a decision regarding the appropriate time to admit a child to the Eucharist. The authors of this book are convinced that everything points to the earliest possible time for admission. The arguments *against* early communion stand equally as arguments against infant baptism. The arguments *for* infant baptism are arguments for communion of the youngest members of the church. Just as an infant is fed by its natural family from the beginning, so an infant member of the church should be fed by the family of God from the beginning. Practical considerations might conceivably favor some delay, just as practical considerations point to a delay in bringing younger children to the table for family meals. Children are surely to be included with joy as soon as possible, however, and the rest of the family gladly makes some adjustments to their capabilities.

In any case, is it not anomalous that children should be admitted to hearing the first part of the service, the lessons and the sermon, which require some rational understanding—a great deal, in the case of some biblical passages—and should then be sent out for the Eucharist, at least some of whose levels of meaning—love and nature—can be grasped experientially even by an infant in arms?

To be sure, it is important to understand Christian faith and Christian ethical teaching as profoundly as one can. Confirmation must be encouraged as the sign that the process of learning has begun. But understanding is never complete this side of heaven.

Meanwhile, would it not be impossible to specify exactly how much knowledge one must have in order to participate in the mysteries of Christ? The clearest message of the Gospel is that God freely gives love and care and forgiveness to all who come simply and openly, as little children.

PART FOUR

Regular Services: Daily Offices, Holy Eucharist

Introduction

In this section we turn our attention to the services of Morning and Evening Prayer and the Holy Eucharist, "the regular services, appointed for worship in this Church" (BCP, p. 13). These are the services with which most Episcopalians are most familiar. Consequently, they inevitably color what most of us have in mind when we think of the liturgy of the church.

The chief feature of the Daily Offices and of the first part of the Eucharist (subtitled in the current book "The Proclamation of the Word of God") is the reading of the Bible. This section on the regular services begins, therefore, with two introductory chapters, one on "The Word of God and the Bible" (Chapter 10) and the other on "The Word of God in the Liturgy" (Chapter 11). The next two chapters cover "Morning and Evening Prayer in Today's Church" (Chapter 12) and "The Holy Eucharist (I): The Proclamation of the Word of God" (Chapter 13).

Chapter 14, "The Holy Eucharist (II): The Holy Communion," is a study of the sacramental aspect of this service. It includes a brief survey of some of the most important ways in which the Eucharist has been understood in the past and at present, and ends with a careful consideration of the eucharistic prayers in the current Prayer Book, which express the faith and devotion of our church.

Chapter 15, "The Holy Eucharist (III): Theories About the Eucharist," is a brief review of eucharistic theology.

Chapter 16, "The Christian Calendar," examines the development and meaning of the celebrations of the liturgical calendar.

10

The Word of God and the Bible

Immediately after his baptism by John, Jesus was driven into the wilderness where he was tempted by Satan (Mk. 1:12). Satan urged him to turn stones to bread, so that he could break his forty-day fast. "If you are the Son of God," he said, "command these stones to become loaves of bread." Jesus refused. "It is written, 'Man shall not live by bread alone, but by every word that proceeds from the mouth of God'" (Mt. 4:3–4; Lk. 4:3–4). In so spurning this temptation, Jesus not only appealed to the word of God, he also used the same words that Moses had spoken centuries before during Israel's time of testing in the wilderness. Moses too exhorted his people to live by every word that came from the mouth of the Lord (Dt. 8:3). In fact, the Word of God has been one of the most powerful resources for living available to both Jews and Christians down through the centuries. The Word of God comes to us in hearing and reading the Bible, in preaching, and through many other ways in which God speaks to us. The Word was made flesh in Jesus of Nazareth. It is continually defined and clarified for us by the words of Holy Scripture.

Words and the Word

It may seem that such an emphasis on words is quite disproportionate. In days drenched with words, we may find them a helplessly inadequate vehicle to express our relationship to God. And yet, what is the alternative?

WORDS AS SYMBOLS

We must resume the discussion of the words as symbols that began in chapter 3. There we pointed out that most words are arbitrary symbols. There is no inner, necessary connection between the word *table*, for example, and the object with legs and a flat surface that the word describes. Some words, to be sure, are not merely arbitrary symbols. Words that describe sounds frequently make the sound they describe. Words like *moo, baa, chirp, tintinnabulate,* are said to be onomatopoetic. There is a close relationship between such words and their meaning. They *are* what they describe.

Even more significantly for our purposes, words not only name objects, whether arbitrarily or in this latter, more immediate sense. Words also express what is in our hearts and minds. Great poets use words to express meaning in such a wonderful way that it is difficult to imagine that the same idea or emotion could be expressed otherwise.

In some such expressive sense as this, Jesus has been called the Word of God. His living and dying and his living beyond death constitute for Christians a true *expression* of who God is. The connection between Jesus and God is so wonderfully direct and unqualified that Christians could not imagine a more adequate way to speak of God. J. B. Phillips renders the first verse of the Fourth Gospel, traditionally translated, "In the beginning was the Word," with the phrase, "At the beginning, God expressed himself."[1] This reading conveys vividly what we are trying to say about words and the Word of God. Just as carefully chosen words may gather what is within us and transmit that content into the heart and mind of another, so God's Word reveals God himself to those who "hear" it.

THREE FORMS OF THE WORD OF GOD

Christians believe that God was revealed decisively through Jesus of Nazareth, who, for us, is the "Word made flesh" (Jn. 1:14). He is the primary Word of God for us, the Word of God in its *first* form. We also believe that this revelation was not a flash of lightning, breaking the prevailing darkness for only the length of his lifetime. The God who is revealed in Christ did "not leave himself without witnesses" (Acts 14:17). God spoke "in many and various ways . . . to our fathers by the prophets" (Heb. 1:1). God revealed himself in the generations before Jesus by giving his word to the prophets. "The word of the Lord came to me . . ." is a standard formula for the introduction of prophetic oracles in the Old Testament.[2] God is said to have written the words of the Ten Commandments on stone tablets brought by Moses to Mount Sinai (Ex. 34:1).

The Bible is a collection of words that have been received by the community of faith as the word of God. It is a *record* of God's revealing of himself to his people. But it is more than a record. In returning to the Bible, God's people keep on hearing God's word spoken through it. Because God inspired the authors of the biblical words to write in the first place, and because God still speaks to us through the Bible when our ears are open to hear, we may say that the Scriptures are the Word of God, a *second* form.

Moreover, God has not stopped revealing himself. God's self-giving was most perfectly expressed in Christ Jesus, our Lord. But that same giving goes on, and God continues to be shown forth in the words as well as in the deeds of human beings whom God commissions to act and speak. One form of the proclamation of that word is preaching, although proclamation has many other forms as well. Proclamation is a *third* form of the Word of God.

The Word of God has been a central idea in Christian theology. Many theologians would agree that the Word is a synonym for God as revealed or for God as made manifest. These three forms of the Word of God are of particular significance: the Word incarnate in Jesus Christ, who is the form of the Word by which all other forms must be judged; the written Word, the Scripture, which communicates to us all that we know about the incarnate Word; and the preached or proclaimed Word, which asserts the contemporary power and meaning of the incarnate Word.[3]

It is important to devote so much attention to the relation between the Bible and preaching on the one hand and Jesus Christ on the other in order to avoid two pitfalls in the succeeding pages. One mistake would be to identify the Bible as the Word of God without qualification. We are not likely to make the same mistake about preaching! Against this point of view we should want to say that Jesus is the unique Word of God. He is the standard by which every other word is judged, whether in Scripture or outside Scripture. The words that do not communicate the quality of love that Jesus revealed cannot be the word of God to us. Those passages of the Old Testament that breathe violence and hate cannot be the word of God to us. One thinks of phrases like "the LORD is a man of war" (Ex. 15.3), or of stories like the slaughter of the Shechemites by Jacob, Simeon, and Levi (Gen. 34). In some passages of the New Testament, moralism almost conquers forgiveness. The Letter of Jude speaks of "hating even the garment spotted by the flesh" (v. 23). Such words, when measured by Christ, seem to fall short of the Word of God. Once they were undoubtedly the Word of God to someone, and under other circumstances, perhaps hard to imagine, may be the Word of God again. All preaching lies under the judgment of Christ's truth and love. Jesus alone is the Word of God in its fullness.

On the other hand, apart from some words written and proclaimed, it is difficult to see how we could know Christ at all, or make him known. And if there are many occasions when human words fail abysmally to express and communicate the wonder and mystery of God's presence, nevertheless, in passages like St. Paul's hymn to love in the thirteenth chapter of First Corinthians, in the Song of the Suffering Servant in the fifty-third chapter of Isaiah, in the four Gospel accounts of our Lord's crucifixion and resurrection, we surely come close to an expression of ultimate reality. And every generation has produced its preachers who know how to speak the words of life to their own generation. To those words a throng usually finds its way.

What Is the Bible?

Since the Bible is used so extensively in worship, we must consider here some basic aspects of its origin, teaching, and interpretation.

THE INSPIRATION OF THE BIBLE

It is often said that the Bible is an inspired book, meaning that its words are evoked by God's Holy Spirit. The writers or speakers of both the Old and New Testaments were moved by God to speak or write as they did.

Many people who write poetry or music, who paint, or who engage in some other creative activity know the experience of being moved or "inspired" from a source beyond themselves. The experience of the biblical writers was presumably analogous. Their own finite, personal faculties were heightened, and they were able to say and do things that under normal circumstances would have been impossible. Preachers who presume to preach "in the name of the Father, and of the Son, and of the Holy Spirit" are from time to time similarly moved. Spirit impinges upon spirit, Person upon person. In this respect, the influence of God's Spirit is not altogether unlike that of human spirits upon us. One might think of the inspiration of the Holy Spirit in some such way as this.

In the early church and until about two hundred years ago, the inspiration of the Bible was conceived rather differently. It was held that divine Spirit and human spirit could not occupy the same "place." When God's Spirit came, the human spirit left—as when the sun rises the moon disappears. An ancient author described the phenomenon of inspiration in that figure of speech. Or in another figure, God played upon the inspired writer or speaker as a musician upon his instrument (Justin Martyr, ca. 150). Or, in a more extreme figure of speech, the biblical author was a "penman of the Holy Ghost."

From this point of view, the words of the biblical text were directly and absolutely the words of God. They were not only inspired words, but considering their source, had to be inerrant in content. It was not so much that these words expressed the mystery of God. They unequivocally *were* the mystery of God. This "absolute" point of view still persists among Orthodox Jews with respect to the Old Testament, among Muslims with respect to the Quran, and among some conservative Christian groups with respect to the whole Bible.

With the rise of a scientific understanding of natural processes and with the growth of knowledge about the culture and history of Israel, it has been widely acknowledged that some things mentioned in the Bible are mistaken. The words are not inerrant. The sun almost certainly did not stand still for a whole day while Joshua battled the Amorites (Jos. 10:13). The question then arises: In what sense can the Bible be inspired? A frequently given answer runs like this: if one understands that God accepts our human limitations and frailties, and reveals himself *to* human beings and *through* them in spite of such shortcomings, one can continue to speak of the inspiration of the biblical writers despite the appearance of factual errors in their work. The Episcopal Church has never officially accepted *any* particular doctrine of inspiration. Most Episcopalians probably hold to the inspiration of Scripture in this newer sense, rather than in the absolute sense of the earlier teachings on the subject.

But can one believe in the inspiration of the Bible in any sense? It is clear that the mere reading of the Bible is not sufficient to convince people that it is inspired. Otherwise the world would have been converted to Christianity a long time ago. How does one come to the conclusion that the Old and New Testament are inspired writing? An ancient and consistent tradition in the church has understood that this conviction is itself the work of God the Spirit, influencing the hearts and minds of hearers or readers of the Bible. John Calvin crystallized this teaching when he said that the "internal testimony of the Holy Spirit" (*internum testimium spiritus sancti*) was necessary to recognize the Bible as God's Word. This phrase expresses a widely shared conviction: namely, that we do not through the exercise of our unaided human faculties recognize that

God has inspired the Scriptures. It is the work of God's Spirit "bearing witness with our spirit" (Rom. 8:16) by which we acknowledge the Bible to be the Word of God. Similarly, it was by God's Spirit that the prophets and apostles wrote the Word of God in the first place. The Spirit interprets "spiritual truths to those who possess the Spirit" (1 Cor. 2:13).

WHY JUST THESE BOOKS?

A second question that is bound to be asked about the Bible has to do with the selection of the books that comprise it. Why should there be just these books and no others? The question often arises in connection with worship. Why should no other books be read as Scripture in the course of the liturgy? For the Old Testament the answer to the question is different than for the New, although in each case a community decision is involved.

Rabbis representing the scattered Jewish community of the Hellenistic world met at Jamnia in A.D. 90 to regulate and order the life of the far-flung community. It was the Council of Jamnia that determined that the thirty-nine books of our present-day Old Testament were in truth inspired by the Spirit and should be regarded as sacred Scripture. Nevertheless, according to Jewish belief, God's full self-disclosure lies still in the future. The Messiah is yet to come. The revelation recorded in Scripture is incomplete, and the *canon*, or list of scriptural books, *is in principle incomplete*. In fact, from Jamnia until the present, no book has been added. Yet the possibility exists.

In the Christian community, the canon of the New Testament developed differently. Like the Old Testament, the collection of books developed over a long period of time, and when the official list was finally adopted by church councils, the adoption was the recognition of a process selection that had already occurred in the life of the church largely through the use of these books in the liturgy. In this case, the books selected bear witness to Jesus of Nazareth, whom we believe to be the Messiah. He was the full disclosure of God. The choice of the canonical books reflects the fact that the church has found in them the necessary and sufficient witness to Jesus of Nazareth as the Christ. *The canon is in principle closed.*

Why should the closing of the canon be insisted upon in the case of the New Testament? The answer depends on the conviction of the Christian church that in Jesus of Nazareth, God has been fully and decisively revealed. The Word was not only God but was God made flesh; for "in him all the fulness of God was pleased to dwell" (Col. 1:19). The list of New Testament books is closed around those documents that were found, in the experience of the ancient church, to bear adequate testimony to him. Some that were discarded during the early years are still known, the so-called apocryphal gospels and Acts. The difference in vividness and sobriety between apocryphal and canonical books is obvious almost on inspection. This canonical list of New Testament books has become normative. That is, it is the list by which all other writing about Christ is to be judged. If one were seriously to propose the addition of a current book to the

New Testament, judgment would have to be made on the basis of our knowledge of Christ mediated by the existing books. Either it would be found in agreement with existing knowledge, in which case there would be no point in adding it, or it would in some respect go beyond existing knowledge. In this latter case, such new knowledge might be historically significant; but if it were thought to be "necessary for salvation," it would imply that the church of the past had been deficient in saving knowledge. It would mean that the account of salvation now to be accepted was different from what Christians had formally taught and believed. In effect, a new church, a new community of faith, would have been created. *To change the canon of the New Testament is, de facto, to change the church.*

The Christian church has not maintained the limits of the Old Testament with the same tenacity with which they have maintained the limits of the new. At the beginning, the church used a collection of Old Testament writings in Greek that was assembled before the Council of Jamnia had purged them. The books in this Greek Old Testament that were not taken into the Jewish canon are called the *Apocrypha* (the "hidden" or "secret" writings). St. Jerome in the fifth century regarded them with disfavor, but could not persuade the church of his day to drop them. For various reasons, they were dropped by Reformed, Presbyterian, and other Protestant churches at the time of the sixteenth-century Reformation. Lutherans and Anglicans have printed them between the Old Testament and the New.

Of the canonical books of both testaments, Article VI of the Articles of Religion states,

> Holy Scripture containeth all things necessary to salvation: so that whatsoever is not read therein, nor may be proved thereby, is not to be required of any man, that it should be believed as an article of the Faith, or be thought requisite or necessary to salvation. (BCP, p. 868)

Of the Apocrypha, however, it asserts,

> And the other Books (as Hierome [Jerome] saith) the Church doth read for example of life and instruction of manners; but yet it doth not apply them to establish any doctrine. . . . (BCP, p. 868)

The two questions about the Bible that we have now considered—the inspiration of the several books and the limits of the canon—are quite different questions. The church and the canon of Scripture depend on each other. The church decides the canon; the canon constitutes the church. To change the canon is to change the church. On the other hand, it is quite possible to recognize that books outside the canon might be inspired by the Spirit of God. Such a judgment was once widely made about the so-called Apostolic Fathers' second-century writings, some of which are now known to antedate some of the New Testament books.[5] And there is no reason why such judgment might not be made, by individuals if not by the church itself, about later books found to be significant in living the Christian life: Dag Hammarskjold's *Markings*, Bonhoeffer's *Letters and Papers from Prison*, Auden's *For the Time Being*, to risk a few nominations. Such books ought not to be read in the liturgy as if they were Scripture, but reading passages from them might very well have the same status as a sermon.

Is the Bible Still Important?

One may still want to ask whether the reading of the Bible, either in the liturgy or as part of our personal devotions, has any meaning. It was produced in a culture very different from ours. It is often hard to understand. Do most of us have to pay attention to it? Can't we turn it over to professional scholars and expert interpreters, and let them tell us what it has to say?

One must acknowledge the legitimacy and force of the questions. When so many things in our world clamor for our attention and need it so badly, what right does the Bible have to claim such a preeminent place, such a disproportionate amount of effort? In a time when there were not many books, perhaps this one book might deserve special notice. But amid millions of published volumes, why this one? And since many devoted scholars have dedicated their lives to establish its text, writing the history of its times, and understanding the message it communicates, why can we not simply rely on their word?

An answer to these questions might be framed around a verse from the Letter to the Ephesians that speaks of the "power to comprehend with all the saints what is the breadth and length and height and depth" (3:18). According to the text it is God the Spirit who gives us this power. But the dimensions are left undefined. In connection with the Bible, we might try to specify what they are.

The Bible establishes the breadth of the Christian community. All Christians have the Bible in common. The Bible, and the two gospel sacraments of initiation and nurture, baptism and Eucharist, are the things, perhaps the only things, that Christians in all times and in all places share. The Bible is a major part of our inheritance.

The Bible gives us a glimpse into the length of the human story. It contains not only the story of what God has done for us in Christ, but also the long, tortuous development of humanity from its beginnings. Some of the psalms and certain parts of the historical books of the Old Testament seem to be older than the Israelite nation itself. Our biblical roots reach back into some of the earliest expressions of human existence. In it Christians read the long story of how we have come to be who we are, and of what God has done for us at every point along the way.

The Bible gives us insight into the depths of the human spirit. The Bible is realistic about human nature. Our anger, jealousy, hatred, and guilt; our despair, grief, shame, triumph, and joy are all recorded with surpassing eloquence. In the Bible we learn that we are creatures made in God's image and sinners redeemed by his love. In the Bible we learn what we shall one day become, for the risen Lord himself is "the first-born among many" (Rom. 8:29). St. Paul says, "the Spirit searches everything" (1 Cor. 2:10), and the psalmist acknowledges that

God has "searched me and known me" (Ps. 139:1). One of the ways this searching and knowledge occurs is through our encounter with God in the Bible. The experience of finding one's self-understanding deepened by hearing and reading the Scripture is profound and irreplaceable.

Most important, *the Bible gives us a vision into the height, into the mystery of God.* "The Bible is our book about God," as a parish priest once taught his church school class with beautiful simplicity. It is one of the means that God uses to give himself to us continually. In reading or hearing it, one may always expect an encounter with the Ultimate. This experience of transcendence, of height, is an incomparable aspect of hearing and reading the Word of God in the Scripture.

11

The Word of God
In the Liturgy

The Christian movement began as an heretical sect within Judaism: heretical because Christians believed that Jesus of Nazareth was the Messiah. This claim was rejected by orthodox Jews. Yet because Christian community originated within Judaism, any adequate understanding of its worship must keep that fact in mind. Its members continued to worship in the temple (Acts 2:46), and they observed the hours of private prayer as did all pious Jews (Acts 3:1; 10:9). The natural interpretation of Acts 2:15 is to suppose that when the Spirit fell on the disciples gathered to pray on the first Pentecost "at the third hour," they had come together because it was one of the customary Jewish hours of prayer. The first chapters of Acts describe the life of Christians in Jerusalem after the resurrection in a way that suggests that it was organized along the lines of a Jewish synagogue. The later chapters indicate that Christian missionaries made their first appeal in the synagogues of the Gentile cities of Asia Minor and Greece. We have already called attention to the Jewish roots of baptism in chapter 8. The occurrence of the first Eucharists at Jewish meals, and the consequent influence of Jewish table prayers, will be discussed chapter 14.

In view of this situation, it is reasonable to suppose that the worship of the earliest church had affinities with that of the synagogue. In fact, Jewish roots can be traced in almost every aspect of Christian worship. This relationship is particularly true for the use of Scripture in Christian liturgy.

The Jewish Use of Scripture

Many writings of the Old Testament pertain to worship. They were used in the liturgy of the temple in a way that we can no longer construct with absolute certainty.[1] It has been suggested that the creation and Exodus stories were the nucleus around which Israel's worship clustered.[2] A number of the psalms suggest liturgical actions: Psalm 48:12 a procession, and Psalm 118 a ritual combat between the messianic king and the forces of Israel on the one hand and enemy nations on the other. Other psalms apparently accompanied the offering of sacrifices: Psalms 4:5; 20:3; 116:17, for example. The appearance of prophecies "against the nations" in the chief prophetic books, the account of how Micaiah prophesied defeat before Ahab and Jehoshaphat (1 Kg. 22) and the story of Amos prophesying in the king's sanctuary at Bethel (Am. 7:10–17) suggest that the setting of many, perhaps most, of the prophetic oracles was in a liturgy having to do with the warfare of Israel in a struggle with her enemies.

But this use of certain Old Testament writings in the temple liturgy did not involve, as far as we can tell, their collection into a single book, the Old Testament as we know it. In particular, there is no reason to suppose that the liturgy of the temple consisted, even in part, of a systematic reading of the sacred texts in order.

A significant change in Jewish liturgy occurred at the time of the exile, when the temple was destroyed and the ancient pattern of worship came to an end. During these years, 585–520 B.C., the synagogue emerged as an institution. The Greek word *synagoge*, like its Latin counterpart *congregatio*, means literally a "coming together." From its beginning until the present, the synagogue has been a meeting of the Jewish community for worship. In orthodox Judaism, at least, some members of the synagogue still gather together morning and evening for worship, at the time of the ancient temple sacrifices.

A major feature of synagogue worship on Sabbath, Monday, and Thursday was the reading of two lessons: one from the *Torah*, or Law, the first of five books of our Old Testament, the section most sacred to the Jews; and one from the *Nebiim*, or Prophets. The Torah is read consecutively from the beginning to end, "in course" on a three-year cycle. The Prophets are not read "in course" but rather a prophetic passage is chosen to make some apt comment on the assigned reading from the Law. The traditional text of the Hebrew Bible is marked with these divisions for public reading to this day.

The practice of the synagogue implies that at the beginning there were only two major divisions of the Hebrew Bible—the Law and the Prophets. To this twofold division, one of the most familiar New Testament verses testifies: "On these two commandments depend all the law and the prophets" (Mt. 22:40). The present Hebrew Bible, however, consists of three parts. The Writings (*Kethubim*) have been added: Psalms, Proverbs, Job, Esther, and others. It is disputed whether the psalms were used in synagogue worship as they were used in the Temple, but some of the other writings had special liturgical use.[3] One passage of the New Testament indicates that a threefold division of the Old Testament writings was beginning to appear in the first Christian century: the risen Christ says to his disciples, "everything written about me in the law of Moses and the prophets and the psalms must be fulfilled" (Lk. 24:44). The third section, the Writings, was not completed, however, until the Council of Jamnia in A.D. 90.

In the course of time, these collections in their threefold division—Law, Prophets, Writings—came to be regarded as the Word of God, in the absolute sense described in the last chapter. The Old Testament itself does not give any indication about the manner of inspiration, whether God's Spirit spoke through a quiescent and passive human agent, or whether God's Spirit heightened and increased the human capacities of the biblical writers. The freedom with which Jesus himself dealt with "what was said to the men of old" in the

Sermon on the Mount, and his lordly substitution for it of what "I say unto you" (Mt. 5) suggests that our Lord himself had the latter view. But the former view prevailed in the synagogue and in the church, as we have seen. In some New Testament passages Old Testament quotations are attributed to God himself or directly to the Holy Spirit, especially in Hebrew (e.g. Heb. 1:5,10,15). This way of citing the Old Testament Scripture would probably have been used in synagogues also.

Thus the synagogue provided the Christian church both with a pattern for reading Scriptures *as an act of worship* and also with a doctrine of the Scripture to account for the practice. Evidence indicates that the church quickly took over both.

Use of Scripture in Christian Worship

NEW TESTAMENT EVIDENCE

In the New Testament itself there is no clear reference to this synagogue practice. There is no notice that the reading of passages of the Old Testament was part of Christian worship. Perhaps it was simply assumed. There is no detailed account of the worship of a Jewish-Christian synagogue at Jerusalem. The natural inference is that in the meetings of the Christian fellowship morning and evening, synagogue worship went on as usual. The specifically Christian acts of worship went on at other times, under other circumstances.

St. Paul gives a tantalizing but incomplete account of what went on in the liturgy of the Gentile church in Corinth:

> When you come together, each one has a hymn [*psalmos*], a lesson [*didachē*], a revelation [*apocalypsis*], a tongue [*glōssa*], or an interpretation [*hermēneia*] . . . If any speak in a tongue, let there be only two or at most three, and each in turn; and let one interpret. But if there is no one to interpret, let each of them keep silence in church and speak to himself and to God. Let two or three prophets speak, and let others weigh what is said. If a revelation is made to another sitting by, let the first be silent. For you can all prophesy one by one, so that all may learn and all be encouraged; and the spirits of prophets are subject to prophets. For God is not a God of confusion but of peace. (1 Cor. 14:26–33)

One must doubt whether any of the items in St. Paul's list referred to the reading of material already written. The description is rather of spontaneous utterances made by certain worshippers in the power of the Spirit. In the course of time, to be sure, some utterances like these were set down in writing. We have, for example, that document entitled *The Teaching (Didachē) of the Twelve Apostles*, to which we have already referred. The New Testament itself contains several apocalypses, notably the book of Revelation, whose Greek name is the Apocalypse of John. That which was spoken in tongues—presumably a nonrational phenomenon similar to that which charismatics sometimes experience today—was not recorded. *Psalmos* in this passage is rightly translated in most modern versions as "hymn" rather that "psalm" as if it were from the Old Testament. It would be strange if it were the only Old Testament item in the list. The Letter to the Ephesians speaks of "psalms, hymns, and spiritual songs," and gives an example of what must be an early Christian hymn:

> Awake, O sleeper, and arise from the dead, and Christ shall give you light. (Eph. 5:14)

A number of other hymns have been identified in the New Testament (e.g., Phil. 2:6–11; 1 Tim. 3:16; 2 Tim. 2:11–13).

Readers may, in St. Paul's account of worship in Corinth, miss any mention of reading from Gospels or Epistles until they recall that not only was the service that St. Paul describes conceived freely, "in the Spirit," but also that the gospels and most of the epistles (and certainly their collection) had not yet appeared. The earliest Gospel, that of St. Mark, is usually dated at A.D. 65. St. Paul is commonly thought to have written to the Corinthians about A.D. 52.

It seems reasonable to conclude, on the basis of this admittedly sketchy evidence, that the earliest Jewish-Christian communities, like the one in Jerusalem, would have been organized like a synagogue and would have continued to read the Hebrew Scripture as part of their worship. On the other hand, if it is legitimate to infer that the sort of worship described by St. Paul was fairly common in Gentile-Christian communities, spiritually inspired utterances of types known to us in very early writings formed part of this style of Christian worship. Yet the distinction may be too sharp. Perhaps both kinds of worship marked both Jewish-Christian and Gentile-Christian churches.

USE OF SCRIPTURE IN EARLY EUCHARISTIC LITURGIES

What we have found in the New Testament is still far from the reading of an Old Testament lesson and a New Testament lesson, as at our services of Morning and Evening Prayer, or the reading of an Old Testament lesson, Epistle, and Gospel, as at our celebrations of Holy Communion. Nothing in Jewish practice in the New Testament itself is comparable to our Eucharist, where the reading of Scripture is joined to the actions of the Supper, done "in remembrance of me."

In the middle of the second century, Justin Martyr describes a somewhat more familiar service of worship. In his *First Apology* (ca. 150) Justin writes:

> On the first day which is called Sunday, all who live in the cities or in the countryside gather together in one place. And the memoirs of the apostles or the writings of the prophets are read as long as there is time.[4]

Eucharistic prayer and communion in bread and wine follow. We shall give our attention in chapter 14 to this second part of the service Justin describes. As far as the first part is concerned, we notice that "memoirs of the apostles" are read. In the previous chapter the *Apology*, Justin has identified them as Gospels. A strict reading of this text would suggest that only one lesson was used, although it might have two possible sources: the Gospels and "the writings of the prophets." Since the prophets are listed *after* the "memoirs of apostles" it seems likely, especially in view of what we learned about prophets from the passage in First Corinthians discussed in the previous section, that Justin has in mind the writings of New Testament prophets; that is, apocalypses rather than the works of Old Testament prophets.

The first unequivocal mention of the reading of Old Testament lessons at a Christian Eucharist occurs in *The Constitutions of the Holy Apostles* or *Apostolic Constitutions*.[5] This work, which probably originated during the fourth century in the Near East, shows numerous traces of Jewish influence. At one point it stipulates the reading of *two* Old Testament lessons followed by a reading from Acts or the Epistles, and at the end a reading from the Gospel. In the liturgy of St. James, the ancient liturgy of the church in Jerusalem, the following rubric after initial prayers and hymns occur:

> Then there are read in order the holy oracles of the Old Testament, and of the prophets; and the incarnation of the Son of God is set forth, and his sufferings and resurrection from the dead, his ascension into heaven, and his second appearing with glory: and this takes place daily in the holy and divine service.[6]

In order and context of this rubric, "holy oracles of the Old Testament" probably refers to the Law; and "prophets" almost certainly refers to Old Testament prophets. Whether the reading from the New Testament is to come from Gospel, Epistle, Acts, or Revelation is not clear. Perhaps more than one reading is envisaged. The rubric does make clear that the New Testament reading proclaims the incarnate Word, an insight of abiding importance.

We may conclude that by the fourth century at the latest, Old Testament readings in the style of the synagogue had been combined with New Testament readings. As time went on, the Gospels were emphasized more and more. It would be tedious to trace the details of subsequent developments. By the eighth century or so, when eucharistic liturgies in both Eastern and Western churches were standardized in more or less the forms that they have retained to the present time, there had come to be two readings from Scripture. The second, climactic, reading was invariably from a Gospel. The first reading, as we know, was usually from an Epistle, although occasionally it might come from the Old Testament, or Acts, or the Revelation to John. The use of two lessons had been traditional until the revisions of the twentieth century. The occasional appearance of the other readings in place of Epistles is an echo of that earlier day when three or perhaps even more lessons were read at length—"as long as time permits," as Justin put it. The retention of a few Old Testament lessons served to remind worshipers that Christian liturgy had its roots in the synagogue, with its intensive reading of the Word of God. In fact, part of the Eucharist, customarily referred to as the Service of the Word, is technically know as the *synaxis*. The word means "public meeting" and is etymologically related to *synagogue*. We can see that synagogue services are the source of the structure of the synaxis and, for a while after the fourth century, of a good deal of its content. In the forms of the eucharistic liturgy that became traditional in both Eastern and Western churches, however, the Old Testament was virtually silenced, except for a few Eastern rites. And since the Eucharist was in the service that most Christians attended most of the time, the characteristic message of the Law and the Prophets was almost never heard: its understanding of God's judgment on the nations, it celebration of his grace manifested in history and hoped for beyond history, its unflinching condemnation of the disobedience of God's own people, and its account of Israel's preparation to receive the incarnate Word.

Nor was this situation remedied at the time of the sixteenth-century Reformation. In many respects, the Reformation succeeded in making the Scripture accessible to the people. It was translated into the vernacular so that once again men and women could hear the words of life in their own tongue. In the Daily Offices, Old Testament as well as New Testament lessons of substantial length were provided. But in English Prayer Books from the beginning, the Eucharist retained the shape and, in the Service of the Word, most of the content of the Latin Mass. Two readings were provided: the second was always a Gospel; the first was usually an Epistle, with the same occasional variants we have noted in the earlier Latin liturgy. And those provisions have remained unchanged through all the revisions of English and American Prayer Books prior to the present revision.

The silencing of the Old Testament in the Eucharist was a major loss. It was reintroduced in the current Prayer Book in a way which we shall examine in a later chapter. A similar recovery is also going on in a number of other churches, including the Roman Catholic and Lutheran. This renewed attention to the message of the Old Testament is one of the most significant features of the liturgical renewal of our time.

USE OF SCRIPTURE IN THE DAILY OFFICE

Like the Service of the Word in the Eucharist, the Daily Offices (Morning and Evening Prayer) have their roots in the practice of the synagogue. Their development, however, involves a very different story from the one we have just traced, particularly with regard to the readings.

We have already noticed that in New Testament times, pious Jews of the synagogue met morning and evening to pray and read the Scripture. In addition, the third hour (about 9 A.M.), the sixth hour (noon), and the ninth (about 3 P.M.), were hours of private prayer. The congregation of the synagogue did not assemble at these times, but pious Jews prayed wherever they were.

From the *Apostolic Tradition* of Hippolytus we know that these same hours of prayer were observed in Rome early in the third century. Parts of the description are worth citing:

> Let all the faithful, whether men or women, when early in the morning they rise from sleep and before they undertake any task, wash their hands and pray to

God; and so they may go to their duties. . . .

If at the third hour thou art home, pray then and give thanks to God; but if thou chance to be abroad at that hour, make thy prayer to God in thy heart. . . .

At the sixth hour likewise pray also, for after Christ was nailed to the wood of the cross, the day was divided and there was a great darkness. . . .

And the ninth hour let a great prayer and a great thanksgiving be made, such as made the souls of the righteous ones, blessing the Lord. . . .

Pray again before thy body rests on thy bed. . . .

At midnight arise, wash thy hands with water and pray. And if thy wife is with thee, pray both together; but if she not yet a believer, go into another room and pray, and again return to thy bed; be not slothful in prayer. At cockcrow rise up and pray likewise. . . .[7]

Not only were the five traditional Jewish hours of prayer observed during the day, as this citation indicates, but also two nighttime hours: midnight and cockcrow. These night hours were the time when the Christian community watched for the coming of the Lord. They were a time of vigil. "Watch, therefore," the admonition runs in the Gospel according to St. Mark, "for you do not know when the master of the house will come, in the evening [sunset], or midnight, or at cockcrow, or in the morning—lest he come suddenly and find you asleep. And what I say to you I say to all: Watch" (Mk. 13:35–37).

The early Christian community must often have met at night. St. Paul "prolonged his speech until midnight" with the members of the church at Troas. Eutychus sank into a deep sleep and fell out the window! (Acts 20:7–12). About the year 112, Pliny the Younger wrote to ask the advice of the Emperor Trojan about handling the troublesome sect of Christians who would not burn incense to the emperor. Pliny reported that "on an appointed day they were accustomed to meet before daybreak."[8] It is perhaps a reference to cockcrow. Christians thus met as circumstances permitted.

From these various sources of the first two centuries there emerged the growth of a rigorous daily discipline of prayer: five times during the day, and twice at night. Sometimes there seems to have been a continuous vigil for a number of hours during the night. This scheme of prayer and praise was amplified and regularized by the monastic communities that sprang up during subsequent centuries.

The monastic rule now most familiar to Western Christians is that devised by St. Benedict of Nursia in the sixth century. He increased the number of daytime hours from five to seven. For it is written in the Psalms, "Seven times a day do I praise thee, because of thy righteous judgments" (Ps. 119:164, KJV). He also provided a single nighttime office, during which there were extensive readings from the Bible, the lives of the saints, the histories of the martyrs. After all, the psalmist also says: "At midnight I will rise to give thanks unto thee, because of thy righteous judgment" (Ps. 119:62, KJV). The night office was called *Matins* (or *Mattins*). The daytime offices were called *Lauds*, at daybreak; *Prime*, at the first hour after sunrise; *Terce*, at the third; *Sext*, at the sixth, usually reckoned as noon; *None*, at the ninth; *Vespers*, at sunset; and *Compline*, completing the day, at bedtime.

The reading of Scripture at these services has had a complex history. Following the synagogue pattern, the Bible seems to have been read twice a day, at Lauds and Vespers. At certain periods of the development, there were not only these two readings at Lauds and Vespers, one from the Old Testament and one from the New, but also at least one reading, sometimes of considerable length, at each of the other hours. The lengthy, often nonscriptural readings at Matins have already been noted.[9]

The church has never been able to sustain such extensive reading of the Bible. In the course of decades and centuries, the number of readings would grow less and their length shorter. Then a reformation, like that which proceeded from the monastery of Cluny in France in the eleventh century, would establish an ampler schedule of readings. In turn the new list would not endure.[10] On the eve of the sixteenth-century Reformation, lessons were read at Matins and Vespers. There were traces of lessons in other services, the so-called chapters, single verses of the Bible, usually the same each day. The service of Compline in the current Prayer Book has such a chapter (pp. 131–132). The regular reading of the Bible was frequently interrupted by the observance of saints' days and other holy days, and for these observances, nonscriptural material was often appointed. The whole was in Latin, a tongue unintelligible to the large majority of the population of Europe.

Cranmer's treatment of the canonical hours in the Prayer Books of 1549 and 1552 was a piece of brilliant simplification. In place of the eight offices of the *Breviary* (the name of the book that contained the Daily Offices in the late Middle Ages) Cranmer provided two offices. In the first book, of 1549, they were called Matins and Evensong. In the second book, of 1552, they received the names that have lasted to the present—Morning Prayer and Evening Prayer. Morning Prayer contains elements from the Latin services of Matins, Lauds, and Prime. Evening Prayer borrows from Vespers and Compline. The minor hours, Terce, Sext, and None, which were originally hours of private prayer, have made no contribution to our Daily Offices.

As for the readings from Scripture, the sixteenth-century Prayer Books provided that a full chapter should be read from the Old Testament and a full chapter from the New both morning and evening. By this means, the New Testament was read in its entirety three times a year, and the most significant parts of the Old Testament once a year. The amplitude of the scheme is admirable, even heroic. But in the plan of lessons (lectionary) that Cranmer provided, the readings moved forward inexorably, making no distinction between Sunday and weekday services and taking little note of the seasons of the Christian year. He used nothing but scriptural material.

Successive revisions of the Prayer Book, both in England and throughout the Anglican communion, have considerably altered Cranmer's lectionary. In the American book of 1928, to use a typical and familiar example, the lessons on weekdays are readings "in course." That is, a book is read in order from beginning to end, sometimes with omissions. The order in which the books are read is chosen with an eye to seasonal appropriateness: for example, the prophesies of Isaiah in Advent; Ephesians, with its emphasis on the revelation of God's mystery in Christ, during Epiphany. On Sundays a different plan is followed. No effort is made to preserve continuity with weekdays. Lessons may be chosen to amplify themes in the Epistle or Gospel read at the Eucharist, or in the long Trinity season, certain books may be read more or less in course from Sunday to Sunday. The length of the lessons is usually far shorter than a full chapter. The 1928 Prayer Book permits the reading of only the Old Testament lesson at Morning Prayer when the Eucharist follows at once, and of only one lesson at Evening Prayer.

It seems to be a fact that the desire to magnify the importance of the Word of God by reading long lessons struggles continuously with a realistic estimate of what can be usefully contemplated and absorbed. The resolution of that tension has always been uneasy and temporary. The current Prayer Book represents a fresh approach to the problem. We shall turn to it in the next chapter.

12

Morning and Evening Prayer in Today's Church

In the last two chapters, we have examined the theological and historical background of the use of Scripture in Christian worship. The reading of psalms and lessons lies at the heart of Morning and Evening Prayer. Yet the Daily Offices consist of more than psalms and lessons. In this chapter we shall consider these services as a whole.

The Structure of Morning and Evening Prayer

The two services have the same structure. The outline is familiar:

I. Introduction
    Opening Sentences
    Confession of Sin
        Exhortation
        General Confession
        Absolution
II. The Main Body of the Office
        Invitatory and Psalter
        The Lessons, each followed by a Canticle
        The Apostles' Creed
    The Prayers
        The Lord's Prayer
        Versicles and Responses
        Collects
III. The Conclusion
    Other Prayers

In Section II, from the Invitatory and Psalter through the Collects, the structure of the Daily Offices somewhat resembles that of the medieval canonical hours out of which they grew. This middle section constituted the whole of the Daily Offices in the first English Prayer Book. The second book, of 1552, added Section I as a penitential beginning. Section III was added in the book of 1662 in the form of a group of four concluding prayers that never changed and the

Grace from 2 Corinthians 13:14. The current Prayer Book permits the use of any authorized intercessions in Section III.

Each of these sections deserves further comment.

SECTION I: INTRODUCTION

The service begins with one or more *Sentences of Scripture*. These are selected either to emphasize a season of the Church Year, celebrating a certain aspect of what God has done for us in Christ, or to state a more general aspect of Christian worship. In any case, they summon the congregation to an awareness of God's presence and focus attention on the worshipers' relation to God in a particular way.

The *Exhortation, Confession of Sin,* and *Absolution* may follow. When this section was first added, in 1552, its use was mandatory. It became optional in 1928. The sixteenth-century requirement rested on a profound understanding of the relationship between God and those who would worship him in spirit and in truth. To stand in the presence of the "high and lofty one who inhabits eternity, whose name is Holy" is to be aware of one's finitude and sin. In our discussion of the Holy in chapter 2, we saw how universally the response to the holy God was a feeling of unworthiness, of being undone, an instinct to "fall flat on one's face." The sixteenth-century reformers believed that the only proper way to approach the presence of God was through the confession of sin. By their provision the Daily Offices and the Eucharist both began on this note, and thus both acquired a more penitential character.

Today it would be widely acknowledged that there are other equally valid responses to the divine, other ways to begin worship equally expressive of authentic Christian piety. At times like Easter a congregation might be so filled with joy and thanksgiving for the power and love of God that it would be right to move at once to a song of praise like the *Pascha nostrum* ("Christ our Passover"). But it remains true that on many occasions the adequate approach to worship is to acknowledge sin and repentance in the presence of God.

The longer exhortation that precedes the confession at Morning Prayer (BCP, pp. 41, 79) not only urges us to "kneel in silence, and with penitent and obedient hearts confess our sins," but also provides a succinct outline of the activities to which worshipers are summoned thereafter: "to set forth [God's] praise, to hear his holy Word, and to ask, for ourselves and on behalf of others, those things that are necessary for our life and our salvation" (p. 99). The exhortation thus serves to prepare those who participate in the office for what is about to take place.

The general confession follows. When we say it in the company of our neighbors, we should remember not only our private and personal wrongdoing but also the trespasses of our society against those whom it rejects: its injustice, cruelty, and greed. General confessions were introduced at the time of the Reformation as a substitute for private confession, which was widely abused at the end of the Middle Ages as a means of raising money through indulgences. Today we have begun to appropriate once more the practice of private confession. We have come to appreciate its psychological strength, and we believe that we can avoid its pitfalls. We shall discuss the reconciliation of penitents in chapter 18. Nevertheless, there is no indication that the hearing of private confession is likely to replace general confession completely as the customary was to deal with individual sins; and in any case, only general confession can express repentence for social ills.

Absolution follows confession. The forgiveness of sins is one of the chief items in the good news of Jesus Christ. Christians recognize themselves as sinners, but as forgiven sinners. Therefore they can be thankful. Absolution is pronounced by a priest, the authorized mediator between God and his people. There is a traditionally acknowledged difference between absolution declared by a priest and the simple statement that God forgives our sins, an assurance which any Christian can and should give others. The difference is recognized by the different formula provided in both offices for use when the officiant is not a priest.

SECTION II: THE MAIN BODY OF THE OFFICE

Material taken over from the ancient canonical hours starts with the *Invitatory* and *Psalter*. In the psalms we begin to praise the Lord. "Lord, open our lips." "And our mouth shall proclaim your praise."

An invitatory is a psalm or hymn, often prefaced (and followed) by a seasonal sentence, or antiphon. Then one or more psalms appointed for the day are said or sung. The Venite—part of Psalm 95 and two verses of Psalm 96—is the invitatory with which most American Episcopalians are familiar: "O come, let us sing unto the Lord. . . ." The current book adds as optional alternatives the Jubilate ("O be joyful in the Lord, all you lands. . . ."), and the Easter canticle for the Easter season ("Christ our Passover is sacrificed for us. . . ."). For Evening Prayer, the current book provides an invitatory for the first time, the ancient hymn *Phos hilaron*, "O gracious light."

The recitation of the Psalter was perhaps the most salient feature of the monastic offices, even more prominent then than the reading of the Bible. The whole of one hundred and fifty psalms was read through in a week, not in order but according to a complete pattern. Cranmer designed his two daily offices so that all the psalms would be read through in order once a month. His division of the one hundred and fifty psalms into sixty roughly equal portions, for Morning Prayer and Evening Prayer every day for thirty days, has appeared in all subsequent Anglican books, including the current one. Although to read the Psalter in this way makes it impossible to choose psalms whose themes might illuminate the lessons and prayers, this method has the virtues of simplicity and regularity. Generations of Anglicans have found their hearts deepened and their minds opened to the ways of God, their spirits searched by God's Spirit, through the steady repetition of the laments, the epic narratives, and the praises of the psalms, day after day, month after month, year after year. Some still find Cranmer's scheme a strenuous but rewarding way to appropriate the Psalter.

Enough has been said in the last two chapters about the *lessons*. In the Anglican form of the Daily Offices, hearing of the Word of God is the center and focal point.

Something further does have to be said, however, about the lectionaries of the current Prayer Book. As mentioned in the last chapter, these lectionaries represent a fresh attempt to resolve the tension between reading at worship a large enough portion of the Scripture to represent it fairly and reading only as much Scripture as can be grasped at one time. The current book presents two new lectionaries, one for main services on Sundays and Holy Days (The Lectionary, pp. 887–931), and one for the daily offices (Daily Office Lectionary, pp. 933–1001) providing lessons daily (including Sunday) throughout the year. The new feature of both lectionaries is a cycle of readings that stretch over more than one year. The Lectionary is based on a three-year cycle. It can be more appropriately discussed in the next chapter.

The Daily Office Lectionary is based on a two-year cycle. The lessons are relatively short, but because the cycle now covers two years, a considerably larger amount of Scripture is used in the readings of the Daily Office than was the case in the lectionary of the 1928 Prayer Book.

Three lessons—an Old Testament lesson, an Epistle, and a Gospel—are set for each day in each cycle. If desired, one can read three lessons at each office—and then one must use both years' provisions every year. It seems more reasonable that two of the three lessons will be read at one of the offices each day—say Morning Prayer—and the remaining one lesson will be read in the evening. If one wishes to read two lessons both morning and evening, one must borrow the Old Testament lesson from the second year's cycle to make the necessary four. In any case, the lessons are reasonably short, and the Scripture fairly represented a workable compromise.

Two sets of psalms are provided each day in each year's cycle. They cover most of the psalms on roughly a seven-week course.

Each lesson is followed by a *canticle*. Canticles are hymns of praise or penitence to God. They provide a way for the congregation to make its response of faith to the reading they have just heard. The *Te Deum* ("You are God: we praise you") and the *Gloria in Excelsis* ("Glory to God in the highest") are ancient hymns. The other canticles are from the Bible. The *Te Deum*, the *Benedicite* (A Song of Creation), the *Benedictus* (The Song of Zechariah), the *Magnificat* (The Song of Mary), and the *Nunc Dimittis* (The Song of Simeon), have come into these services by way of the canonical hours. The *Benedictus es* (A Song of Praise) was added in the Prayer Book of 1928. The others—*The Song of Moses* (verses from Exodus 15), the three songs of Isaiah, *A Song of Penitence* (verses from the Prayer of Manasseh in the Apocrypha), *A Song to the Lamb*, and *The Song of the Redeemed* (both the latter from Revelation) were introduced at various stages of trial use in the course of developing the current Prayer Book. There is enough variety now so that judiciously chosen canticles can provide an apt comment on virtually any set of lessons. In the current book, any canticle may be used after any lesson at Morning or Evening Prayer. A period of silence is also permitted.

The *Apostles' Creed* is the customary response to the whole preceding service: psalms, lessons, canticles. In the light of all this material from the Bible, which through the action of the Holy Spirit becomes the Word of God to the participants in the service, the congregation affirms its faith in "God, the Father Almighty, . . . and in Jesus Christ his only Son our Lord, . . . and in the Holy Spirit." It has been so in every Anglican Book of Common Prayer. The Apostles' Creed was originally a baptismal declaration of faith. It takes its name from an ancient legend that told how the first apostles composed it at the Council of Jerusalem (Acts 15), each contributing a clause.[1] Although this story as it stands cannot be regarded as serious history, it does point to the antiquity of the opinion that some form of the creed was handed down from the apostles and their disciples, and to the fact that each clause taken separately refers to a clear teaching of Scripture. The Apostles' Creed is an ancient and venerable summary of the Christian faith. Those who say it in the Daily Offices reaffirm their baptismal profession, joining themselves by reciting this symbol of faith to the swelling throng of Christians down through the ages.

A series of prayers beginning with the *Lord's Prayer* concludes the Offices. Having been nourished by hearing the Word of God and having reaffirmed the faith which that Word engenders and shapes, the congregation expresses its trust in God by prayer. At the head of all the prayers stands the prayer that our Lord himself taught: "Our Father in heaven, hallowed by your Name. . . . " This prayer occurs at the climax of every service of Prayer Book worship. It is followed by a series of *suffrages*, one-line prayers recited alternatively by officiant and congregation. These petitions for church (ministers and people), world, nation, the spread of the Gospel ("Let your way be known upon earth"), the poor, and the congregation itself, make the first set of suffrages, the traditional ones, a cameo of Christian intercession.

After the suffrages come a series of *collects*. In the traditional Anglican form of the Offices, the series consisted of the Collect of the Day and two other invariable collects: at Morning Prayer the Collect for Peace (a "memorial" collect in the Breviary) and the Collect for Grace (from Prime); at Evening Prayer a different "memorial" Collect for Peace and the Collect for Aid against Perils (from Compline). The current Prayer Book presents a series of eight collects at each office: the Collect of the Day, the traditional invariable collects, special collects for Friday, Saturday, and Sunday (those days so crucial for the Christian mystery), and two others. In the current book only one collect need be read from this longer list. With the wider range of choices, the special character of the service may come to more adequate expression. There is a second group of three collects, different in morning and evening, for the mission and ministry of the church. They remind worshipers of matters that must always press on the Christian conscience, and should serve as continual prods to action.

[NOTE] What is a collect? The noun *collect* is derived ultimately from the Latin verb *colligere*, which means to gather, or to collect. Two related Latin nouns, *collecta* and *collectio*, came to be applied to short prayers, by somewhat different routes. The Gregorian Sacramentary, one of the earliest documents of the Latin Mass, referred to an *oratio ad collectam*, or prayer at the gathering. It designated a prayer early in the Mass, like the Collect of the Day at our Eucharist. That collect once referred to the prayer said over the gathered assembly, in that ancient time of small congregations when all the Christians in Rome met at some fixed place before they set out to the site where Mass was to be said—a different site each Sunday, such as the tomb of a martyr. The name of this prayer was eventually shortened to *collectio*, referring to a prayer which gathered together or summarized a preceding devotion. The collect at the end of our Litany is an instance of such a prayer.

In contemporary Anglican usage, collects, which are used in both these cases and many others, have come to be simply prayers with certain formal characteristics. Collects are one sentence in length, with three major parts: (1) an *address* to God (e.g., "whose Son our Savior Jesus Christ is the light of the world"); (2) a *petition* ("Grant that your people, illumined by your Word and Sacraments, may shine with the radiance of Christ's glory"); the petition is often, but not always, followed by a result clause ("that he may be known, worshiped, and obeyed to the ends of the earth"); (3) a *mediation* ("through Jesus Christ our Lord") usually coupled with a *doxology* ("who with you and the Holy Spirit lives and reigns, one God, now and forever"). Like all prayers, it concludes with *Amen*.

SECTION III: THE CONCLUSION

Until 1662 Morning and Evening Prayer ended after these collects. In the book of that year a collection of intercessions was appended to both the Daily Offices: for the King and the Royal Family, for Clergy and People, and the Prayer of St. Chrysostom. In the first American book of 1789, the Prayer for the King and the Royal Family was replaced, of course, by a Prayer for the President; and because of their popularity, the Prayer for all Conditions of Men and the General Thanksgiving were included in both the Daily Offices instead of in the collection of general prayers and thanksgivings. The resulting list of intercessions—for state, church, and all persons in their need—to which a prayer of general thanksgiving is added, covered a remarkably comprehensive group of concerns. They are virtually the same as those mentioned in the Prayers of the People at the Eucharist.

It came to be widely felt, however, that the unchanging use of the prayers printed at the end of Morning and Evening Prayer did not allow worshipers' prayers to be directed toward the vast and fluctuating variety and complexity of things that happen week after week. In the book of 1928, a rubric after the fixed collects at each service states that "the Minister may here end the

Morning [Evening] Prayer with such general intercessions as he shall think fit," thus encouraging variety in the intercessions. In the current book the rubric reads simply: "Authorized intercessions and thanksgivings may follow" (pp. 58, 71, 101, 125). Those who desire to pray "with the church," however, should remember this tradition of fixed prayers and should allow their own prayers to range through these specific areas of public corporate concern—state, church, and all in need—as well as over their own needs and desires.

Other Components of the Daily Office

In the contemporary language section of the current Prayer Book (Rite II), there have been significant extensions of the Daily Office.

First, An Order of Service for Noonday and An Order for Compline fill out the number of offices to four. These additions are brief services, in the manner of the lesser canonical hours. They consist of psalms, chapters (one or two verses of Scripture), and prayers appropriate to the time of day. They are not included among the "regular" services mentioned in the rubrics "Concerning the Service of the Church," but they fill a long-felt need. Noonday services, particularly when they are the occasion of special preaching, as in Lent, require an order of prayer for which neither of the regular Daily Offices is quite appropriate. Conferences and retreats have for a long time made frequent use of unofficial services of Compline. These two additions supply authorized forms for such services. Moreover, if any person or group desires to undertake a discipline of prayer more rigorous than that represented by a regular reading of Morning and Evening Prayer, these two additional services would provide a Daily Office with four Hours.

In addition to these two services, four brief Daily Devotions for Individuals and Families were added at the end of the Daily Office, after Compline. They are designed for use in the morning, at noon, in the evening, and at the close of the day. Each of these devotions consists of a few verses of a set psalm or hymn, a short reading (a chapter) or the reading of Scripture from the lectionaries, and the opportunity to offer prayer spontaneously for one's self and others. Each has its own concluding collect.

The invariable material of these services is so short that it could be easily memorized and would provide a practical way for a busy family to pray together, or individuals to pray on the road or at work. The eloquent services of Family Prayer in older American books were long, and bespoke a pace of life that few enjoy any longer. These forms attempt to provide the framework for organizing a simple life of prayer. Anyone could undertake it without fear of overextension. The profundity of prayer and meditation has no necessary relation to length, in any case; but everything depends on regularity.

The Use of the Daily Offices

The considerations of the foregoing paragraph raise the whole question of the use of the Daily Offices. They are designed to be read either with a congregation or privately.

Public use of Morning and Evening Prayer has been undergoing marked change during the past decades. Evening Prayer has virtually disappeared as a regular Sunday service, although it is widely used in Lent and on special occasions. Until fairly recently, Morning Prayer on three Sundays a month, with Holy Communion on the first Sunday, was the predominant pattern for main Sunday services, the "eleven o'clock" service in the American Episcopal Church, and probably throughout the Anglican communion. For some years past, this pattern too has been changing. Today the Eucharist is the main service every Sunday in a growing number of parishes, and in many more Eucharist is celebrated twice a month, with Morning Prayer on the other Sundays. In the current book, with the emphasis on the Eucharist as "the principal act of Christian worship on the Lord's Day" (p. 13) and with ample provision for the Proclamation of the Word of God (to be discussed in the next chapter), this trend is likely to continue. Since this development may trouble some Episcopalians, it may help to clarify what is going on by setting it into a broad historical perspective.

There can be no question that the Eucharist was the chief Sunday service in the Christian church from the beginning, and remained so both in Eastern Orthodoxy and Roman Catholicism after the Great Schism that divided them. It is also true that in the Middle Ages lay people received the elements quite infrequently. Partly superstitious fear of the Real Presence located in the elements, partly the requirement that baptized Christians could not receive communion unless they had made confession and received absolution led to the result that most of the laity "made their communion" only once or twice a year.

The sixteenth-century reformers, far from wishing to discourage participation in the Eucharist, wished to increase it in both quantity and quality. Calvin wanted a weekly celebration in Geneva.[2] Nevertheless, the habits of centuries could not be changed overnight. In most Protestant parish churches the reformers had to settle for less frequent Eucharists. Yet they did establish one principle: when Eucharist was celebrated, the whole congregation received. "Noncommunicating masses" were abolished. The corporate emphasis of the Eucharist was restored. In the sixteenth century many and perhaps most English parishes settled down to Holy Communion once a quarter. We should realize that this pattern doubled or perhaps even quadrupled the frequency with which most communicants approached the Lord's table.

In 1561 Archbishop Grindal directed that the service every Sunday should consist of Morning Prayer, the Litany, and Ante-communion, which was the communion service as far as the Prayer for the Whole State of Christ's Church.[3] On Sundays when the Lord's Supper was celebrated, the same pattern was to be foowed, except, of course, the communion service was read to the end. These so called "accumulated" services constituted the standard pattern of Anglican cathedrals and parishes, in which communion was celebrated as often as once a month, and in a few, weekly. The pattern of quarterly communions, however, predominated.

The Wesleyan revival in the eighteenth century introduced the custom of monthly communions, although the use of accumulated services continued. Wesley himself desired more frequent communions. The Catholic revival of the nineteenth century encouraged weekly celebrations. Under this influence most Episcopal parishes added a communion service every Sunday—the "eight o'clock." But the pressure of time, as well as the controversy provoked by the Catholic revival, produced a curious change in the pattern of accumulated services at eleven. A few parishes moved to a celebration of the Eucharist every Sunday and dropped Morning Prayer. A larger number retained the monthly pattern inherited from the previous century, but separated the services— others, often Morning Prayer and Litany on the third. In this way, toward the end of the nineteenth century, Morning Prayer came to be the chief Sunday service three-quarters of the time.

The developments of the past few decades indicate that the Eucharist is becoming the central Sunday morning service for a growing number of congregations. Available evidence shows that where this has happened, the whole congregation continues to receive communion. The corporate character of the Eucharist has been preserved. If the church is able to sustain this pattern of eucharistic services, without reverting to noncommunicating celebrations, the dream of the reformers will have been achieved. In that case, Morning Prayer is likely to drop out of view as the service most Episcopalians know best, following the path Evening Prayer has already taken. Yet, for the better part of four hundred years, Morning Prayer has provided the vehicle by which Anglicans were nourished by the Word of God, and obviously it will be called upon to do so for some time to come until the goal of weekly communion by the whole people of God is attained.

Meanwhile, it should be borne in mind that Morning and Evening Prayer are designed to be *daily* offices. Through them worshipers read psalms and the Bible in an orderly and systematic way. They continue to be used fruitfully to this end in cathedrals, some large parishes, seminaries, monasteries, and other institutions where a community gathers to work and pray.

Moreover, individuals can also use the Daily Offices to their great profit. English clergy are enjoined, by the rubrics of all Prayer Books after 1552, to read them. American Prayer Books have never required their use, either by clergy or by lay persons. Nevertheless, the Offices are perhaps the most characteristic Anglican form of private devotions. And with their round of praise, instruction in the Word of God, and eloquent prayers to cover the chief concerns of human life, they commend themselves to all who seriously desire to live their lives with God in Christ. With the various options provided in the current Prayer Book, and with the addition of workable short forms for family and individual use, such a disciplined life is within the reach of us all.

13

The Holy Eucharist (I):
The Proclamation
of the Word of God

Like the Daily Offices, the first part of the service of Holy Eucharist centers on the Word of God. Like the Daily Offices, this part of the Eucharist, the Proclamation of the Word of God, has its roots in the practice of the Jewish synagogue, as we have seen. Like the Daily Offices, it consists of psalms, lessons, canticles, prayers, with a general confession and absolution. In fact, the two Daily Offices and the Proclamation of the Word of God at the Eucharist are, liturgically speaking, so nearly the same that the current Prayer Book permits Morning or Evening Prayer to be substituted for the first part of the Eucharist, "provided that a lesson from the Gospel is always included, and that the intercessions conform to the directions given for the Prayers of the People" (pp. 322–324).

Nevertheless we should notice the particular structure of the Proclamation of the Word of God and examine some of its special features in detail.

The Structure of the Proclamation
of the Word of God at the Eucharist

I. Entrance Rite
    Opening Dialogue
    Collect for Purity
    The Summary of the Law
    Canticles
        Kyrie eleison or Trisagion
        Gloria in excelsis
II. The Collect of the Day
III. The Lessons
IV. The Sermon
V. The Nicene Creed
VI. The Prayers of the People
VII. Confession of Sin

Exhortation
General Confession
Absolution
Comfortable Words
VIII. The Peace

A Penitential Order is provided as an optional beginning. It may also be used as a separate service (BCP, pp. 319, 351). The Penitential Order recalls the beginning of the communion service from 1552 to 1928, with its solemn recitation of the Ten Commandments and the response after each, "Lord, have mercy upon us, and incline our hearts to keep this law." This use of the Ten Commandments served as an examination of conscience for priest and people together and constituted that approach to the holy God in awe and repentance that the sixteenth-century reformers deemed essential. As in the case of the Divine Offices, it has been found devotionally useful to permit a variation in this pattern. In the current Prayer Book, the Eucharist is found with its pre-Reformation nonpenitential beginning as the standard one. It is expected that the Penitential Order, however, will continue to be used on some regular basis to express this different response to the Holy One.

ENTRANCE RITE

As far as the entrance rite is concerned, the *opening dialogues* (one for Easter, one for Lent and penitential occasions, and one for ordinary or "ferial" days) establish liturgy as the mutual task of priest and people from the outset. The *Collect for Purity*, "Almighty God, unto whom all hearts are open, all desires known, and from whom no secrets are hid . . ." has opened all Anglican eucharistic liturgies after 1549. At the beginning of this central Christian act, we acknowledge that God "searches us out and knows us" better than we know ourselves, and that apart from this, we have no worthiness and no ability to praise or worship God.

The *Kyrie* ("Lord, have mercy") and *Trisagion* ("Holy God, Holy and Mighty, Holy Immortal One . . .") are ancient hymns of acclamation. The use of the Kyrie is traditional in Anglican and Roman Catholic liturgies; the Trisagion comes from the Orthodox liturgy being sung during the Little Entrance as the deacon carries the Gospel book. It was introduced into our worship during the period of trial use that preceded the adoption of the current Prayer Book.

The *Gloria in excelsis* is also an ancient hymn, ultimately of Greek origin, used in both Eastern and Western churches. It served to move the Latin liturgy forward in a paean of praise and thanksgiving after the Kyrie. It was transferred to its more familiar place at the end of the service by Cranmer in 1552, in line with his instinct to keep a penitential note at the beginning. In the current Prayer Book its return to the introduction at certain appointed times makes it possible once again to begin the service, when appropriate, in a burst glory (p. 406, rubric 5).

The *Collect of the Day*, which was discussed in the last chapter, draws the entrance rite to a close.

THE LESSONS

Although enough has been said also concerning the reading of lessons at the Eucharist, we must give some attention to the main service lectionary, called in the current Prayer Book simply The Lectionary. It determines which lessons shall be read Sunday by Sunday at the Eucharist, or at Morning Prayer if it is in fact the main service (pp. 889–931). Like the Daily Office Lectionary, it seeks to resolve the tension between hearing a large part of the Scripture in the course of a complete cycle and keeping the lessons on each day reasonably short. It accomplishes this end by the device of extending the cycle of readings from one year to three.

Its use at the Eucharist restores an Old Testament lesson, as well as providing an Epistle and Gospel. One is not required to read both Old Testament lesson and Epistle, although experience suggests that three lessons are frequently being used. The possibility of hearing the characteristic message of the Old Testament at eucharistic celebrations restores a lack that began at a very early date. This feature of the Proclamation of the Word of God allows the Eucharist in the current book to be as faithful and ample in presenting the Word of God as the Daily Offices are.

The Lectionary appoints a psalm and three Scripture passages for every Sunday, as well as for Holy Days and certain special occasions. It is an ecumenical venture. Roman Catholics, Lutherans, Presbyterians, the United Church of Christ, and Methodists use lectionaries very similar to it, although the churches that do not have a fixed liturgy may not use a lectionary as regularly as the Lutherans, Roman Catholics, and Anglicans do. Still, the possibility exists, firing one's imagination, that on a given Sunday, the same readings from the Word of God will be heard in nearly every church in Western Christendom and in their counterparts around the world.

THE SERMON

A sermon is mentioned in the text of the Eucharist, as it is not in the Daily Offices (p. 142, rubric 5). An Additional Direction permits a sermon at Morning or Evening Prayer, but there is no provision for it in the structure we examined in the last chapter. There was no provision for preaching in the Breviary nor in the Daily Offices of prior Anglican books. The combination of Morning Prayer and sermon is a juxtaposition of two independent liturgical actions that has become standard fare. On the other hand, a sermon belongs in the Eucharist. It is mentioned by rubric in earlier English and American Prayer Books (BCP 1928, p. 71). In the current Prayer Book, the sermon has a subtitle of the same prominence as those for the Collect of the Day, Lessons, the Creed, and the Prayers of the People. What of preaching?

In an earlier chapter, we examined three interdependent forms of the Word of God: the Incarnate Word, our Lord Jesus Christ; the written Word, the Scripture; and the proclaimed Word. We must turn our attention now to the third of these forms.

The Incarnate Word is crucified and risen. Under the form of flesh and blood, he is not here. The written Word is contained in a book. Under the form of paper and ink, it is here with us. Yet its words come from a distant past. It does not always yield its meaning directly or easily. The proclaimed Word, however, is spoken to us by persons like ourselves. The words of a preacher are words out of our time and culture. The preacher lives and moves as one of us. There is an immediacy in preaching, an embodiment in it, and a confronting quality to it, all of which make it a unique form of the Word of God.

To be sure, not all preaching becomes the Word of God for each hearer. Just as the Scripture has been inspired by the Spirit, and the hearers of the scriptural word must receive "the internal testimony of the Spirit" to hear God's Word through the scriptural words, so the preacher must receive the gift and bear the weight of the Spirit in order to preach God's Word, and hearers must have their ears opened by the Spirit in order to hear God's Word in the preaching.[1] Only those with "ears to hear" can hear (Mt. 11:15).

"Does a love like this come into the heart of the hearer from the *mouth* of him who sings the other's praise?" asked St. Augustine in his *Confessions*. "Not so. Instead one catches the spark of love from one who loves." Preaching too, is an affair of the heart. One catches the spark of faith not so much from the preacher's words (although not without them) as from the faith from which those words proceed.

Like the reading of Scripture as an act of worship, preaching as an act of worship had its beginnings in the life of Israel. The early chapters of Deuteronomy (chapters 1–12) are probably examples of ancient sermons, preached at covenant-renewal ceremonies on Mount Schechem. The speaker of the occasion addressed the assembly of Israel as if the present generation of Israelites were the generation that came out of Egypt. "The LORD our God made a covenant with us in Horeb. Not with our fathers did the LORD make this covenant, but with us, who are all of us here alive this day" (Dt. 5:2–3). These addresses or sermons have two centers of interest: they rehearse the story of the Jews' flight from Egypt and their wanderings through the wilderness; they also exhort the people to obey "the statutes and the ordinances which I teach you" (Dt. 4:1). Sermons in the book of Acts are thought to be modeled on synagogue sermons of the century before Christ. In them, too, there are both narrative and ethical elements. There is a recital of the story of God's gracious dealing with the Israelite people, concluding, usually, with an exhortation to repentance, baptism, and obedience (Acts 2:38; 10:42), or a reproach for disobedience (Acts 7:51).

Preaching is far more prominent in the New Testament than in the Old. The word appears nearly fifteen times more often in a book only one-third as long. The conclusion seems clear, and the experience of the church bears it out: the most effective way to communicate the fact of God's reconciling work in Jesus our Lord, and the implications of it for our living, is for one who knows about it to tell one who doesn't. One hungry man tells another where to find bread, as someone has said. How else can we find it?

Preaching has three aspects. We have encountered two of them already. One is the telling of "the old, old story" of God's gracious dealing with his people, culminating in Christ, and in his overcoming of sin and death for us. The reading of passages from the Gospel and the Old Testament every week gives the preacher a springboard into some aspect of the story, different every week, encompassing the whole drama year by year.

A second aspect of preaching concerns our response to the story. What shall we do? How are we to be faithful? This ethical dimension of preaching also appears in the sermons we considered in the Old Testament and in Acts. Readings from the Epistles (and sometime the Old Testament) give the preacher his text in these matters.

A third feature of preaching is disclosed in the account of St. Paul's night of worship with the elders at Troas. We read that he "prolonged his speech until midnight" (Acts 20:7). The Greek text suggests a much less formal utterance, a discussion, a sharing of experience in a small group of Christians. We might call it *dialogue*.

It is surely not necessary to choose among these three aspects of preaching. Certain situations call for one emphasis or one style more than another, but the full proclamation of the Word of God sooner or later surely involves them all: the story, dialogical engagement, ethical exhortation. Nor is it essential that the proclamation of the Gospel should be a sermon in the conventional sense of the word. The Word of God is greater than any human words, and may choose to come clothed in quite different ways. He who was once "veiled in flesh" does not now have to be veiled by human discourse. If the Spirit of God can inspire preachers and writers with the word of life that puts fire in our bones and music in our hearts, so can he inspire dance, drama, music, and art. And if the Spirit can open our ears to hear the truth of God in the Bible and in preaching, so we can be opened to see it and hear it in the work of Rembrandt, Mozart, and Milton; or Picasso, Auden, and Britten; or thousands of others.

The Order for Celebrating the Holy Eucharist has this rubric under the heading, "Proclaim and Respond to the Word of God":

> The proclamation and response may include readings, song, talk, dance, instrumental music, other art forms, silence. A reading from the Gospel is always included. (BCP, p. 400)

The thoughtful and imaginative use of such forms in the proclamation of the Word of God in the liturgy will immeasurably enrich our worship; and by their use as vehicles for God's Word in the liturgy of the church, these art forms may be consecrated to become vehicles for the communication of God's Word in the world; for those whose eyes and ears are opened by the Spirit of God, the heavens themselves declare God's glory, and all his works praise him and magnify him forever.

RESPONSE

The response to the proclamation of the Word in lessons and sermon is the recitation of the creed, prayer, and confession of sin. These liturgical acts have been discussed in the previous chapter, in connection with the Daily Offices. Only a few additional remarks need to be made.

The Nicene Creed is used at the Eucharist, rather than the Apostles' Creed of Baptism and the Daily Offices. It has been so in both Eastern and Western Christendom since the fifth century, when this creed was first introduced into the eucharistic liturgy as a symbol of orthodox faith.

This creed should properly be called the Nicene-Constantinopolitan Creed, for it is the version of the credal text authorized by the second General Council of Constantinople rather than that of the first Council of Nicaea. The difference lies in the addition of all the words after the clause, "We believe in the Holy Spirit," where the creed of the first council ended. The elaboration of the doctrine of the Spirit came at Constantinople.

This text has been the official creed of the Christian church, Eastern and Western, Protestant and Catholic, for the intervening 1600 years. It stands for what the church believes. To recite it is to confess one's faith in Christ as the church has always held it and continues to do so. One believes with the church and hence confesses faith in the words "We believe," as the original text runs, restored in the current Prayer Book. (Rite I retains the "I believe" form as an alternative.) It is a corporate action, just as the confession of sin is a corporate action.

The Western church added one phrase to the original text. After the clause about the Holy Spirit, "who proceeds from the Father," the Western church inserted "and the Son." The reasons, both historical and theological, are complex. The phrase was intended to elucidate the meaning of the original text, although Eastern churches have always claimed that the added words distort that meaning. A move to eliminate them from the current Prayer Book, and to return to the exact text of the Council of Constantinople, was narrowly defeated at the Minnesota Convention in 1976. The phrase remains, an issue to be resolved in further discussions with Orthodox churches.

The *Prayers of the People* are intercessions for the "whole state of Christ's Church and the world." These prayers are the classic and full form of intercessions, on which the intercessions at Morning and Evening Prayer are modeled. They include prayers for the universal church, the nation, the welfare of the world, the concerns of the local community, for those who suffer or are in trouble, and for the departed. A number of different forms are provided in the current book.

Prayers have been made for the church at the Eucharist from the time of the *Didache*, in the first or early second centuries. Justin Martyr mentioned them. Eucharistic liturgies from the fourth century on include extensive intercessions, usually within the eucharistic prayer itself. The intercessions were removed from the eucharistic prayer in the book of 1552, to make the action of the second part of the service more direct; they remain outside the eucharistic prayer in the current book. In this place they can best be understood, like the intercessions in the Daily Offices, as a response to the Word.

After all discussions about the content and placement of these prayers, one question remains outstanding. Why pray at all? What good does it do to ask God to do things for one's self or one's neighbors?

In chapter 4, we pointed out that prayer expresses our relationship with God in Christ, and that special prayers articulate that relationship at special times under special circumstances. When we pray for ourselves or for others, in the Eucharist or at any time, we express what it means to have a relationship with the God who was in Christ reconciling the world to himself in the face of some special need or some particular situation.

To pray, therefore, requires us to be as aware as we can of how we feel, and allows us to admit our feelings honestly. Especially in the Eucharist, in the presence of him "to whom all hearts are open, all desires known, and from whom no secrets are hid," we must be honest if we want to be related to God in Christ; and therefore we must be honest with ourselves. Prayer brings us to self-understanding.

Prayer also helps us to see the situation for which we pray, in our own lives or in the church or in the world, in the light of Christ crucified and risen. If God's own son suffered rejection, pain, and death, we are not likely to do better. "As he is, so are we in this world," wrote St. John (1 Jn. 4:17). Our suffering may acquire meaning in the light of his suffering, and indeed we may be called upon to "complete what is lacking in Christ's afflictions for the sake of his body, that is, the church," in St. Paul's overwhelming phrase (Col. 1:24). Moreover, prayer in the name of Christ not only brings understanding of the agonies and contradictions of our individual and corporate life in this way, but it also brings hope. For God raised Christ from the dead, and showed himself triumphant over the last and fiercest enemy of human existence. Deliverance is at hand for those who trust God. We may share that deliverance. Christian prayer, as we have already observed, is marked by its certainty of being heard.

In prayer, moreover, we offer ourselves to accomplish God's purposes. One of the ways in which God's will is done on earth is through the men and women who freely obey what they understand God's will to be. To pray for the need of another person, or for the solution of a problem in our nation or community, involves Christians in allowing themselves to be the instruments of God's action; and to pray without holding ourselves ready to act in the matter for which we pray is less than Christian prayer.

Prayer has a still deeper level, however. After these preliminary levels have been reached and crossed, after those who pray have learned and expressed their true feelings, after we have understood the situation in terms of the cross and the resurrection, after we have done all that we can do in obedience to God, then, in prayer, we put the situation into the hands of a loving and omnipotent

God, "who is doing for us better things that we can desire or pray for." Such prayer, in Christian experience, is always answered, either in fact or in hope. Such prayer always strengthens our relationship to God, and therefore is always worth doing—especially in the Eucharist, but indeed at all times and in all places.

Confession of Sin is a third response to the Proclamation of the Word. We confess our sin as we confess our faith. We have already discussed his liturgical element in chapter 12.

The Proclamation of the Word of God concludes with the *Peace*. This action does not appear in the daily offices, nor in earlier Anglican eucharistic liturgies. It was introduced into our service during the period of trial use which preceded the publication of the current Prayer Book. It is an exchange of greeting between ministers and people, and among the people, a liturgical way of expressing that we are in love and charity with our neighbors.

The Peace was mentioned in very early liturgical texts. Over the years, it has occurred at different moments in the course of the eucharistic action. In the late Latin liturgy it had become a purely formal verbal exchange between priest and congregation just before the act of communion itself. It dropped out of Anglican Prayer Books.

As it appears in the current Prayer Book, after the Absolution, it means that the power of God's forgiveness that we have received enables us to offer reconciliation to our neighbors and to receive forgiveness from them. Our defenses are down. We are open to one another. The Peace is thus a liturgical symbol of renewed relationships within the Christian community. And it is the apt introduction to the section that follows—the Offertory. For our Lord himself taught,

> So if you are offering your gift at the altar, and there remember that your brother has something against you, leave your gift there before the altar and go; first be reconciled to your brother, and then come and offer your gift. (Mt. 5:23–24)

OTHER SERVICES OF THE WORD

We have analyzed the Proclamation of the Word of God at the Eucharist. A similar proclamation occurs as the first part of Baptism, Confirmation, Holy Matrimony, the Ministration to the Sick, the Burial of the Dead, and Ordination services. All these rites had a service of the Word in earlier Anglican books except Holy Matrimony, where no Scripture was read. In the earlier books, however, the parallel to the service of the Word at the Eucharist was implicit. In the current book the form is identical in each case. Baptism, marriage, ministry to the sick, burial, ordination—all of these crucial actions are to be seen as our responses in these different circumstances of life to the Word of God.

THE MINISTERS OF THE WORD

The Proclamation of the Word of God at the Eucharist and in these other services provides a significant instance of the shared ministry that is such a noteworthy development in modern liturgical practice. As the directions "Concerning the Service" in the BCP make clear, the bishop should be the celebrant at the Eucharist if he is present (pp. 322, 354). Otherwise the celebrant is to be a priest, assisted by other priests in the actions of Holy Communion, assisted by a deacon in reading the Gospel and in preparing the bread and wine at the Lord's Table, assisted by lay persons in reading the Old Testament lesson, the Epistle, and the Prayers of the People. This shared liturgical ministry is significant chiefly as an outward expression in the gathered church of the shared ministry of the people of God as they go about their work in the world, in obedience to Christ. Each baptized Christian is given both a ministry and gifts to perform it. The sum of these ministries constitutes the liturgy of the church. Our lives lived in accordance with the self-giving love of God revealed in Christ, expressed in the worldly decisions we make daily, are the shared ministry of the church in the world. This ministry is reflected in the shared ministry of the people of God at worship, where each baptized person also has a ministry. In order to actualize this shared ministry most effectively, as many different individuals as possible, lay and ordained, share the reading and the prayers.

14

The Holy Eucharist (II):
The Holy Communion

The liturgy of the Holy Eucharist consists of two primary parts: the Proclamation of the Word of God and the Holy Communion. In trying to understand the second part of the Eucharist, Holy Communion, we shall be involved, as we were in the case of baptism and the use of Scripture, in an exploration of the Jewish background of this central Christian act, in a brief survey of the historical development that the service has undergone, and in an examination of the liturgy that we use today in the American Episcopal Church.

The Jewish Background of Holy Communion

THE LAST SUPPER

The New Testament presents four rather different accounts of the Last Supper: in the Gospels according to Matthew, Mark, and Luke (Mt. 26:26–29; Mk. 14:22–25; Lk. 22:14–22); and in St. Paul's First Letter to the Corinthians (11:23–26). What really happened? Careful comparison of these four narratives has led scholars to conclude that there are in fact two very old forms of the story, one represented by St. Mark and one represented by St. Paul. St. Matthew agrees with St. Mark, almost word for word. St. Luke combines the two traditions and adds material not found in the others. He speaks of two cups of wine, for example, one distributed before the bread and one after.

All of these texts, taken together, add up to extremely complicated evidence for what happened on that "night before he was betrayed." We will not be able to do justice to the vast amount of scholarly work that has been done to clarify this subject, nor to the variety of opinions that still exists. What follows represents one possible and reasonable way to understand the Last Supper, with a glance at some alternative possibilities.

The striking difference between St. Mark's version and St. Paul's is in the commandment of Jesus to his disciples to repeat the Supper in the future. In St. Mark's account, Jesus' closing words are, "Truly I say you, I shall not drink again of the fruit of the vine until that day when I drink it new in the kingdom of God" (Mk. 14:25). St. Paul, unlike St. Mark, puts the familiar words, "Do this

128

in remembrance of me," after the distribution of both the bread and the cup, and concludes "For as often as you eat this bread and drink the cup, you proclaim the Lord's death until he comes" (1 Cor. 11:26). St. Mark's version, in other words, envisions no repetition of the Supper. St. Paul's version does. According to St. Mark, Jesus expected that the end of the world would come quickly and that his fellowship with his disciples would be reestablished in the kingdom of God, whose nearness he had proclaimed and whose immediate coming he apparently now anticipated. The end of human history was near. This attitude is consistent with everything else we know of Jesus' teaching and preaching.

St. Paul's version, on the other hand, assumes that there will be some indeterminate time before the Lord comes again in majesty. In the meantime, the Supper will continue to be celebrated in order to proclaim the Lord's death. This attitude is consistent with everything else we know about St. Paul's teaching: his continual efforts to account for the fact that the Lord had not returned, for the fact that the general resurrection of humanity seemed as far in the future as ever, for the fact that human history continued, and for the fact that life apparently went on as before in spite of the cross of Christ. The church began to prepare for the long haul.

It seems likely, though by no means certain, that St. Mark's account of the Last Supper is closer to the historical reality of what happened than St. Paul's. On the one hand, if the command, "Do this," had actually been spoken by Jesus in history on the night before his death, how can we account for the fact that none of the Gospels records it? On the other hand, if the Supper in fact continued to be celebrated after the first Easter, and if Jesus continued to "make himself known in the breaking of the bread," as he did in the upper room in Jerusalem and in the inn on the road to Emmaus on the days after the first Easter, surely it would have occurred to someone sooner or later—perhaps to St. Paul himself or to someone else who shaped the tradition St. Paul reports—that the repetition of the Supper was precisely what the risen Lord willed his church to do, to "proclaim the Lord's death until he comes." So St. Paul begins his account of the Last Supper with the words, "I received from the Lord what I also delivered to you . . ." (1 Cor. 11:23).

In any event, Jesus ate the Last Supper with his disciples in Jerusalem. He knew he would be betrayed. He faced death. It was Passover time.

During the mid-decades of the twentieth century, there was considerable discussion about whether or not the Last Supper was a Passover meal. Three of the evangelists—Matthew, Mark, and Luke—write as if it were. John writes as if it took place on the night *before* the Passover meal would have been eaten (cf. Jn. 19:31). Dom Gregory Dix in his famous book, *The Shape of the Liturgy*, argued that St. John's chronology was the accurate one. On the other hand, Joachim Jeremias, in *The Eucharistic Words of Jesus*, argued that the Last Supper *was* a Passover meal.[1] Many others have taken up each side of the discussion. The argument has been inconclusive. In either view, Passover was in the air, the time of remembering God's deliverance of the chosen people from Egypt, and of hoping for final establishment of God's rule of justice and peace over all the earth. Passover provides the background for the Last Supper.

One of the well-known features of the Passover Seder (the liturgical order recited at the family meal on that night) is the identification by the host of some of the food that the family eats: "This is the bread of affliction which your fathers did eat when they came out of Egypt. . . ." Whether or not the Last Supper was a Passover meal, this action would have been in everyone's mind. When Jesus took the bread and made a *different* identification, its significance would not have been lost on the Twelve. This is my body . . . This is blood of the covenant which is poured out for many. Truly I say to you, I shall not drink again of the fruit of the vine until that day when I drink it new in the kingdom of God." The old Passover celebration is not to usher in the kingdom, but rather a new celebration, in the body and blood of Christ. The death of Christ will initiate the kingdom of God. After it is established, the Lord will feast with his faithful followers in God's presence.

From this point of view, expressed by St. Mark, the Last Supper is a sign of the kingdom, a prophetic sign, similar to many occasions in the Old Testament when prophets *acted out* the word of the Lord in addition to speaking it. Once Jeremiah, for example, took a pottery flask and broke it in the presence of the elders of the city of Jerusalem. He announced the breaking as a sign that the city would be destroyed by the approaching Babylonians. It was a sign, of course, in the "participating" sense that we examined in chapter 3. God disclosed his will ahead of time to the prophets; and because God was with them, their words and deeds were filled with God's own power. The breaking of the flask was connected with the approaching fate of Jerusalem. God was the source of both events. When the flask broke and Jeremiah prophesied, the city's destruction was surely to be expected. If the prophet was a true prophet, his signs and words entailed the future event, as all who were caught up in the events of those days knew. That is why the elders imprisoned Jeremiah for breaking the flask (Jer. 19). Similarly, at the Last Supper, Jesus, filled with the power of God, believing and trusting that the salvation of the world would come through his death, broke bread and poured out wine as a sign of his death and the consequent establishment of God's kingdom. No repetition of the Supper was expected. The end was at hand. For those who believed that God was with Jesus, Immanuel, the sign entailed the event.

EARLY EUCHARISTS

But the end did not come. The crucifixion of Jesus did not bring the kingdom of God in any obvious way. Yet in the days following the crucifixion, a marvelous thing happened. Jesus showed himself to be alive. Many of the occasions of his appearing were at the meals of his faithful and expectant disciples: to two disciples on Easter afternoon, on the way to Emmaus, when they met a stranger and broke bread with him; to the Twelve, now eleven without Judas, probably in the same upper room in Jerusalem where the Last Supper was eaten; to seven who had returned to their fishing on the shore of the Sea of Tiberia as they ate fish and bread. How often the risen Christ revealed himself at a common meal!

Whether or not Dom Gregory Dix is correct in his contention that the Last Supper was not a Passover meal but an ordinary Jewish meal eaten the night before the Passover, he did draw attention in a remarkably influential way to what common Jewish meals were like. And whether or not the Last Supper was a Passover, these subsequent meals when Christ's presence was known cannot have been the Passover. They all took place within a few days of the Passover; and Passover recurs but once a year. After the death of Jesus, the disciples continued to eat together, as Jewish religious fellowships, or *chaburoth*, were accustomed to do. As they ate together, recalling the many occasions when the Lord had broken bread with them before his crucifixion, they found that he was with them still. Precisely because he was with them still, particularly at these common meals, someone—was it St. Paul himself?—finally understood that the continuation of these common meals was the means by which the Lord intended to give his disciples a sign of his presence and a foretaste of the kingdom of God, until in God's good time it would be established in its fullness. "Do this in remembrance of me. For as often as you eat this bread and drink the cup, you proclaim the Lord's death until he comes." In some way like this, the Eucharist must have become an institution.

THE EUCHARIST: FOCUS OF CHRISTIAN LIFE

It is easy to see why the Supper became the characteristic liturgical expression of the life of the earliest church. For the Supper brought into one focus a great many facets of Christian belief and expectation. It was a reminder, of course, of the Last Supper that Jesus shared with the Twelve. Beyond that, it recalled all the meals he had eaten with them in the course of his ministry. The feedings of multitudes in the wilderness were also meals of thanksgiving. At those meals too, Jesus took bread, broke it, and gave thanks (Mk. 6:41; 8:6).

The Eucharist, moreover, was always much more in the life of the church than a meal of recollection. The Last Supper was a prophetic sign of the cross, as we have seen. Subsequent Eucharists, by the same token, were signs of the coming kingdom of God. They enabled the company of faithful Christians to stand in that single full moment of time between the death of Jesus in the past and the fulfillment of God's purposes in the future. It was one of the chief ways in which the mystery of Christ became actual.

The Eucharist was even more. For the Lord was present at these meals. Through him, communion with God had been restored. Therefore, the death of Christ was recognized as a sacrifice. Consequently the Eucharist, the way of realizing again and again this opening of communion between God and his people, could be recognized as being in some sense a sacrifice, because it participated on the one, perfect once-for-all sacrifice of Jesus' obedient life and death. Furthermore, the Eucharist was the celebration of the new covenant, long expected by the prophets, a covenant written on the hearts of faithful people, based on the forgiveness of sins (Jer. 31:31–34). "This cup is the new covenant in my blood" (1 Cor. 11:25).

No, the kingdom did not come in its fullness. Yet the Eucharist is a foretaste of the kingdom to come. It is a memory of those mighty acts that God did for us in Christ, giving us our present hope. It is a way by which Christ is present among us in the meantime.

The Form of the Eucharistic Prayer

JEWISH TABLE PRAYERS

Through the Talmud, a post-biblical collection of Jewish teaching and practice, we know something about the liturgy used at Jewish meals. From present Jewish practice, more can be inferred. The tractate *Berakoth* ("Blessings") mentions table prayers used at a date not very long after the New Testament. Jesus and his disciples would have used such prayers as they ate, and the meals after the resurrection that turned into joyful encounters with the risen Lord would have been accompanied by similar prayers. Those would have concluded with a dialogue between host and guests. The content of that dialogue has changed little during the intervening centuries.

> The host begins: "Let us give thanks . . ."
>   (if there should be a hundred present
>   he adds, 'unto our God.')
> The guests answer: "Blessed be the name of
>   the Lord from this time forth forevermore."
> The host: "With the assent of those present
>   (they indicate their assent)—we will
>   bless Him of Whose bounty we have partaken."
> The guests: "Blessed be He of Whose bounty
>   we have partaken and through Whose goodness
>   we live."

Prayers follow, giving thanks to God for food, for the deliverance of his people from Egypt, for the giving of the Law.

> The host: "Blessed art Thou, O Lord our God, eternal king, who feedest the whole world with thy goodness, with grace, with loving kindness and tender mercy . . . We thank Thee, O Lord our God, because Thou didst give as an heritage to our fathers a desirable, good and ample land, and because Thou didst bring us forth, O Lord our God, from the land of Egypt, and didst deliver us from the house of bondage, as well as for Thy Covenant which thou hast sealed in our flesh; for Thy law which Thou hast taught us; Thy statutes which Thou hast made known unto us . . ."[2]

The dialogue between host and guests expressed their mutual intention to bless the Lord; then together host and guest gave praise and thanksgiving to

God for his goodness and mercy, both in providing food through a generous creation, and in delivering his people from their enemies: that is the structure of Jewish table blessings. At this period in history, the host apparently expressed himself with a certain freedom in Jewish as in Christian worship. In spite of this spontaneity, however, the outline of the prayer would have been kept. In Christian congregations, too, it seems likely that a comparable outline remained in the celebrant's mind but that he varied and extended his thanksgiving to God to include the work of Christ in overcoming sin and death.

We do not have the *text* of any eucharistic prayer for nearly two hundred years; but in the middle of the second century, about A.D. 150, Justin Martyr wrote a description of a Eucharist. We have used his description in chapter 11 for its information about the reading of the Scripture. The service no longer took place on Saturday night, the beginning of the First Day for the Jews, but on Sunday morning, the beginning of the day for Gentiles. "Over all," he writes, "we make a blessing to the Creator of all things, through his Son Jesus Christ and through the Holy Spirit." After the reading and a discourse by the president, the service continues:

> Then we all stand up together and offer prayers. And as we mentioned before, when we have finished the prayer, bread is presented, and wine with water; the president likewise offers up prayers and thanksgivings according to his ability, and the people assent by saying, Amen.[3]

By Justin's time, the service had moved from night to morning. We observe also that the setting was no longer a full meal. St. Paul tells us about the difficulties that the Corinthians had already found in celebrating their Eucharists at a regular supper. The congregation divided into dissenting cliques, gathering around their own food. Some had too much, some had too little. "Your meetings tend to do more harm than good," the apostle told them (1 Cor. 11:17). One concludes that in the Gentile world, the full meal gradually disappeared as the setting for the Eucharist. The prayers remained, however, and the bread to be broken and the cup of wine. Justin Martyr's description of the prayers would fit a Christianized version of Jewish table blessings.

This conclusion is confirmed when we look at the eucharistic prayer in the *Apostolic Tradition* of Hippolytus. It begins with a dialogue between bishop and congregation:

> The Lord be with you.
> *And with thy spirit.*
> Lift up your hearts.
> *We lift up unto the Lord.*
> Let us give thanks unto the Lord.
> *It is meet and right.*[4]

The echoes of the dialogue between host and guests at a Jewish table blessing are clear. As is easily recognized, the same dialogue has begun the eucharistic prayer throughout Christendom from that day to this.

A prayer of thanksgiving for God's work in Christ follows.

> We give thee thanks, O God, through thy beloved Son Jesus Christ, whom at the
> end of time thou didst send to us a Saviour and redeemer of thy counsel. Who
> is thy Word, inseparable from thee; through whom thou didst make all things
> and in whom thou art well pleased. Whom thou didst send from heaven into
> the womb of the Virgin, and who, dwelling within her, was made flesh, and was
> manifested as thy Son, being born of [the] Holy Spirit and the Virgin. Who, ful-
> filling thy will, and winning for himself a holy people, spread out his hands
> when he came to suffer, that by his death, he might set free them who believed
> in thee. Who, when he was betrayed to his willing death, that he might bring to
> nought death, and break the bonds of the devil, and tread hell under foot,
> and give light to the righteous, and set up a boundary post and manifest his
> resurrection . . .[5]

Does it stretch imagination too far to see in this prayer a Christianized version
of the Jewish thanksgiving for creation, deliverance from Egypt, and the giving of
the Law? Here the Christian congregation gives thanks for God in Christ, his
work in creation (shortened to a single phrase, it is true), and his work in setting
his people free from death and the devil. None of the words are the same, but the
rhythm of the dialogue, the tone, and the intention of the prayer are the same. It
seems reasonable to think that the nucleus of Christian eucharistic prayers is the
dialogue and prayer of thanksgiving spoken at Jewish table blessings. We shall
call this part of the eucharistic prayer the *Prayer of Blessing*.

APOSTOLIC TRADITION OF HIPPOLYTUS

The eucharistic prayer in Hippolytus continues, however, with three sections
that have no counterpart in Jewish table blessings. These sections have
appeared in most subsequent eucharistic prayers, including those in the present Prayer Book. The first addition is an account of the institution of the supper in words similar to St. Paul's in 1 Corinthians.

> . . . taking bread and giving thanks to thee, [he] said: "Take, eat, this is my body,
> which is broken for you." And likewise also the cup, saying: "This is my blood,
> which is shed for you. As often as ye perform this, perform my memorial."[6]

It is not surprising to find these words. They explain what the Christian community means by its meal. This section is the charter and authorization of our
celebration of the Supper. This part of the prayer became particularly important in the Gentile world, where the practice of Jewish *chaburah* meals was
unfamiliar and the Jewish background of the eucharistic liturgy not known.
This section of the eucharistic prayer is known as the *Institution*.

The Institution is followed by a succinct recital of the acts of God in Christ
for the salvation of the world as bread and wine are offered.

> Having in memory, therefore, his death and resurrection, we offer to thee the

bread and the cup, yielding thee thanks because thou hast counted us worthy to stand before thee and minister to thee.[7]

This part of the eucharistic prayer calls to mind our earlier discussion of the transformation of time as a key for understanding the action of God in the Christian mystery. By remembering in God's presence what has been done for us through the power of the Spirit, we participate in those events. They are present for us. Our time is that time. We are there. This section of the prayer is entitled the *Oblation* in the 1928 Book of Common Prayer and in the earlier American and English books. Its technical name is the *Anamnesis*, or the Memorial.

The third of these sections in the prayer of Hippolytus refers to the work of the Holy Spirit. There is considerable debate about the original text of the prayer at this point. If one were to accept the shorter reading, which is quite possibly the original, it runs:

> And we pray thee that thou wouldst grant to all thy saints who partake to be filled with the Holy Spirit, that their faith may be confirmed in truth, that we may praise and glorify thee. Through thy Servant Jesus Christ, through whom be to thee glory and honour, with [the] Holy Spirit in the holy church, both now and always and world without end. Amen.[8]

In this form, the prayer asks that all who share the eucharistic gifts may thereby be filled with the Holy Spirit for the confirmation of their common faith. The use of *saints* is a reference to all Christian people, just as in the New Testament. This element in the eucharistic prayer, generally called a *Communion Epiclesis* or *Communion Invocation*, eventually gave rise to the incorporation of intercessions for the church within the text of the prayer. In the course of time these intercessions became quite lengthy.

The longer version of this part of the prayer has a somewhat different focus, although it is still concerned with the activity of the Holy Spirit. The text runs:

> And we pray thee that thou wouldst send thy Holy Spirit upon the offerings of thy church; that thou, gathering them into one, wouldst grant to all thy saints who partake to be filled with [the] Holy Spirit. . . . [The text continues as cited above.][9]

Here it is a question of an invocation of the Holy Spirit upon the material offerings of bread and wine. The thrust of this form of the prayer is that the divine activity is directed toward the gifts of bread and wine that, in being shared by the communicants, brings about their unity and also fills them with the Holy Spirit. The technical name for this form is a *Consecratory Epiclesis* or *Consecratory Invocation* because of its focus upon the bread and wine. This longer version combines both *consecratory* and the *communion* aspects of this traditional element in the prayer. The Invocation has had a complicated history in the evolution of the eucharistic prayer in the various Christian traditions. In a more emphatically consecratory form, it became an essential characteristic of the Eastern Orthodox eucharistic rites. As we noticed in our discussion of the history of the American Book of Common Prayer in chapter 7, this element has been a part of every American eucharistic prayer, including those of the current book.

Thus, the first form of the eucharistic prayer that has come down to us contains all the fundamental elements that have appeared, in one form or another, in subsequent forms. In summary, the prayer of Hippolytus contains the following elements:

> Dialogue (Lift up your hearts . . .)
> Thanksgiving: Prayer of Blessing
> Memorial: (*Anamnesis*) Institution and Oblation
> Invocation: (*Epiclesis*) Prayer for the Church

The prayer concludes with an Amen, spoken by the entire congregation to express and affirm its participation in what has been proclaimed in the prayer. The only familiar element that is missing is the *Sanctus* (Holy, Holy, Holy Lord . . .), which has been a standard part of all subsequent forms.

Holy Communion in the Current Book of Common Prayer

In the current Prayer Book, the eucharistic prayer is called *The Great Thanksgiving*. It constitutes the central part of the second half of the Holy Eucharist, the part entitled Holy Communion. The Great Thanksgiving is preceded by the Offertory. It is followed by the Lord's Prayer, then by the Breaking of the Bread and the distribution of bread and wine, and then by post-communion prayer, a blessing, and a dismissal.

THE OFFERTORY

In chapter 7 we discussed the checkered career of the offering as part of the Eucharist. Popular late medieval theology of the Eucharist made of it a new offering of Christ himself, and each Mass came to be regarded as something offered to God for the sins of the people. The once-for-all character of Christ's dying, and the basic point that in the Eucharist Christ is offered *by* God *to* us, became obscure. In English Prayer Books after 1552, as we have seen, all mention of the offering was eliminated in order to correct what the reformers regarded as a complete distortion of biblical faith. As a result, not even money, bread and wine were regarded as offerings. From 1552 until 1662, money was put in the "poor box" and bread and wine were placed on the Holy Table before the beginning of the service. In 1662, we noted, bread and wine were to be put on the table at the time of the offering; and in the American book of 1928, it was directed that money should be presented and placed on the Holy Table, and that bread and wine should be *offered* and placed on the Holy Table.

The rubric of the current Prayer Book makes the Offertory more explicit and joins the money and the bread and wine together as part of one action:

> Representatives of the congregation bring the people's offerings of bread and
> wine, and money or other gifts, to the deacon or celebrant. The people stand
> while the offerings are presented and placed on the Altar.

The restored Offertory is thus in no sense a new offering of Christ. It is the representative gift of the baptized and forgiven people of God. In placing on the altar money and bread and wine, the congregation offers *itself* and *its world*. Money represents the work of the congregation. As in every sacrificial act from time immemorial, a part stands for the whole. We give part of what we make. That part stands for "our selves, for our souls and bodies." Otherwise the meaning of the gift becomes distorted. Symbolically, we offer bread to become the body of Christ. But the underlying reality of the action is that we offer our lives, individually and corporately, to become his body in this world. We acknowledge that what we offer to God is, in a certain sense, not ours but his all along, given to us in trust as his stewards of creation. We should recognize also that in a dramatic way, the act of *securing* bread and wine for offering involves the whole structure of a society: it implies the agricultural enterprise, industry (in the manufacture of what is used to harvest wheat and grapes), and the system of transportation and distribution. In offering bread and wine, a congregation offers not only itself in a limited and individual way, but also the world of which it is a part. (It is significant that in contemporary slang "bread" means "money.")

THE GREAT THANKSGIVING

There are eight eucharistic prayers in the current book: Eucharistic Prayers I and II in Rite I; Eucharistic Prayers A, B, C, and D in Rite II; and Forms 1 and 2 in the Order for Celebrating the Holy Eucharist. Each of these prayers will be found to exhibit the same basic parts that were identified in the prayer from the *Apostolic Tradition* of Hippolytus. We shall comment in this section on Eucharistic Prayer I from Rite I and on Eucharistic Prayer D from Rite II. Eucharistic Prayer I has been used in all American Books of Common Prayer since 1789. It was taken from the Scottish liturgy, as we saw, at the insistence of Bishop Seabury. This prayer is the one most familiar to the greatest number of Episcopalians today. Eucharistic Prayer D was produced in 1976 under ecumenical auspices. It is significant not only because of its eloquence and fullness of expression, making unmistakably clear the emphases and trends present in all the new eucharistic prayers, but also because of its acceptability by a number of different denominations. It has an Eastern Orthodox Prayer of Thanksgiving as its model.

We have chosen to study Eucharistic Prayer I and Eucharistic Prayer D for these reasons. Readers of this book can easily apply the same kind of analysis to the other six prayers. The following arrangement in parallel columns will disclose the significant features of these prayers, and their similarity to the prayer of Hippolytus.

This comparison reveals at a glance both the continuities and discontinuities among these prayers. The fundamental structure of the prayer is preserved in each case. Verbal similarities are strongest in the ancient dialogue in the Words of Institution. The similarity of thought in the Prayer of Blessing, the Oblation, and the Invocation is evident. The power of the tradition that surrounds the encounter of the Christian community with its risen Lord in the breaking of bread is strikingly attested by the common features of these three prayers, springing from such different times and places.

Yet the differences are also noteworthy, and the developments that they imply are worth comment.

1. Both Eucharistic Prayer I and Eucharistic Prayer D contain sections of praise to God the Father, culminating in the familiar hymn, "Holy, holy, holy Lord, God of power and might," the Sanctus. It is not clear why the prayer of Hippolytus does not contain praise to the Father, although in the section that follows, of praise to the eternal Word, some of the same material is covered. The hymn of praise to the Father did, in fact, appear in other early eucharistic prayers, and their presence has been continuous. This element, like the opening dialogue, is reminiscent of the Jewish *chaburah* meal.

As part of the Prayer of Blessing, Eucharistic Prayer I, like most of the eucharistic prayers in the current Prayer Book, provides a Proper Preface, which expresses some particular aspect of God's action on our behalf. Proper prefaces are used every Sunday; every day during the seasons from Advent to Pentecost, and on other special occasions. Form 1 and 2 in the Order for Celebrating Holy Communion do not provide a special proper preface because it is intended that this whole part of the prayer be especially prepared for the occasion. The whole is a "proper preface," so to speak. Prayer D has no proper preface, following its Orthodox model, but gives a very full description of God's saving activity.

2. Eucharist Prayer D and the prayer of Hippolytus, in their different ways, make much more of God's work in creation, of the creation of human beings in the divine image, of the fall, and of the coming of Christ in the flesh than does Eucharistic Prayer I. Eucharistic Prayer I focuses all its attention on the sacrificial death of Christ: ". . . for that thou, of thy tender mercy, didst give thine only Son Jesus Christ to suffer death upon the cross for our redemption . . . ." In the other prayers the death and resurrection of Christ is the climax of the recital of a much longer history of salvation. In an age like the sixteenth century, when the longer history was perhaps better known, the readings in the service of the Word might serve as sufficient reminder of the total biblical perspective. In our day, as in the earliest situation, the continual rehearsal of these elements in the prayer itself served to put the climactic event in its necessary setting. All the new prayers in the current Prayer Book provide for this broader perspective, although none expresses it as fully as Prayer D.

3. In each case, the oblation or anamnesis contains the three significant ele-

	APOSTOLIC TRADITION OF HIPPOLYTUS	EUCHARISTIC PRAYER I	EUCHARISTIC PRAYER D
DIALOGUE	The Lord be with you. *And with thy spirit.* Lift up your hearts. *We lift them up unto the Lord.* Let us give thanks unto the Lord. *It is meet and right.*	The Lord be with you. *And with thy Spirit.* Lift up your hearts. *We lift them up unto the Lord.* Let us give thanks unto the Lord our God. *It is meet and right so to do.*	The Lord be with you. *And also with you.* Lift up your hearts. *We lift them to the Lord.* Let us give thanks to the Lord our God. *It is right to give him thanks and praise.*
PRAYER OF BLESSING (Preface) *Praise for the work of God the Father*		It is very meet, right, and our bounden duty that we should at all times, and in all places, give thanks unto thee, O Lord, holy Father, almighty, everlasting God. (A Proper Preface follows if provided.)	It is truly right to glorify you, Father, and to give you thanks; for you alone are God, living and true, dwelling in light inaccessible from before time and forever. Fountain of life and source of all goodness, you made all things and fill them with your blessing; you created them to rejoice in the splendor of your radiance.

APOSTOLIC TRADITION OF HIPPOLYTUS	EUCHARISTIC PRAYER I	EUCHARISTIC PRAYER D
	Therefore, with Angels and Archangels, and with all the company of heaven, we laud and magnify thy glorious Name; evermore praising thee, and saying,	Countless throngs of angels stand before you to serve you night and day; and beholding the glory of your presence, they offer you unceasing praise. Joining with them, and giving voice to every creature under heaven, we acclaim you, and glorify your Name, as we sing,
	Holy, holy, holy, Lord God of Hosts: Heaven and earth are full of thy glory. Glory be to thee, O Lord Most High. (Blessed is he that cometh in the name of the Lord. Hosanna in the highest.)	Holy, holy, holy Lord, God of power and might, heaven and earth are full of your glory. Hosanna in the highest. Blessed is he who comes in the name of the Lord. Hosanna in the highest.
		We acclaim you, holy Lord, glorious in power. Your mighty works reveal your wisdom and love. You formed us in your own

APOSTOLIC TRADITION OF HIPPOLYTUS	EUCHARISTIC PRAYER I	EUCHARISTIC PRAYER D
		image, giving the whole world into our care, so that, in obedience to you, our Creator, we might rule and serve all your creatures. When our disobedience took us far from you, you did not abandon us to the power of death. In your mercy you came to our help, so that in seeking you we might find you. Again and again you called us into covenant with you, and through the prophets you taught us to hope for salvation.
	All glory be to thee, Almighty God, our heavenly Father, for that thou, of thy tender mercy, didst give thine only Son Jesus Christ	Father, you loved the world so much that in the fullness of time you sent your only Son to be our Savior. Incarnate by the Holy Spirit,
Praise for the work of God the Son		
We give thee thanks, O God, through the beloved Servant, Jesus Christ, whom at the end of time Thou didst send to us a Saviour and		

APOSTOLIC TRADITION OF HIPPOLYTUS	EUCHARISTIC PRAYER I	EUCHARISTIC PRAYER D
Redeemer and Messenger of thy counsel; who is thy Word inseparable from thee; through whom thou didst make all things, and in whom thou art well pleased; whom thou didst send from heaven into the womb of the Virgin, and who, dwelling with her, was made flesh, and was manifested as thy Son, being born of [the] Holy Spirit and the Virgin. Who, fulfilling thy will and winning for himself a holy people, spread out his hands when he came to the supper, that by his death he might set free them who believe on Thee.	to suffer death upon the cross for our redemption; who made there, by his one oblation of himself once offered, a full, perfect, and sufficient sacrifice, oblation, and satisfaction for the sins of the whole world; and did institute, and in his holy Gospel command us to continue, a perpetual memory of that his precious death and sacrifice, until his coming again.	born of the Virgin Mary, he lived as one of us, yet without sin. To the poor he proclaimed the good news of salvation; to prisoners, freedom; to the sorrowful, joy. To fulfill your purpose he gave himself up to death; and, rising from the grave, destroyed death, and made the whole creation new. And that we might live no longer for ourselves, but for him who died and rose for us, he sent the Holy Spirit, his own first gift for those who believe, to complete his work in the world, and to bring to fulfillment the sanctification of all.

	APOSTOLIC TRADITION OF HIPPOLYTUS	EUCHARISTIC PRAYER I	EUCHARISTIC PRAYER D
INSTITUTION *The word over the Bread*	Who, when he was betrayed to his willing death, that he might bring to nought death, and break the bonds of the devil, and tread hell under foot, and give light to the righteous, and set up a boundard post, and manifest his resurrection, taking bread and giving thanks to thee, said: Take, eat; this is my body, which is broken for you.	For in the night in which he was betrayed, he took bread; and when he had given thanks, he brake it, and gave it to his disciples, saying, "Take, eat, this is my Body, which is given for you. Do this in remembrance of me."	When the hour had come for him to be glorified by you, his heavenly Father, having loved his own who were in the world, he loved them to the end; at supper with them he took bread, and when he had given thanks to you, he broke it, and gave it to his disciples, and said, "Take, eat: This is my Body, which is given for you. Do this in remembrance of me."
The word over the Cup	And likewise, also the cup, saying: This is my blood, which is shed for you. As often as ye perform this, perform my memorial.	Likewise, after supper, he took the cup; and when he had given thanks, he gave it to them, saying, "Drink ye all of this; for this is my blood of the New Testament, which is shed for you, and for many, for	After supper, he took the cup of wine; and when he had given thanks, he gave it to them, and said, "Drink this, all of you: This is my Blood of the new Covenant, which is shed for you and for many for the

	APOSTOLIC TRADITION OF HIPPOLYTUS	EUCHARISTIC PRAYER I	EUCHARISTIC PRAYER D
		the remission of sins. Do this, as oft as you shall drink it, in remembrance of me."	forgiveness of sins, Whenever you drink it, do this for the remembrance of me."
OBLATION (Anamnesis) *Remembering* *Offering* *Thanking*	Having in memory, therefore, his death and resurrection, we offer to thee the bread and the cup, yielding thee thanks because thou hast counted us worthy to stand before thee and to minister to thee.	Wherefore, O Lord and heavenly Father, according to the institution of thy dearly beloved Son our Savior Jesus Christ, we, thy humble servants, do celebrate and make here before thy divine Majesty, with these thy holy gifts, which we now offer unto thee, the memorial thy Son hath commanded us to make; having in remembrance his blessed passion and precious death, his mighty resurrection and glorious ascension; rendering unto thee most hearty thanks for the innumerable benefits procured unto us by the same.	Father, we now celebrate this memorial of our redemption. Recalling Christ's death and his descent among the dead, proclaiming his resurrection and ascension to your right hand, awaiting his coming in glory; and offering to you, from the gifts you have given us, this bread and this cup, we praise you and we bless you. *We praise you, we bless you, we give thanks to you, and we pray to you, Lord God.*

	APOSTOLIC TRADITION OF HIPPOLYTUS	EUCHARISTIC PRAYER I	EUCHARISTIC PRAYER D
INVOCATION (Epiclesis)	[The longer reading] And we pray thee that thou wouldst send thy Holy Spirit upon the offerings of thy holy Church;	And we must humbly beseech thee, O merciful Father, to hear us; and, of thy almighty goodness, vouchsafe to bless and sanctify, with thy Word and Holy Spirit, these thy gifts and creatures of bread and wine; that we, receiving them according to thy Son our Savior Jesus Christ's holy institution, in remembrance of his death and passion, may be partakers of his most blessed Body and Blood.	Lord, we pray that in your goodness and mercy your Holy Spirit may descend upon us, and upon these gifts, sanctifying them and showing them to be holy gifts for your holy people, the bread of life and the cup of salvation, the Body and Blood of your Son Jesus Christ.
Prayer for the unity of the church	That thou, gathering them into one, wouldst grant to all thy saints who partake to be filled with [the] Holy Spirit, that their faith may be confirmed in truth, that	And here we offer and present unto thee, O Lord, our selves, our souls and bodies, to be a reasonable, holy, and living sacrifice unto thee; humbly beseeching	Grant that all who share this bread and cup may become one body and one spirit, a living sacrifice in Christ, to the praise of your Name.

	APOSTOLIC TRADITION OF HIPPOLYTUS	EUCHARISTIC PRAYER I	EUCHARISTIC PRAYER D
	we may praise and glorify thee. Through thy Servant Jesus Christ [*The shorter reading*] And we pray thee that thou wouldst grant to all thy saints who partake to be filled with [the] Holy Spirit . . . [*The text continue as above*]	thee that we, and all others who shall be partakers of this Holy Communion, may worthily receive the most precious Body and Blood of thy Son Jesus Christ, be filled with thy grace and heavenly benediction, and made one body with him, that he may dwell in us, and we in him.	Remember, Lord, your one holy catholic and apostolic Church, redeemed by the blood of your Christ. Reveal its unity, guard its faith, and preserve it in peace. [Optional intercessions and a conclusion follow.]
INTERCESSION	[The intercessions are not fully developed in this prayer, but are implied in the *Epiclesis*, and were amply developed in later forms of the eucharistic prayer.]	[The intercessions have been removed from this prayer, and from most of the eucharistic prayers in the current Prayer Book, and are found elsewhere in the service, as previously discussed.]	
THE CONGREGATIONAL AFFIRMATION	Amen.	Amen.	Amen.

ments of offering, remembering, and giving thanks. Prayer D, like its Orthodox model, heightens the future thrust of the prayer by including among the significant events in the saving work of Christ his "coming in glory." And since future expectation cannot intelligibly be counted as *remembering* in modern English, the coming in glory, as well as resurrection and ascension are said to be "proclaimed." Proclamation, of course, is the purpose of our recollection.

4. On the prayer of Hippolytus, the Holy Spirit is involved in the "offerings of thy holy Church"; similarly in Eucharistic Prayer I, "thy Word and Holy Spirit" are called to bless and sanctify "these thy gifts and creatures of bread and wine." As our earlier discussion has led us to anticipate, Eucharistic Prayer D calls the Holy Spirit to "descend upon *us*, and upon these gifts." Only as participants are illuminated by the Spirit can they perceive the new identity of bread and wine that the Spirit creates. To be sure, all baptized persons have been illuminated by the Spirit, and consequently it is not absolutely necessary to express this dimension of the eucharistic action. However, misunderstanding at this point is so easy that it seems desirable to do so. Nearly all the eucharistic prayers in the current book express the invocation of the Spirit upon the congregation as well as the bread and wine.

5. Eucharistic Prayer I makes no provision for explicit intercessions. In fact, among the eucharistic prayers in the current book, only Prayer D contains such a section. As we have seen in chapter 13, the current book in particular and the Anglican liturgical tradition in general have made other provisions for intercessions at the Eucharist. In Prayer D, the section of intercessions may be omitted if they have been included elsewhere; but for the sake of those churches in the group that have adopted the prayer and do not make another provision for a Prayer for the Church and the World, this paragraph is included.

The Lord's Prayer

In both Rite I and Rite II, the Eucharistic Prayer is followed by the Lord's Prayer said by the congregation. The Lord's Prayer appears at a climactic point in every Prayer Book service of worship. For American Episcopalians, this is the accustomed place for this most familiar, best loved, and most important Christian prayer. The eucharistic context emphasizes the well-known petitions for daily bread in the expectation of the coming kingdom of God, for forgiveness, and for deliverance from evil. The final act of praise seems especially appropriate: "For the kingdom, the power, and the glory are yours, now and forever."

THE BREAKING OF THE BREAD

In silence, consecrated bread is broken. The action reminds us that all participants receive from one loaf of bread. They are made one by their participation in the one Christ. The breaking of the single loaf is a sign of the unity of Christians in their Lord.

Distribution of the Bread and Wine

First bread and then the cup are distributed to communicants. According to Catholic custom, they normally go to the altar or to some other station in the church where a priest, often assisted by a deacon or lay person, administers the elements. The administration is accompanied by a short sentence, spoken to each communicant individually. One hopes that communicants will learn to respond with a firm "Amen," to signify that they receive Christ "by faith with thanksgiving."

This receiving of Christ through the sacramental elements is at once the most personal and the most corporate action of the church. When the congregation moves together to the designated place for distribution, the corporate nature of the action is emphasized. The receiving of bread and wine individually, and the prayer, meditation, and reflection that usually follow, bring into focus the personal and individual dimension of communion. Participation in the Eucharist has both these dimensions. It is easy to neglect one in favor of the other. Christian life in general and eucharistic piety in particular have in the recent past erred on the side of individualism. Religion was what one did with one's solitariness, a famous definition ran. One often took communion with no sense of the surrounding community, like a horse wearing blinders. In correcting this situation, we should be careful not to lose the dimension of the private in overcompensation. We best discover and enter into the depths of our own private, unique existence before God in the company of our neighbors. Holy Communion is a deepening of all our personal relationships: with God first, but with our neighbors also, as an inseparable part of the same action.

Post-Communion Prayer, Blessing, Dismissal

After the act of communion, anything else is almost certain to be anticlimax. The service should come to its end as quickly as possible. The post-communion prayer brings the congregation together after its period of private devotion. It briefly expresses appreciation and thanks for God's gracious acceptance of us and asks for his help to serve him in the world. The bishop or priest gives his blessing, according to Rite I; in Rite II, the blessing is optional. It was added to the eucharistic liturgy late in time, apparently being a formalized version of the spontaneous blessing that a bishop might give as he walked through the congregation at the close of the service. After the immeasurable blessing of God's own presence in the act of Holy Communion, it adds nothing essential.

The service ends with a dismissal, traditionally given by the deacon. By the dismissal, the congregation is sent forth to do God's work in God's world. It is an act of *sending*, or *mission*. Both dismissal and mission are derived from the same Latin verb, *mittere*, which means "to send." The dismissal marks the Eucharist as a missionary service, commissioning and empowering all of us to be missioners and ministers of the Gospel of Christ.

"Go in peace," says the deacon, "to love and serve the Lord." The congregation responds, "Thanks be to God." Mission and Eucharist are opposite sides of one coin.

15

The Holy Eucharist (III):
Theories about the Eucharist

The description of the Holy Eucharist that has occupied us in the foregoing chapters has avoided explanations. We have not tried to give a rational account of how Christ makes his presence known to us, or of when bread and wine become for believing communicants his body and blood. In these matters, the authors of this book have adopted a traditional and characteristic Anglican posture of reverent agnosticism. Our church has consistently refused to give an official answer to these speculative questions.

Nevertheless, in the course of Christian history, a number of influential theories have been advanced. They continue to be discussed. Individual Anglicans may entertain one or another of them as giving an intellectually satisfactory account of this central Christian mystery. The task of theology is to provide just such reasons as *aids* to faith. Especially in regard to the Eucharist, however, our church refuses to require its members to believe any particular theory, for all have been tried and found wanting. They easily become stumbling blocks to faith and the cause of great dissension.

This chapter is written to describe some of the most frequently encountered of these theories, so that readers will be able to gauge their strengths and weaknesses, and perhaps to "add understanding to their faith." That famous definition of theology, given by St. Anselm, expresses the purpose of all theories about the Eucharist.

How Is Christ Present?

In connection with the fundamental question of eucharistic theology—How is Christ present in this service?—it is important to recognize the continuous experience of the Christian church from the first Easter afternoon to the present; namely, that Christ *is* present when the church gathers to "do this in remembrance" of him and to make Eucharist, to give thanks. The power of this experience does not depend on our being able to explain why or how it happens.

Nevertheless, the power of that experience has always invited attempts to explain it. When Sir Edmund Hilary was asked why he wanted to climb Mount Everest, he gave the classic reply: "Because it's there." Just because the eucharistic experience is so vivid, just because "he is there," one is driven to ask *how* he can possibly be present. The resulting explanations depend on the philosophical assumptions of those who give them. What you see depends on where you start—in theologizing as in mountain climbing. When a theologian begins where most of his contemporaries are, with the assumptions that his generation takes as common sense, the resulting eucharistic theory will be helpful to many. When the common-sense assumptions of a generation or an era change, the explanation will no longer make sense to those who are expected to accept it. In the new situation, people will begin from a different starting place. They recognize few of the landmarks or vistas that had been opened up by the earlier theologian who had set out from a different base camp. Then the older theory is no longer helpful.

TRANSUBSTANTIATION

The doctrine of transubstantiation provides an example of this course of events. For hundreds of years, the attempt made by Thomas Aquinas to explain Christ's presence in bread and wine by means of Aristotle's philosophical categories of accidents and substance helped countless Christians to understand what they already believed. Aristotle argued that every physical object, like bread or wine, presented its reality to our physical senses through properties such as shape, size, color, and taste. These sense-perceived qualities Aristotle called *accidents*. At the same time, every object had a fundamental underlying reality—*in* the thing—that the mind could understand. This intellectually understood aspect of reality Aristotle called *substance*. Thomas Aquinas developed an elaborate and subtle eucharistic doctrine, *transubstantiation*, which allowed him to say that by the power of God, the substance of bread and wine became in the Eucharist the body and blood of Christ, while the accidents remained those of bread and wine. To the physical senses, no change had occurred. For the believer, in faith, the great miracle happened. As Thomas's familiar hymn runs:

> Word made flesh, true bread he maketh
> By his word his Flesh to be
> Wine his Blood; when man partaketh
> Though his senses fail to see,
> Faith alone, when sight forsaketh,
> Shows true hearts the mystery.[1]

This account of the presence of Christ slowly lost its hold on many believers because Aristotle's categories of substance and accidents gradually appeared to thoughtful persons less and less adequate to deal with everyday reality. Already in the sixteenth century, the Protestant world—the Church of England with it—rejected the doctrine of transubstantiation as an official statement of belief. Today, a number of Roman Catholic theologians, though they continue to use the word, argue with considerable force that its use in official Roman Catholic documents has lost the technical Aristotelian meaning that it had in the thought of Aquinas, and now merely describes the fact of Christian experience, that Christ is present. If so, their position is close to the one Anglicans prefer, although we usually use the phrase "real presence" to express the great eucharistic reality.

TRANSESSENTIATION

Eastern Orthodox theologians go to considerable trouble to distinguish the eucharistic teaching of their churches from that of the Roman Catholic Church. The underlying philosophical assumptions of Orthodox theory are Platonic, rather than Aristotelian. Translating the Greek word used to describe it, we may call this teaching *transessentiation* (in Greek, *metaousités*).

Plato thought that every object, such as bread or wine, presented to the physical senses a derivative reality, which was the outward symbol or sign of the true reality, or idea, of the object. The physical object was a participating symbol of the reality, to be sure. Yet the idea, or the reality, of the object was in a different realm, that is to say, in heaven, not in the object itself, as Aristotle held. When one's sense registered bread and wine, for example, the sensation in the body triggered a "memory" in the mind, a memory of real, true bread and wine, with which one's soul had had contact in heaven but with which it had lost contact through being embodied in flesh.

When Christian theologians applied this understanding of reality to the Eucharist, they held that when priest and congregation uttered the prayers of the Eucharist, God brought about a change in the heavenly reference of the bread and wine. At the outset, the physical objects were symbols of true bread and wine, and brought those who experienced the physical symbols to knowledge of the intellectual reality. By the action of God's Spirit, the physical objects became participating symbols in the body and blood of the risen and ascended Christ, and brought those who received these symbols to the knowledge of this much greater spiritual reality.

As in the doctrine of transubstantiation, no change in the physical properties of the bread and wine is involved; but unlike the doctrine of transubstantiation, the change involved does not occur in the bread and wine, but in the heaven of God and his archetypal creatures.

This doctrine brings into focus a different way of understanding the Eucharist. It is the first theory of sacramental presence to be elaborated by Christian theologians, and it continues to have many advocates. To the extent that "all Western philosophy is a series of footnotes to Plato," as Whitehead put it, it can make sense of the eucharistic experience to modern men and women far beyond the bounds of Eastern Orthodoxy. But its dualism of soul and body, and its implicit downgrading of sense-experienced reality in favor of an intangible idea, make it inaccessible to many others. Most readers of this book will probably find it strange.

MEMORIALISM

Early in the sixteenth century, the Zürich reformer Huldrich Zwingli suggested another theory, as closely in tune with the prevailing nominalism of his age (and ours) as these other theories have been with other philosophical world views. Nominalism has already been described in chapter 1. It is based on the premise that a thing really and fundamentally *is* what appears to our physical sense. In this respect, Zwingli's theory is unlike both transubstantiation and transessentiation, both of which make a sharp division between what the physical senses grasp and what the mind understands. In much modern thought, "a rose is a rose is a rose," as we have had occasion to observe before. Such an assumption leaves no room for a theory of the Eucharist which holds from some change or conversion of the object. According to Zwingli, Christ was truly present, by the power of God, when a Christian congregation remembered with solemn intensity those events that happened in the upper room in Jerusalem "in the night in which he was betrayed." In Zwingli's view, however, Christ's presence was a spiritual one, not attached in any way to the bread and wine. Eucharistic bread and wine, to be sure, are symbols; but they are not participating or communicating symbols. There is no inner connection between them and the reality of Christ, crucified and risen.

Dom Gregory Dix dubbed this a theory of "real absence," a charge that is obviously and grossly unfair. Zwingli understood God's power to be truly at work, and he truly acknowledged Christ presence. The action of the congregation is one of remembering, and so this theory may be called *memorialism*. Yet it is not the remembering of the congregation that is thought to actualize the presence of Christ. God brings it about. He is the actor. Thus it is not quite right, either, to say that this teaching about the Eucharist makes it a "mere memorial," although this charge is often made. It is not simply a humanistic or secular teaching. God's power is sovereign. Like each of the other doctrines, this one brings new dimensions of the Eucharist into view; and it has genuine power, not least because it is so accessible and seems so reasonable to many of our contemporaries. There is every reason to suppose that Thomas Cranmer himself held a view not very different from Zwingli's, and it seems likely that something like memorialism still commends itself to some Episcopalians.

Nevertheless, Anglican theologians after the sixteenth century have been notably unwilling to adopt or advance this theory. The fact that it breaks the connection between the presence of Christ and the sacramental elements makes it seem particularly inadequate, for that connection seems so firmly established by the words of Scripture and so deeply congruent to the action of God in assuming the human life—the flesh—of Jesus of Nazareth. To reject this connection seems to do violence to an essential aspect of Christian faith.

Among them, these three theories have probably claimed the allegiance of the largest number of Christians in the Western world down through the centuries. Many Episcopalians even today adopt one or another of them in order to increase their understanding of this central act of Christian worship. But none of the three, nor any of the several others that have been developed in order to understand Christ's presence in the Eucharist, is finally adequate to the enduring mystery.

THE EUCHARIST AS A MYSTERY OF TIME

The reality of worship is a mystery of time, given to us by God in the Spirit. We have returned to this point of view again and again in these pages. God gives his presence to us, and in God's presence, all times—past, present, and future—are one: "We *were* there when they crucified our Lord." He is with us now, and even his future coming in power and great glory is a present reality. Such affirmations are true especially about the Eucharist, although they pertain to all acts of Christian worship. To speak in this way seems to a number of scholars the best interpretation of the whole biblical attitude toward worship, as we have seen. From this point of view, we can see that it is not so much the substance of sacramental elements that is changed; rather that the whole sacramental moment—including priest, congregation, bread, wine, and all—is transformed. Our moment of time *becomes* that moment. It was so in Old Testament worship. It is so in the worship of the church. The transformation of time is the heart of liturgical reality.

Yet we must acknowledge that this way of understanding the Eucharist is also a theory. It may be the best that we can do. But it is not a substitute for the basic reality that we are trying to communicate in this whole book: in Christian worship, God gives himself to us continually as he did in Christ; and that self-giving of God is the power by which Christians live their lives.

When Is Christ Present?

Another question that is often asked in connection with the Eucharist has to do with the moment at which the bread and wine become Christ's body and blood. St. Augustine asked himself once what God was doing before he created heaven and earth, and, in frustration, answered that he was making hell for minds that pry. The question about a moment of consecration has been equally frustrating.

From one point of view, it is an eminently reasonable question. If at the beginning of the liturgy, bread is bread and if, when we receive it, it is the Lord's body, a transformation must have occurred. When? The question has often been asked in this form. It has been answered differently in different traditions.

If one were to follow Zwingli, and sever any connection between the sacramental elements and Christ's body, the question becomes meaningless. For the Eastern Orthodox, who maintained the connection, the movement of consecration is associated with the *epiclesis*, the invocation of the Holy Spirit, to "show these gifts . . . to be holy gifts for your holy people, the bread of life and the cup of salvation." For Roman Catholic eucharistic piety, at least of the style current before the Second Vatican Council, the moment came to be associated with the words of institution: "This is my Body . . . This is my Blood."

It would carry us too far afield to trace the growth of these divergences, for in this matter, as in the question of how Christ is present, Anglican churches have maintained their characteristic agnosticism. "The whole service consecrates," is a customary expression among us. No one part of the eucharistic prayer, no one part of the eucharistic liturgy, is considered to be more effective or more sacred than another. When the Christian community meets to do the whole eucharistic action in obedience to the risen Lord, he comes. He gives himself to us, again and again. It is part of the mystery of time.

To say anything more than this in the name of the church would, we believe, transgress Anglican restraint.

Queen Elizabeth I is said to have written the following quatrain:

> He was the Word that spake it,
> He took the bread and brake it;
> And what that Word did make it,
> I do believe and take it.

Both in what it affirms and in what it leaves unsaid, it is an epitome of Anglican eucharistic theology.

16

The Christian Calendar

One outstanding feature of the regular services of Anglican worship has not yet been discussed. It has to do with the way our life regularly makes contact with Word and Sacrament as time runs through its recurring cycles. The emphases of the Daily Offices and the Holy Eucharist change as day succeeds to day and season follows season. These alterations bring into focus different aspects of the work of God and the life of Christ. The patterns shift slowly and gradually, and keep the repetition of the regular services from being dead or from sinking into the rut of mere routine.

The Time Crystal

Again and again in this book we have referred to the relationship between Christian worship and time. We have said that past, present, and future are aspects of the eternal presence of God, to which God's Spirit lifts us in worship. In this paragraph we shall develop one implication of this relationship: namely, that every unit of time is an occasion for meeting God. Consequently, every unit of time expresses the character of God, which Christians believe to have been most perfectly revealed in the death and resurrection of Christ.

Time has a crystalline character. Crystals are a mineral formation that have a unique property. No matter how small or how large the crystal, it always has the same shape, the same number of facets, the same angles between the facets. We are coming to a similar understanding of time itself, as a result of our experience in Christian worship. Every time is a time to observe, celebrate, and participate in the great mystery of Christ. The mystery can be known in every unit of time, no matter how long or short. It would carry us to absurd lengths to speak about our liturgical encounter with the mystery in each second or minute or hour, although it is important to remember the reality of such encounters in the course of our daily lives, as we live the liturgy. For the purpose of worship, however, the significant blocks of time are days, weeks, perhaps months, and, most of all, the year.

The Day

In connection with our examination of the Daily Offices, we learned that the Jewish custom of marking each day by communal prayers at sunset and sunrise, and by private prayers at the third, sixth, and ninth hours, was taken up by the Christian community and transformed into the monastic Hours. These services lie behind Anglican Morning and Evening Prayer, and also the Noonday and Compline services in the current book. It remains to observe that in the Offices a connection is drawn between morning and new life, and therefore resurrection; between evening, rest, and death. The noonday hour is the hour when Jesus hung on the cross, and at mid-afternoon he was buried. The day is a crystal of the great mystery. We must admit that this relationship is not a major aspect of our present liturgy for the Daily Offices. Nevertheless, it is observable. The Collect for the Renewal of Life and the more familiar Collect for Grace remind us that in a sense life starts afresh each morning. God has "brought us in safety to this new day." God "divides the day from the night and turns the shadow of death into the morning." In the Noonday service, we find the collect, "Blessed Savior, at this hour you hung upon the cross, stretching out your loving arms. . . ." In Evening Prayer the second set of versicles and responses, marked B, makes the connection most explicit:

> That there may be peace to your Church
> And to the whole world,
>> We entreat you, O Lord:
> That we may depart this life in your faith
> And fear, and not be condemned before the
> Great judgment seat of Christ. . . . (p. 122)

In our hymns for morning and evening, the relationship is often quite plain. In the morning, John Wesley's hymn,

> Christ, whose glory fills the skies,
> Christ, the true, the only Light,
> Sun of Righteousness, arise! . . .[1]

and in the evening, the familiar words,

> Guard us waking, guard us sleeping,
> And, when we die,
> May we in thy mighty keeping,
> All peaceful lie. . . .[2]

make the same point. Examples could be multiplied.

The Week

The death and resurrection of Christ is more prominent as the pattern for the Christian week than as the pattern for the day. Fridays are a commemoration of the crucifixion, and except in the seasons of Christmas and Easter they are to be observed "by special acts of discipline and self-denial" (BCP, p. 17). Every Sunday is a "little Easter," as it is often put.

SUNDAY AS THE DAY OF THE RESURRECTION

The articulation of the calendar into seven-day weeks is part of our Jewish heritage. Neither the Babylonian calendar nor any of the others known to us from antiquity displays this feature. In Jewish practice, to be sure, the climax of the week was on the seventh day, the Sabbath, when God looked upon his creation, saw that it was very good, and rested. Observance of the Sabbath by worship and by stopping work is one of the chief features of Jewish religion to this day.

For Christians, the first day of the week has replaced the seventh as the time for celebration and worship. Although Sunday is often popularly called "the Sabbath," this usage represents considerable confusion and distortion. The celebration of the first day rather than the seventh discloses both the power and the special character of the Christian message. We keep the Lord's Day.

Every one of the four Gospels asserts that the resurrection of Christ occurred on the first day of the week (Mt. 28:1; Mk. 16:2, Lk. 24:1; Jn. 20:1), and other indications in the New Testament make it clear that the first day became the day when Christians broke bread. He appeared in the upper room to Thomas, with the others, "eight days later" (Jn. 20:26); and it was on the night of the first day that Paul spoke at such length to the members of the church of Ephesus (Acts 20:7ff). The objective power and reality of the resurrection are eloquently attested by the fact that the first day has replaced the Sabbath for Christian worship. Members of the Society of Friends still speak of Sunday as "the first day."

The days of the week, numbered from one to seven, recall the story of creation in the first chapter of Genesis: " . . . and there was evening and there was morning, the first [or second, or sixth] day." To speak of the resurrection on "the first day" is thus to proclaim the beginning of the new creation in Christ. The world has a new start, marked by the events of Easter Day. Moreover, on a seven-day scale, the eighth day repeats the first. The eighth day had therefore become a symbol for the completion of the new creation in the kingdom of God, as early as the Epistle of Barnabas (15:8) written early in the second century. Baptismal fonts traditionally have eight sides to remind us that baptism is our introduction to the new creation, symbolized by the term "the eighth day."

The first day came to be called "the Lord's Day" at an early date. The apocalyptic visions recorded in the Revelation to John came to the seer on "the Lord's day" (Rev. 1:10), when he was "caught up by the Spirit." In Romance languages, Sunday is still a variant of this name: *domencio* (Italian), *domingo* (Spanish), *dimanche* (French). Scholars have pointed out that "the Lord's day," by an insignificant change in order of words, becomes "the Day of the Lord." We remember the vivid associations of this phrase in Old Testament expectation. On the Day of the Lord, God would come in power and great glory, he would assert his role, judge finally and decisively between the faithful and the wicked, overthrow powers of evil, and establish his kingdom of righteousness and love. All of this Christians believe to have happened, in principle, "in power and beginning," at the resurrection of Christ. To speak of Sunday as the Lord's Day, or the Day of the Lord, reminds us of this whole complex of events and hopes.

Sunday itself, of course, is a pagan name: the day of the sun. As early as the middle of the second century, Justin Martyr, in a passage we have already cited, applied this name to the day of Christian worship; and it has become the name of the first day of the week in most northern European languages: *sunday* (English), *sonntag* (German), *zontag* (Dutch). In using it, we should find a way to remind ourselves continually that it is the day of resurrection, of the beginning of the new creation, of hope for fulfillment, of judgment, and of the establishment of the kingdom of God. If we could remember all of this, the very act of worshiping God on Sunday would be a full confession of the Christian faith.

OTHER DAYS OF THE WEEK

Once Sunday was established as the primary day for Christian worship because of the resurrection, it did not take long to provide a commemoration of Jesus' crucifixion on Fridays. Friday was already a day of fasting—along with Wednesdays—in the *Didache*.[3]

Saturday as a day of rest for Christians has had a rather spottier and less straightforward history. In some communities, at a fairly early date, it was recognized alongside Sunday as a day of leisure and religious instruction.[4] Of course, as long as Christianity was a minority religion in a pagan world, it could not require general cessation of work; and even when Christianity was recognized as the official state religion, not Saturday but Sunday attracted to it the Old Testament prohibition of labor.

Modern life has made leisure more and more a possibility. Most working persons spend at least two days a week away from work. Under these circumstances it seems highly desirable to reclaim in some fashion the distinction between Sunday on the one hand, with its joy in the resurrection of the Lord, and, on the other hand, the Sabbath. On the Sabbath, God rested from the six days of work in creation. That is to say, creation is not all there is to God. He has power and being to spare. He is not identical with the universe, as pantheism would have it. He would *be* even if the known world ceased to exist. In this sense, the Sabbath expresses God's transcendence. Human beings, we believe, are made in the image of God. When they rest from their labors, they too show that they are not identical with their work or defined by it. The Scottish epitaph, "Born a man, died a green grocer," should not be spoken of anyone who lives by the biblical understanding of the Sabbath. We have being and meaning beyond what we do at work, or in any of our this-worldly relationships. The Sabbath expresses human transcendence as well as God's. We Christians need to find our way of observing it by "resting from our labors." But we should not confuse the Sabbath with the day of resurrection.

The Month

There are virtually no liturgical observances of passing months. None displays any relationship between the Christian mystery and a thirty-day unit of time.

As we have already mentioned, the current Book of Common Prayer, like all previous Anglican Prayer Books, provides for the monthly recitation of the Psalter "in course," that is, read through in order from beginning to end. The psalms are divided into sixty sections, marked, for example: First Day: Morning Prayer (Psalms 1, 2, 3, 4, and 5), or Thirtieth Day: Evening Prayer (Psalms 147, 148, 149, and 150). One way of reading the Daily Offices is to use this scheme, repeated every month. This monthly plan has nothing to do with the Christian mystery, with the death and resurrection of Christ, but it does bring an enviable familiarity with the psalms to those hardy enough to persist in it.

The Christian Year

By all odds the most striking application of the Christian mystery to the cycle of time occurs in the case of the year. In a way that we shall describe, the whole year, from its beginning on the First Sunday in Advent (four Sundays before Christmas Day) to its close at the end of November, has been arranged and presented to assist worshipers to devote their attention in succession to the salient aspects of the Christian mystery: preparation, incarnation, revelation, the life and death of Jesus of Nazareth, his resurrection and ascension, the coming of the Holy Spirit, and the life of the church and of Christians in the world.

Two major cycles of observances span the year: the resurrection Cycle, which was, as a matter of historical fact, the first to develop; and the Nativity Cycle, observances connected with the birth of Jesus. In addition to these two cycles, there are a number of other days marked in the calendar: days of saints and Christian heroes and heroines, rogation days, ember days, and national days. We shall discuss each of these groups in turn.

THE RESURRECTION CYCLE: EASTER
AND ITS RELATED DAYS

We have already pointed out in chapter 14 the close connection between the death and resurrection of Christ and the Jewish Passover. Not only did the crucifixion of Jesus happen at Passover time, but in a remarkable way, his resurrection brought to fulfillment the successive victories of God over the enemies of human existence. Thus Easter was first celebrated as the Christian Passover, the Christian Pasch, as it is sometimes called. *Pascha* is Greek for Passover. The death and resurrection of Christ is often spoken of as the *paschal* mystery.

The Twofold Significance of the Passover

The Jewish Passover itself was already a complex observance. At one level, the historical level, Passover was the annual remembrance of God's deliverance of the Israelites from the bondage in Egypt, when they were led safely across the Red Sea.

> I will sing to the Lord, for he is lofty and uplifted;
>> the horse and its rider has he hurled into the sea.
> The Lord is my strength and my refuge;
>> the Lord has become my Savior." (BCP, p. 85)

as Moses and the Israelites sang in triumph on the far bank, and as we still sing as a canticle in the Daily Offices during the Easter Season. In Hebrew liturgical devotion, moreover, Passover was not only a remembrance of a past event, but also the expectation of that future victory when all of Israel's enemies would be vanquished. "This year in exile, next year in Jerusalem," proclaims the Passover Seder.

Further examination of the Old Testament accounts of the institution of the Passover reveals a striking fact. Passover itself occurred at a time when there was already a liturgical celebration, the Feast of Unleavened Bread. Passover includes a prior celebration of the first fruits of the crop. It is a spring celebration, a fertility celebration. The time when Israel celebrates God's victory over the tyranny of Pharaoh and all *historical* bondage is also the time of celebrating God's victory over the death of winter and the *natural* enemies of humanity. No effort was made to eliminate this underlying agricultural spring festival in the later provisions for Passover. Passover is a two layered, double-tiered celebration.

> You shall keep the feast of unleavened bread; as I commanded you, you shall
> eat unleavened bread for seven days at the appointed time in the month of Abib,
> for in it you came out of Egypt. (Ex. 23:14–15)

the ancient Code of the Covenant says tersely.

Easter as a Three-layered Festival

When we view our celebration of the resurrection of Christ in this perspective, we can see that Easter adds a third level to the existing two levels of Passover. Sin and death have *also* been vanquished, and God's power over what we may call our *spiritual* enemies is acknowledged as well as his power over historical and natural foes. "The last enemy to be destroyed is death."

The very name the English language has supplied to this festival underlines the same point. Eostre was the name of an Anglo-Saxon fertility goddess, the goddess of spring. The Christian Easter is the transformation of her festival, celebrating the power of new life in the springtime. It is also the transformation of the Jewish Passover, celebrating the power God gives to people who seek freedom from political tyranny. These earlier levels are caught up and transformed by the God who is supremely powerful over sin and death.

One of the most familiar Easter hymns, by St. John of Damascus, expresses the Christian's sense of triumph and release on all three levels:

> Come, ye faithful, raise the strain
>   Of triumphant gladness;
> God hath brought his Israel
>   Into joy from sadness;
> Loosed from Pharaoh's bitter yoke
>   Jacob's sons and daughters;
> Led them with unmoistened foot
>   Through the Red Sea waters.
>
> Tis the spring of souls today;

Christ hath burst his prison,
And from three days', sleep in death
　As a sun hath risen;
All the winter of our sins,
　Long and dark is flying
From his light, to whom we give
　Laud and praise undying.[5]

The Date of Easter

The date of Easter depends on the date of the Jewish Passover. It consequently rests on a lunar rather than a solar calculation, since the Jewish calendar is based on the moon. Easter Day is always the Sunday after the full moon that occurs on or after the spring equinox on March 21. Easter Day cannot be earlier than March 22 or later than April 25 (BCP. 880). This dependence on a lunar date, with its allusions to fertility rites of ancient peoples, reminds us, perhaps better than any other single feature of Easter, of the primordial depth of this celebration. Both Easter and Passover are more than historical commemorations.

The Development of the Great Fifty Days

In Jewish custom, the Passover was brought to completion at the Feast of Weeks, seven weeks after Passover. Seven weeks after the feast of first fruits comes the celebration of the harvest—the wheat-harvest. What was started at Passover was brought to its completion at Pentecost—a Greek term for fiftieth—the fiftieth day after Passover. In earliest Christian custom, the celebration of the death and resurrection of Christ, a Christianized Passover, went on for "the great fifty days." At the beginning, no effort was made to differentiate the separate events: the Last Supper on Maundy Thursday, the crucifixion on Good Friday, the resurrection on Easter Day, the ascension forty days after Easter, and the coming of the Holy Spirit fifty days after Easter. The whole undifferentiated mystery was observed for all fifty days. "A unitive feast," someone has called it, or "the feast of an idea." Pope Leo I called it "the feast of feasts." This way of looking at the Easter events would fit the chronology of the Gospel according to St. John, where resurrection, the gift of the Spirit, and ascension are all described as having happened on Easter Day.

However, in the Third Gospel and the Book of Acts (two parts of a single history by St. Luke), the more familiar chronology is presented. Jesus ascended on the fortieth day, and the Spirit descended on the apostolic band in the upper room on Pentecost. It seems likely that the liturgical possibilities inherent in the association of these separate events with separate days were first developed in Jerusalem in the fourth century, while Cyril was bishop of that city. Whether or not he was the originator of this scheme, he indicates in his cathechetical lectures that some such provision was made in Jerusalem during Holy Week and the fifty days. A contemporary of his, the pilgrim nun Etheria (or Egeria), describes how the pilgrims to Jerusalem during Lent and Easter season went to the shrines built on the sites connected with these events, on the particular day associated with each in the New Testament account. From Jerusalem the custom spread rapidly and widely and is now virtually universal.

Lent

A forty-day period of fasting and preparation, Lent, also dates from the fourth century. It was in particular a time of special discipline for those who were to be baptized at Easter. For them it heightened and brought to its climax a much longer period of training and learning. After infant baptism became the common practice of the church, Lent nevertheless remained as an observance undertaken by all the baptized. Its association with the forty days that Jesus spent in the wilderness, fasting and undergoing his Satanic temptations, was inevitable and has been long-lasting. For as long as we have records, the passage read as the Gospel for the First Sunday in Lent has been the account of Jesus' temptations.

The current Prayer Book says that Ash Wednesday and the other weekdays of Lent are to be observed by "special acts of discipline and self-denial" (p. 17). It does not specify fasting, which means doing without food or eating only a small amount of food. A systematic and carefully considered fast has much to recommend it as an aid to clarifying mind and spirit. The psychosomatic unity of human beings makes it inevitable that a physical glut will cloud mind and spirit. Even if fasting as such is not possible or desirable in some cases, positive actions undertaken in the name of Christ, or some deprivations to remind us continually of his suffering, are enjoined on us by the Prayer Book provision.

Ash Wednesday

The first day of Lent is the fortieth weekday before Easter. (Sundays, days of the resurrection, have priority even over a Lenten fast, and so are not counted in the forty days of Lent.) The imposition of ashes on Ash Wednesday is an ancient biblical sign of desolation of spirit and repentance. In the current Prayer Book, their use is optional. When they are imposed, it signifies the continuance of this ancient tradition, making one's inward disposition outwardly visible. When they are not used, it is in respect to Jesus' own words in the Sermon on the Mount, the Gospel appointed to be read on this day.

> And when you fast, do not look dismal, like the hypocrites, for they disfigure their faces that their fasting may be seen by men. Truly, I say to you, they have received their reward. But when you fast, anoint your head and wash your face, that your fasting may not be seen by men but by your Father who is in secret; and your Father who sees in secret will reward you. (Mt. 6:16–18)

Proper Liturgies for Special Days

Thus the period from Ash Wednesday to Pentecost depends on the life, death, and resurrection of Christ, not so much as historical events but as events in the spiritual world, as mysteries that impinge directly on our lives in their depth and power. Over the centuries, certain of the days in the Easter cycle have acquired special liturgical observances that express their significance for us with great power and beauty. Contemporary forms of some of these proper liturgies are included in the current Prayer Book in the section entitled Proper Liturgies for Special Days (pp. 264–295). Here are to be found services for Ash Wednesday, including its optional imposition of ashes and a litany of penitence; for Palm Sunday, with provision for a procession with palms; for Maundy Thursday, allowing a foot-washing ceremony; for Good Friday, with its moving solemn intercession for church and world and three of its traditional anthems; a bare liturgy for Holy Saturday; and the Great Vigil of Easter, with its lighting of the new fire and the paschal candle, the reading of the Old Testament lessons that root the Christian mystery firmly in the life of old Israel, and the baptism of new members (or at least the renewal of baptismal vows) at the ancient time for baptism.

Before Lent

For a while, Lent was extended to a seventy-day length. The three Sundays before Lent—Septuagesima, Sexigesima, and Quinquagesima—were the marks of this longer preparation for Easter. The word *septuagesima* means seventieth and denotes the seventieth day before Easter. Once included in Lent itself, these three Sundays came to be pre-Lenten season, in both Roman Catholic and Anglican practice. One prepared to prepare, so to speak. Because they were not really part of Lent, these Sundays have now been included, both in the Prayer Book and in the liturgical regulations of the Roman Catholic Church, in the preceding Epiphany season. Their names have been dropped.

After Pentecost

The doctrine of the Trinity has been celebrated on Trinity Sunday, the Sunday after Pentecost, beginning at a relatively late date in the Middle Ages. It is the only day in the liturgical cycle that does not call to mind one of God's mighty acts for us. It was much loved by Thomas à Becket, and one of the consequences of his martyrdom seems to have been the custom of naming subsequent Sundays as Sundays *after Trinity*. The current book continues the observance of Trinity Sunday on its traditional day, but reverts to the more ancient and ecumenical custom of naming subsequent Sundays as Sundays *after Pentecost*. Sundays after Pentecost continue until the First Sunday in Advent, when the Church Year begins anew.

Rogation Days

Another medieval addition to the Easter cycle were the Rogation Days, the three days before Ascension Day. The Latin word *rogare* means to pray. Rogation Days were at first observed with prayer for the crops, at a time in the spring crucial for their well-being in the northern temperate zone. Since these days are always on a Monday, Tuesday, and Wednesday and cannot fall on Sunday, and since for some time past, the life of Western people has been dependent on other forms of economic activity in addition to agriculture, Rogation Days have not been considered as "major holy days observed in the Church" (BCP, pp. 31–32; compare the 1928 book, p. li). Propers are provided for these days in the current Prayer Book (pp. 258–259; 930) with a note that they may be used "on the traditional days or at other times"; and their focus has been expanded to include commerce and industry (Proper II) and the steward- ship of creation (Proper III), in addition to prayer for fruitful seasons (Proper I).

The Nativity Cycle: Christmas and Its Related Days

The second cycle of days and seasons that comprise the Christian year is the Nativity Cycle, observances dependent on the date of Christmas.

THE DATE OF CHRISTMAS

The date assigned to the birth of Jesus is December 25. That date is probably the best-known fact in the whole field of liturgical study. What may not be so well known, however, is the fact that there is no shred of historical evidence to support the date. The New Testament is completely silent about it, and for sev- eral centuries the documents of early church history contain no reference to a celebration of the birth of the Lord. At least we know that the resurrection happened at Passover time. In the case of Jesus' birth, we are not certain even about the season.

When the church first began to celebrate the birth of Christ, the date was connected with the winter solstice, in somewhat the same way that the date of Easter was connected with the spring equinox. At the winter solstice, the sun— in the northern hemisphere—reaches its southernmost point in the sky. The days are shortest. The sun seems to have fled. Thereafter it turns north. Days begin to get longer. One might say, with a poetic flourish, that the light has been born. To be sure, the winter lies ahead. Cold will increase. But the princi- ple of the return of life in the spring has been asserted, in spite of all appear- ances. "If winter comes, can spring be far behind?"

By some such reasoning as this, there came to be in many parts of the ancient Mediterranean world a fertility celebration at the time of the winter solstice. In Egypt, at the beginning of the Christian era, astronomical calcula- tions were so out of phase with the actual performance of the sun that the fes- tival fell on January 6. In Rome, the Julian calendar was somewhat more accu- rate. There it fell on December 25. But even the Julian calendar had to be cor- rected in the eighteenth century. According to our present Gregorian calendar, the winter solstice falls on December 21. These other dates aim at the same event.

Thus Christian celebrations at the winter solstice are the counterparts of pagan festivals having to do with the birth of light. They are not so much developments of the pagan observance as theological correctives to it. Easter was a development of the Jewish Passover, as well as a corrective. We have called it a three-layered festival. Christmas, on the other hand, constitutes a theological and polemical thrust against surrounding pagan culture. Christians celebrate not the birth of light in the sky but rather the birth of the Son of God, the light of the world.

EPIPHANY AS A UNITIVE FEAST

Christian observance of the winter solstice apparently arose first in Egypt and was there called *Epiphany*, a Greek word that means "showing forth," or "manifestation," or, to give it a more theologicallysignificant name, "revelation." Epiphany is the season that celebrates the revelation of God in Christ. It was first conceived as a "unitive" rather than a historical festival, as Easter was. Combined into a single undifferentiated whole were the eternal "begetting" by the Father of the Word of God (that Word who was "with God and who was God," and "whose life was the light of men"), the birth of Jesus of Nazareth, the incarnate Word; the baptism of Jesus by John the Baptist, the occasion where Jesus "went public" and made his appearance to his own people; and the turning of water to wine at Cana of Galilee, which was "the first of his signs [that] Jesus did at Cana in Galilee, and manifested his glory." (Jn. 2:11). This later aspect of the celebration had special force in Egypt, where one of the chief celebrations at the winter solstice was in honor of Dionysius, god of wine.

ROMAN DESIGNATION OF CHRISTMAS

The celebration of December 25 as the birth of Jesus of Nazareth began in Rome somewhat later. Records discovered only in this century allow us to pinpoint, within a few years before 336, the time when Christmas began to be officially observed.[6] The situation seems to have been parallel to that in Egypt. The popular festival in Rome, however, was the *Natalis Solis Invicti*, the birthday of the Invincible Sun, a significant celebration in the cult of Mithras. To this observance, the church opposed the birth Jesus of Nazareth in the stable at Bethlehem, as recorded in the Gospel according to St. Luke.

THE DEVELOPMENT OF THE CHRISTMAS SEASON,
THE EPIPHANY, AND SUNDAYS AFTER EPIPHANY

In these early years in the life of the church, there was neither hostility on the part of one church for another, nor a particular desire to impose a rigid uniformity in all parts of the Christian community. In this case, the Eastern churches borrowed from the West, and the Roman church accepted the observance of Epiphany in addition to its own Christmas celebration. To this day, Eastern Orthodoxy has a preliminary observance on December 25, although its chief festival of the incarnation is January 6. The Western church, on the other hand, began to sort out certain events for commemoration on certain days. It historicized the celebration of the incarnation. Thus in the West, the unitive character of the Nativity Cycle was lost at a fairly early time. December 25 was associated with the birth of Jesus of Nazareth (although the reading of the first chapter of the Gospel according to St. John on Christmas Day is a powerful reminder of the eternal revelation of God through his Word). January 6 came to be associated with the coming of the Wise Men to Bethlehem, "guided by a star," the "Manifestation of Christ to the Gentiles," as our Prayer Books subtitle it. The days from December 25 to January 6 are the Christmas season, the "twelve days of Christmas" famous in song.

In the current Prayer Book, the weeks after the Feast of the Epiphany have been extended through the omission of the three pre-Lenten Sundays that developed during the highly penitential medieval period and that had been retained in all previous versions of the Prayer Book. Their omission now offers us through this longer period of post-Epiphany Sundays ample time to delineate Jesus' revelation of himself to his own people. His baptism by John the Baptist is always observed on the First Sunday after Epiphany. On subsequent Sundays, his miracles of healing and his teachings are read in the appointed Gospel, and on the last Sunday after Epiphany there is a fixed observance of the transfiguration of Christ, that moment in the Gospel narrative when at last Peter, James, and John saw Jesus in the light of his divine glory.

To this day, Epiphany season remains a time for recalling the birth of the light of the world in the ministry of Christ, a time also for rededicating ourselves to our own missionary task of continuing the spread of light.

ADVENT

The four Sundays before Christmas have been devised as a season of preparation for the coming of Christ. The Latin word *adventus* means "coming." The First Sunday in Advent is the beginning of the Christian year.

Although Advent has some similarity to Lent—in that both are times to prepare for occasions of great festivity and both are times for repentance and renewed commitment—there are also great differences between them. The background of Advent is the kingdom of God, the rule of God over his creation, which is said to be "at hand." One prepares for judgment in the presence of the great king, and when Advent is over, one confronts the child in the manger. In Lent, one is asked to share the sufferings of the Lord, and at the end confronts the mystery of the empty tomb. In the first case, awe and quiet wonder; in the second, agony, compassion, and triumph. Advent and Lent represent different effects that different aspects of the Christian mystery have upon those who live into it. It is useful to distinguish them.

Thus the part of the year from the fourth Sunday before Christmas—which in fact turns out to be the Sunday nearest November 30—to Ash Wednesday takes its character from the birth of Jesus and the incarnation of the Word of God.

OTHER DAYS DEPENDENT ON CHRISTMAS

Other events in the Gospel narratives having to do with the incarnation have been assigned dates in our calendar related to Christmas day. These are as follows:

The Annunciation of Our Lord Jesus Christ to the Blessed Virgin Mary, on March 25, nine months before Christmas. It is an appropriate date, since the story in St. Luke of Gabriel's visit to Mary relates: "And the angel said to her, 'The Holy Spirit will come upon you, and the power of the Most High will overshadow you; therefore the child to be born will be called holy, the Son of God . . .'" (Lk. 1:35). It is the celebration of the conception of Jesus.

The Holy Name of Our Lord Jesus Christ, on January 1, one week after Christmas. St. Luke tells us: "And at the end of eight days, when he was circumcised, he was called Jesus, the name given by the angel before he was conceived in the womb" (Lk. 2:21). This day was called the "Circumcision of Christ" in earlier Prayer Books. The point of the celebration is twofold: In the first place, from the beginning, Jesus' life was lived as Jewish law required, including circumcision on the eighth day; in the second place, in accordance with Jewish custom, he received his name, Jesus, which means "God will save." An anticipation and summary of the whole Gospel drama is implied on this day.

The Presentation of Our Lord Jesus Christ in the Temple, also called *The Purification of St. Mary the Virgin*, on February 2, forty days after Christmas. Again it is St. Luke who reports that Mary took Jesus to the Temple as the law requires. "And when the time came for their purification according to the law of Moses, they brought him up to Jerusalem to present him to the Lord. . . ." (Lk. 2:22). On this occasion, Mary met the old man, Simeon, on whose lips are put the familiar canticle *Nunc Dimittis*, "Lord, now lettest thou thy servant depart in peace," uttered when he beheld Jesus, who should be "a light to lighten the Gentiles and . . . the glory of thy people Israel." Again the celebration involves an anticipation of the drama yet to come.

The Nativity of St. John the Baptist, on June 24, was most likely determined by the phrase in the Gospel according to St. Luke (1:36), which speaks of John's conception as six months prior to that of Jesus. Yet, this date may also be a subtle astronomical reference to the verse in the Gospel according to St. John, "He must increase, but I must decrease." John was the Lord's herald and forerunner, even while he remained in his mother Elizabeth's womb.

Other Holy Days

RED-LETTER DAYS AND BLACK-LETTER DAYS

One of the most significant features of the reform of worship in England in the sixteenth century was the drastic reduction in the number of holy days. In the Prayer Book of 1549 only saints of the New Testament period were acknowledged in addition to the recognition of All Saints on November 1. The first three American books of 1789, 1892, and 1928 followed this usage. These days have come to be called red-letter days, because in early Prayer Book calendars they were printed in red, like the rubrics. (Those feasts of our Lord whose date is fixed and dependent on Christmas, described in the preceding section, also count as red-letter days, as do all the days in the Easter cycle.)

In 1567 some sixty-seven more holy days were added to the calendar of the English Prayer Book. For the most part they honor saints of the early, undivided, church and a number of English men and women. No Proper Collects, Epistles, and Gospels were supplied for these celebrations, and no indication is given in the English Prayer Book of how the day is to be observed, or even whether it is to be observed. These days, or some of them, are in fact celebrated with a special Eucharist in places where there is a daily service or where there is some special interest in a particular person. A parish named for St. Giles, for example, might have its "patronal festival" on St. Giles Day, September 1. Propers are frequently drawn from traditional, pre-Reformation material. These days have come to be called black-letter days, because in Prayer Books printed in two colors, they appear in the calendar in black ink, to distinguish them from red-letter days, whose observance is assumed.

The current Prayer Book introduced black-letter days into the American calendar. The list is quite different from the old English list. It contains outstanding men and women recognized by the universal church before the Reformation. After the Reformation, only persons in the Anglican tradition appear; after 1789 they are chiefly Americans.

Observance of the days is optional, but proper collects and lessons are provided in an auxiliary volume, *Lesser Feasts and Fasts*, together with brief historical notes about the persons and events commemorated. The men and women dignified by black-letter days are not called saints. There is no procedure in the Anglican communion for recognizing sainthood. We have, on the whole, preferred the New Testament understanding of a saint as any Christian believer. "The saints who are at Corinth" is for St. Paul synonymous with the Christian congregation at Corinth. In the Old Testament the saints are *hasidim*, those who belong to the covenant people and are bound to God and to each other by the covenant loyalty (*hesed*), which God requires of us and himself gives. All baptized Christians are saints in this sense.

Black-letter days, then, commemorate not saints, but great persons in the Christian tradition, or, to be precise, some notable persons particularly important in our tradition. We do speak of those persons given red-letter days as "saints," in a significant exception to the general principle. The twelve apostles (excluding Judas but including Matthias, his successor); the four evangelists; Mary and Joseph, Mary Magdalene, Stephen, the first martyr; James, the Lord's brother; Michael, the archangel—these are recognized as saints in a special though not exclusive sense, in much the same way as the books of the Bible are recognized as inspired in a special but not exclusive sense.

In the current Book of Common Prayer, the calendar lists some two dozen red-letter days in addition to the days related to Christmas, and one hundred nineteen black-letter days.

EMBER DAYS

Four times a year, the calendar recognizes a Wednesday, Friday, and Saturday as Ember Days. Ember days fall in each of the four seasons: in spring after the First Sunday in Lent, in summer after Pentecost, in the fall, after Holy Cross Day (September 14), and in winter after December 13. The origin of these days is not certainly known. The meaning of the word *ember* is disputed. Some take it as a corruption of the Latin phrase *quattuor tempora*, "four seasons." Others understand it to be related to an Anglo-Saxon word *ymber*, which means "running in a cycle." The days have become traditional times for ordinations and for prayer for the ministry of the church.

NATIONAL DAYS

American Books of Common Prayer have always included Thanksgiving Day, but Independence Day only since 1928. Each has its Proper Collect, Epistle, and Gospel. In a somewhat analogous way, the Anniversary of the Day of the Accession of the Reigning Sovereign is counted as a "solemn day" in the calendar of the English book, and a special service is appointed for it. It is quite true that such observances do not bring into focus an aspect of the Gospel story. These days are not particular times of illuminating or communicating the Christian mystery. They are not holy days, like those we have discussed in the earlier parts of this chapter.

Nevertheless, these celebrations are appropriate in the church. One of the chief points that we have been concerned to make in this book, and to which we have returned a number of times, is that Christian worship is corporate as well as individual. It concerns our life together as well as our private spirituality. The nation is one of the most significant groups in which we live. The quality of its corporate life, its ethos, its acts, its fate, determine our private and family lives to a remarkable degree. It is therefore both necessary and good that we should bring our life as a nation into the presence of God, both to give thanks for it and to hear the word of God's judgment upon it. The naturally convenient times to do so are our great national holidays. Thanksgiving Day has been conceived from its outset as a day to give thanks to God for his blessings upon the nation; and the Declaration of Independence, commemorated on Independence Day, makes such an appeal to Providence and to Deity that to commemorate the day with a religious observance simply continues to express its inherent significance.

Since successful nations are even more readily infected with overweening pride than individuals, there is always a danger that such observances should turn into self-congratulatory and chauvinistic occasions, and that we should approach God as if he should do our will rather than as if we, being his servants, should do his. The service of the Word on both these occasions, therefore, speaks a clear warning. On Independence Day, the Old Testament lesson reminds us that we Love the sojourner therefore; for you were sojourners in the land of Egypt. You shall fear the LORD your God; you shall serve him and cleave to him, and by his name you shall swear. (Dt. 10:19–20)

The Gospel appointed, from the Sermon on the Mount, reminds us that even in the context of our national existence, "But I say to you, Love your enemies and pray for those who persecute you" (Mt. 5:44). And on Thanksgiving Day, the Gospel, also from the Sermon on the Mount, cautions:

> Therefore, do not be anxious, saying, 'What shall we eat?' or 'What shall we drink?' or 'What shall we wear?' For the Gentiles seek all these things; and your heavenly Father knows that you need them all. But seek first his kingdom and his righteousness, and all these things shall be yours as well. (Mt. 6:31–33)

A NOTE ABOUT COLORED VESTMENTS

It is customary in most Anglican churches to mark changing seasons and occasions by changing the color of altar hangings and of some of the vestments of officiating clergy. In the American Episcopal Church, no rubric or canon law requires such a practice or specifies what it should be. Among us it is a matter of tradition and taste.

An Anglican liturgical classic book titled *The Parson's Handbook*, by Percy Dearmer, describes the rich and imaginative use of color and the large number of different colors used in some medieval English cathedrals and churches. It was glorious, elaborate, and complex. The use of colors varied considerably from place to place. The Protestant Reformation simply abolished the use of colored vestments. For the better part of three hundred years most holy tables had only a linen cloth; perhaps a full velvet tablecloth-like hanging, usually red, was placed under the linen. Contemporaneously, the Roman Catholic Church in its sixteenth-century Counter-Reformation simplified and codified the use of color: white for occasions of joy and festivity, such as Easter and Christmas; red for feasts of the Holy Spirit or for martyrs; purple for penitence; black for the departed; green for all other items. It is a clear, simple, and practical scheme, which combines aesthetic and teaching values. This use of color was reintroduced into Anglican churches during the nineteenth century as part of the Catholic revival. It has spread so widely that it is now no longer a matter of partisan debate.

In recent years, a movement away from such a rigid color sequence has developed, and an attempt has been made to recover some of the freedom and spontaneity of the Middle Ages in the use of color design. Such a development clearly moves within the limits of Anglican canon law and the long tradition that we have indicated.

PART FIVE

Other Liturgies: Pastoral Offices and Episcopal Services

Introduction

We turn now to the remaining services of worship provided in the current Prayer Book. A glance at the index of that book will show that these other rites fall under two headings: Pastoral Offices and Episcopal Services. A closer examination of the rites themselves will show that all but one of the Pastoral Offices and all of the Episcopal Services are designed to be incorporated into the service of the Word at the Holy Eucharist or, less usually, into Morning or Evening Prayer. Thus all the material that we covered in Part IV of this volume is implied in the material of this section. Certain events in individuals' lives are so significant, however, and touch us so deeply, that it seems necessary or at least highly desirable at these times to focus the Christian mystery by a special liturgical act. We have in mind events like marriage, death, or ordination.

When we discussed the Christian calendar, we remarked that time has a "crystalline" structure, so that each unit, no matter how small or how large, has the same quality—the quality of the death and resurrection of Christ. This part of our study might be considered as an extension of the same point. The whole time of a person's life, from beginning to end is marked by that same quality. In particular, these special critical events have that character. These events are especially illuminated by the paschal mystery.

Part V consists of three chapters, in chapter 17, "Pastoral Offices (I)," we shall examine liturgical provisions for marriage, for the birth or adoption of a child, for sickness, and for death. These might be called "natural" events. They are experiences that we may expect whether or not we are members of the Christian community. Birth and death are inevitable, sickness nearly so. Marriage is a universal human institution. The Christian faith has its characteristic interpretation of each and expresses that interpretation in these rites.

Chapter 18, "Pastoral Offices (II)," examines our liturgical provision for commitment and reconciliation. These services are not Christian interpretations of "natural" events, but rather applications of the Gospel messages of trust and forgiveness at certain crucial points of a Christian believer's life. Christian liturgies for marriage, birth, sickness, and death make Christian interpretations of universal human experiences. Liturgies of commitment and reconciliation, on the other hand, are based on Christian experience. They express our response to God's work in Christ in terms of commitment and trust when we enter a new phase of life, or they claim the promised forgiveness of God when we have sinned. From one point of view this response and this claim are continuously repeated, and they are given continuous expression in the regular services, as we saw in Part IV. Yet the lives we live are not simply repetitive cycles. Extraordinary things happen, which move us profoundly to special acts of commitment, or drive us anxiously to seek special assurance of God's mercy. The liturgical provisions for such times are the subject of Chapter 18.

In Chapter 19, "Episcopal Services," we consider ordination to the three historic orders of ordained ministry—bishop, priest, and deacon—as well as the provisions for celebrating the beginning of a new ministry and for consecrating a church or chapel.

17

Pastoral Offices (I):
For Marriage, Birth,
Sickness, and Death

In this chapter we shall deal with the ministration of the Gospel in marriage, birth, sickness, and death—"natural" occasions of extraordinary joy or sadness. We shall approach them in the order in which they appear among the Pastoral Offices, both in the current book and in the book of 1928. Family life begins with marriage. Birth is an event within an existing family. It leads on to sickness and the grave. We confront the solemn cycle of human existence.

Marriage

MARRIAGE AS AN INSTITUTION

Marriage is a relationship between a man and a woman for the creation and nurture of new life, and for mutual support and enjoyment. It is established by an act of intention in accordance with some custom and tradition. It constitutes families as the basic unit of society, the context for expressing the deepest of human relationships, and the normal structure within which children are born and raised. It is a completely *human* institution, which can be distinguished from the mating of animals. Some animals, too, apparently establish a relationship of relative permanence in order to raise their young. In this case as in so many others, it is impossible to make an absolute distinction between the realm of the human and that of other creatures. Yet there is an absolutely crucial difference. The marriage of a man and a woman, though rooted in the natural urges of sex, is transformed by human will and culture.

It would obviously take us far beyond the limits of this book to examine marriage customs of different cultures and different times. They vary widely. At the beginning of Old Testament history, for example, the patriarchs practiced polygamy, as has been done in many cultures outside Israel. Jacob married two wives—Leah and Rachel—and, in accordance with the widespread custom of the day, and apparently with God's blessing, took two concubines as well—Bilhah and Zilpah (Gen. 30:1-13). Solomon's seven hundred wives are legendary (1 Kg. 11:3). One may even suspect some Oriental hyperbole!

Within the Old Testament, the understanding of human sexuality and marriage deepened under the influence of two leading Old Testament convictions: that creation is good, and that God's Covenant with its people sets the standard for all relationships within the covenant, including the relationship between husbands and wives. In the first place, sex is a good part of God's work. In the second place, husbands and wives are to be related to each other with loyal love (*hesed*) of the same quality as God's loyal love to Israel.

The story of creation in the first chapter of Genesis puts an extraordinarily high value on human sexuality. We read: "God created man in his own image, in the image of God he created him; male and female he created them" (Gen. 1:27). Sexual union is created to be one means by which human beings realize and participate in the image of God. (It is not the only one, to be sure. Marriage is not necessary to salvation.) Sexuality is therefore a matter of greatest concern for Christian faith.

On the other hand, what is designed to be a great good is often, in sin-ridden human life, a source of evil and distortion. The corruption of the best is the worst, as a familiar proverbs puts it. Our sexuality is no exception. It brings soaring joy. It can also bring frustration and bitterness. In the biblical understanding of the conditions of human existence after the Fall, the relationship between man and woman comes under the curse that affects all things. What was designed as a blessing and as an expression of deepest human mutuality becomes, time and time again, a frustration and an opportunity of one partner to dominate the other. "Your desire shall be for your husband, and he shall rule over you," the Genesis account reads (3:16).

Under these circumstances, the understanding of marriage in Israel grew with the developing knowledge of God's ways with his people. It came to be recognized that the sexual bond between husband and wife was most secure, satisfying, and fulfilling when it was maintained in the context of a relationship marked by the kind of loyalty and faithfulness that God showed to Israel. *Loyal love* (hesed) *is the decisive factor in the biblical understanding of marriage.* An examination of Old Testament laws, for example, would show that if a man had sexual relations with a woman married to someone else or with one engaged to be married, both man and woman were put to death. If the woman were not married or engaged, the man had to pay her father a sum of money and marry her, but the couple were not punished as criminals (cf. Dt. 22:23–29). The violation of a pledge makes the difference.

Today, we surely find these laws grotesquely severe, and we probably regret that their provisions did not fall more equally on man and woman. Nevertheless it is clear that in its time, the Old Testament sought to uphold faithfulness in marriage; and when God taught the prophet Hosea about God's faithfulness to the covenant by requiring him to be faithful to Gomer, "a worthless woman," faithfulness (*hesed*) began to be grasped as a man's responsibility in marriage, as well as a woman's (Hos. 1:2–4; 3:1–5).

MARRIAGE IN THE NEW TESTAMENT

The New Testament develops these Old Testament insights. Jesus himself regarded marriage not only as monogamous but as lifelong. In this view, a husband should not be able to rid himself of his wife simply by giving her a "bill of divorce," as contemporary Jewish practice was. No, said Jesus,

> "For your hardness of heart [Moses] wrote you this commandment. But from the beginning of creation, 'God made them male and female.' 'For this reason a man shall leave his father and mother and be joined to his wife, and the two shall become one flesh.' So they are no longer two but one flesh. What therefore God has joined together, let no man put asunder." (Mk. 10:5–9)

This teaching not only establishes the permanence of the marriage bond in Christian understanding, but also underlies the Christian conviction that the relation between husband and wife is, humanly speaking, their *primary* relationship and takes precedence over all human relationships, including those to parents and the parental family. All other ties become subordinate to the new one established by the marriage vow. This aspect of Christian marriage brings it into conflict with many alternative understandings of marriage, where the parental family, usually of the husband, occupies first place, and the new relationship is subordinate.

Two thousand years of Christian experience have taught us that despite the best of intentions, some marriages are not healthy. Some way has to be provided to dissolve them. In these cases, the break-up of a marriage may be the least of evils, but it is a defeat for the Christian vision of what marriage can be. A couple who undertake Christian marriage must intend it to be permanent when they exchange their vows.

They are also bidden to model their married love on the love of God for his people. The obligation to do so has rarely been more movingly expressed than in the Letter to the Ephesians:

> Wives, be subject to your husbands, as to the Lord. For the husband is the head of the wife as Christ is the head of the church . . . Husbands, love your wives, as Christ loved the church and gave himself up for her . . . Even so husbands should love their wives as their own bodies. (Eph. 5:22–23, 25–28)

Many modern Christians will especially regret the lack of mutuality between man and woman expressed in this passage. Many of us today would say that husbands and wives should be subject to *each other* and should give themselves to *each other*, as Christ loved the church and gave himself up for it. We believe that this mutuality is an implication of Christian love, which has gradually become clear as Christian people have lived into the meaning of the Christian mystery.

In any case, there can be no mistake that the model for Christians of love in marriage is Christ's total self-giving—his *agape*. When Christians try to understand the implications of Christ's life for their lives, they realize that his steadfast love for his church involves, in the case of marriage, the complete loyalty of the man to the woman, and of the woman to the man, for life. The chief reason Christians have for claiming that marriage is an exclusive and permanent relationship is the unswerving faithfulness, revealed by Christ, that God has for his people. When this religious conviction weakens, our understanding of marriage will be correspondingly insecure. The love of God in Christ, *agape*, which is faithful to death, redeems sexual love, *eros*, and makes it capable of bearing the meaning it was designed in creation to have; capable of making the union of male and female to be the image of God. This capacity of Christian marriage to be a communicating symbol of God's own life is so potent that marriage is commonly called a sacramental act.

THE DEVELOPMENT OF CHRISTIAN MARRIAGE RITES

There is no service of marriage recorded, or even mentioned, in the Bible. Even after Christianity moved into the Gentile world, there was no special Christian marriage service. In the second century Ignatius required a couple seeking marriage to get the bishop's permission,[1] and Tertullian in the third century indicated that a couple's marriage would be blessed at a celebration of the Eucharist.[2] In each case the implication is that the actual marriage ceremony took place in accordance with existing local customs. That ancient practice expresses the consistent teaching of Western churches ever since. A couple pledge themselves to each other and observe the legal requirements of the place where they live when they do so. The church then blesses the union.

Until well into the Middle Ages, there was no expectation that a Christian marriage should take place in a church. The first full description of a Christian marriage liturgy is found in the ninth century.[3] When the church at last did take over the marriage ceremony, it really functioned as the civil authority, church and state being coterminous at this period of history. The priest was understood to function as a *witness* of the couple's vows as well as the church's representative to bless the couple. The marriage rite itself embodied local customs. Some of the features of the Prayer Book service most familiar to Episcopalians originated in northern England. The father's giving away of the bride, for example, belongs in this category. The giving of a ring as the symbol of the vow is a widespread European custom, but it is by no means universal.

Since the eighteenth century, the principle of separation of church and state has gained ascendancy in Western Europe and North America. As a result of the American Revolution, there is no religious establishment among us. Ordained Christian ministers are nevertheless regularly permitted to function as civil officers in this one instance, officially witnessing the exchange of the vows in accordance with a license issued by the state. Thus in the United States a marriage ceremony can still take place altogether in the church building. On the other hand, the revolutions that occurred in many European nations during the nineteenth century established a wider gulf between church and state.

In France, for example, there now must be two complete ceremonies: a civil ceremony at a town registry and the blessing of the marriage in the church. The practice of early Christianity has virtually been reestablished.

THE CELEBRATION AND BLESSING OF A MARRIAGE

In the current Prayer Book, the liturgy for a wedding is entitled "The Celebration and Blessing of a Marriage." The two parts of the title corresponds to the two parts of the ceremony that have characterized Christian marriage from the beginning: the exchange of vows and the blessing. The whole rite is embedded in a service of the Word identical with the Proclamation of the Word of God at the Eucharist.

The service begins with an *exhortation* that affirms the biblical teaching about marriage that we have already examined and states the purpose of the marriage bond:

> The bond and covenant of marriage was established by God in creation, and our Lord Jesus Christ adorned this manner of life by his presence and first miracle at a wedding in Cana of Galilee. It signifies to us the mystery of the union between Christ and his Church . . .

> The union of husband and wife in heart, body, and mind is intended by God for their mutual joy; for the help and comfort given one another in prosperity and adversity; and, when it is God's will, for the procreation of children and their nurture in the knowledge and love of the Lord. (BCP, p. 423)

The Declaration of Consent follows, in which each partner promises the other "to live together in the covenant of marriage . . . and forsaking all others, be faithful unto him (or her) as long as you both shall live." Marriage is presented as a covenant relationship that is exclusive and lifelong, and takes precedence over any other human relationship ("forsaking all others . . .").

The congregation then promises to uphold the couple in this relationship, expressing by this commitment the often overlooked fact that the expectations of a community have a great deal of influence on the stability of the marriage.

The "giving away" of the bride has become optional. It is a vestige of a time when women were considered to be property.

After the lessons, which introduce some of the biblical material that we have discussed, the couple make their promises by taking each other's right hand and repeating the age-old words "To have and to hold from this day forward, for better for worse, for richer for poorer, in sickness and in health, to love and to cherish, until we are parted by death." These mutual vows constitute the marriage.

It has become possible for both husband and wife to give rings as a symbol that "with all that I am, and all that I have, I honor you." This mutual exchange is a further sign of the complete equality of the man and the woman. Since the exchange of rings is in origin local and not universal custom, provision is also made to allow some other symbolic exchange at this point (p. 437).

The concluding *Prayers* and *Blessing* take the place of the Prayers of the People in a regular service of the Word. The blessing of the couple by the officiating priest constitutes the irreplaceable action of the church at this service. The exchange of the *Peace* brings the marriage service to a close. The couple first exchange the peace with each other, and then in a custom of growing popularity, may move through the congregation to greet with the peace those who have come to share this celebration. The Eucharist may follow, in accordance with ancient tradition.

The current Prayer Book provides a service titled "The Blessing of a Civil Marriage" (pp. 433-434). It is a sign of the fact that in our society, as in many others in the Western world, civil marriages are becoming more frequent.

The Birth or Adoption of a Child

The service of "Thanksgiving for the Birth of a Child" in the current Prayer Book corresponds to the service of "Thanksgiving of Women after Child-birth, commonly called the Churching of Women" in the 1928 American Prayer Book and in earlier books from 1552 on. In 1549 the corresponding service was called "The Order of the Purification of Women."

This service in the current Prayer Book is the modern development of a Jewish rite for the purification of women after childbirth. Ritual purification was required by Old Testament law (Lev. 12:1-8), and Christian attention was drawn to it because, as we have already pointed out, Jesus' mother observed these requirements. A woman was believed to be unclean after giving birth. In Israel, she had to offer sacrifices for purification before she could be readmitted to the congregation. A Christian service of purification has been known since the fifth century, although the New Testament itself makes no mention of such a ceremony. The first English Prayer Book simply adopted traditional practice.

In the course of time, this rite has been completely transformed. At an early date, thanksgiving for safe delivery became one emphasis of the service. In the second English book the phrase, "Thanksgiving of Women after Child-birth," was added to the title, and thanksgiving became the exclusive content of the service itself. There was no thanksgiving, however, for the birth of the child; and the action of the service still suggested the reintroduction of the woman to the congregation after a period of separation, for the priest went through the service with the woman alone at the door of the church.

Advances in medicine have nearly eliminated the dangers of childbirth. As a result, the Prayer Book service had been widely ignored. The current book provides what amounts to a new service to mark the occasion of the birth of the child. It contains some traditional materials, but its focus has completely shifted.

THE SERVICE IN THE CURRENT PRAYER BOOK

In the current Prayer Book, the emphasis is on thanksgiving for the gift of the child. A new life has been entrusted to a family and a congregation. It is an occasion for solemn rejoicing.

No longer is it a service for a woman alone. The service is to be set within Morning or Evening Prayer or the Eucharist. Both parents are involved. They may express their thanksgiving in their own words, and at the appropriate time they present themselves together at the altar. The whole congregation shares their joy, in keeping with one of the familiar features of the contemporary liturgical renewal.

The chief liturgical element in the act of thanksgiving is the Magnificat (the Song of Mary), or either Psalm 116 or Psalm 23. The recitation of Psalm 116 is traditional at the churching of women, and its verses,

> What shall I render to the LORD
>   for all his bounty to me?
> I will lift up the cup of salvation
>   and call upon the name of the LORD.

are appropriate either in the older setting or the new. The traditional prayer of thanksgiving for the safety of the mother is used here, along with prayers for the parents and the child.

One feature of the current service is its provision for the *adoption of a child*. Adoption, like marriage, is an act of human purpose and will. It involves something like a covenant. The adopting parents are asked to signify their intention of taking the child as their own; and the child, if old enough to answer, is asked to signify that he or she takes the woman and man as mother and father. The celebrant concludes this exchange of promises by saying: "As God has made us his children by adoption and grace, may you receive N. as your own son (daughter)" (p. 441). The quality of life in the New Covenant is determinative for this relationship, as in all others.

Sickness

One of the chief pastoral functions of the church is to minister to the sick, as Jesus himself did.

Sickness is a universal human predicament. There may be a few fortunate people who have "never been sick a day in their lives"; but most people sooner or later learn the pain and anxiety of illness, if not in themselves, at least by watching the suffering of those they love. What place can sickness have in the economy of an all-powerful and loving God?

INTERPRETATIONS OF SICKNESS

Probably no completely satisfactory answer can be given to this question, but several answers have been influential in forming Christian attitudes. They represent at best partial and incomplete understandings of sickness; but in coming to terms with them, we shall put ourselves in a better position to understand the bearing of the Christian mystery on the relief of disease.

Sickness as Retribution

Perhaps the earliest religious interpretation of illness, at least in the biblical tradition, is the theory of retribution. According to this theory, God sends illness, like all evil, as a punishment for disobedience. If this interpretation be true, sickness requires us to examine ourselves, to correct our way of life, and to throw ourselves on the mercy of God.

It is easy to find fault with this interpretation of sickness. If it stood by itself as an adequate theory, it would make God a tyrant rather than a loving parent. The Old Testament itself, however, calls this theory into question. The Book of Job presents us with a righteous man who suffers both loss and sickness. His three friends keep trying for chapter after chapter to convince Job that he must have done something wrong to deserve so much suffering, but they never shake his conviction that he has been upright. After Job, the retribution theory never recovered its former hold on Israel's faith. Jesus himself did not entertain it (Lk. 13:1–5).

Modern understanding of disease confirms the conclusion. There is far, far more than moral failure involved when an individual contracts a disease. Yet it would be foolish to rule out this element completely. There are some instances when illness comes as a direct result of foolishness or foolhardiness. If we expose ourselves to the cold or to others who already have a contagious disease, we usually get sick. Those examples are trivial. Less trivial ones could be found. There is some evidence to suggest that, at a certain deep level of the complex structure of human beings, it is possible to *will* to be sick. The moral retribution theory as the sole factor to account for sickness has been generally discredited. Yet it may be a factor, and the need for self-examination, repentance, and acceptance of God's mercy is always in order. The acceptance of forgiveness can be a significant factor in recovery.

Sickness as Discipline

Both the Old and the New Testaments indicate that sickness may be understood, if not as God's punishment, then as his discipline. The Lord chastens those whom he loves (cf. Pr. 3:11–12; Heb. 5:8). Sickness, in bearable amounts, like other trials, may train us to endure in a world where there is much inexplicable pain and suffering, and where without such discipline, it would be easy to lose faith in the goodness of God.

This interpretation, too, has something to commend it. Even if one can't be convinced that sickness is intended as retribution, it might be helpful on occasion to regard it as training for the long, hard, pilgrimage of life. Yet the truth is that this interpretation does not take us very far either. Some sickness is so severe and protracted that to insist that it is somehow disciplinary would distort any understanding of God as loving and righteous.

Sickness as the Power of Satan

Jesus himself regarded sickness as a mark of Satan's rule over the world. When Jesus or his disciples healed the sick, he took those events as signs that the power of Satan's rule was broken in principle. The rule of God over his creation was asserted in making the sick whole. This understanding of sickness lay behind Jesus' word about the man blind from his birth. "It was not that this

man sinned, or his parents," Jesus answered (rejecting any simple theory of retribution), "but that the works of God might be made manifest in him" (Jn. 9:3).

It seems like a harsh saying. Jesus doesn't claim, of course, that God made
the man blind in order to cure him. In this verse, he gives no reasons for blind-
ness or disease at all. However, he boldly proclaims the power of God to set
these things right. That proclamation is surely the best word in the Christian
tradition on the subject. When all is said and done, when all preliminary religious interpretations of sickness are examined and taken for what they are
worth, the existence of sickness is an unresolved enigma. It is a power hostile to
us, and stronger than we. Only God's power to cure it is certain. That power is
an integral part of God's kingdom, of his rule over the world disclosed in the
Christian mystery—the death and resurrection of our Lord.

Faith and Medicine

None of these interpretations of sickness, including the last, are substitutes for
the treatment of disease by the best methods that modern medicine affords.
Faith in the Christian mystery establishes an attitude of confidence in the face
of sickness. That confidence is part of the cure. It establishes the avenue
through which God's healing power gains access to our bodies and spirits. But
the means of that healing may be medical science or the prayer of the church.
We should not overlook either one, for God uses both. Prayer, to be sure,
accomplishes what nothing else can, but it is neither inimical nor alternative to
modern scientific methods. Faith makes us expect to get well. Without such
expectancy, cure is often impossible, no matter what the means.

Sickness as Sharing the Suffering of Christ

Sometimes the most elaborate and sophisticated medical treatment and the
most urgent prayers seem to have no result. After every effort has been made,
incurable sickness remains. Only then may a Christian appeal to St. Paul's
almost incredible interpretation of suffering, that it "makes up what is lacking
in the suffering of Christ." Under circumstances of ultimate extremity, this
interpretation confers meaning on sickness in a powerful way and enables us to
endure when everything else fails. For if one shares Christ's suffering now, one
looks forward in hope and confidence to sharing his victory in God's good time.

THE MINISTRATION TO THE SICK

Jesus healed the sick with a word and a touch. According to the Letter of James,
the elders of at least one early congregation used prayer and anointing with oils
(Jas. 5:14). Liturgies for the ministration to the sick have made use of similar
resources from that day to this. The provisions of the current Prayer Book continue to do so (pp. 453–461).

Three major parts comprise the Ministration to the Sick: Part I. Ministry of
the Word, Part II. Laying on of Hands and Anointing, and Part III. Holy
Communion. Any one or more parts may be used.

Part I. Ministry of the Word needs little comment. It is a simplified service of the Word, like the ones we have already discussed. The lessons emphasize the importance of faith and trust, and God's power to heal. A special series of lessons may be chosen if it seems appropriate to emphasize penitence. A rubric (p. 454) urges a special act of confession, as has been done in the services for Visitation of the Sick in all earlier English and American Prayer Books (cf. BCP 1928, p. 313). There are also special lessons for use when anointing is to follow, and others when communion is to follow.

Part II. Laying on of Hands and Anointing provides the words to accompany these ancient and traditional actions.

The churchly gesture of laying one's hands on another is an act of claiming and blessing. When a priest lays hands upon a sick person, the sick person is claimed for the Kingdom of God and brought into the domain of God's rule. Laying one's hands on another establishes contact and lets power flow. New Testament accounts of Jesus' healing indicate that touch accomplished some transference of energy (Lk. 8:46). Modern testimony points in the same direction. To be touched often means to experience an accession of energy or power. Laying on of hands is thus a symbol, even a communicating symbol, of the coming of the Spirit. The act is a blessing.

Oil provides a similar symbolic content, often with the same effect. As we have noticed in connection with confirmation (chapter 9), oil was a sign of the richness of the Spirit in biblical times. Its use in connection with the ministry to the sick continued to be meaningful to many Episcopalians. In fact, the anointing of the sick with oil, or unction, has been such a powerful means of displaying and communicating the power of God over sickness that it is commonly called a sacramental rite.

Part III. Holy Communion provides for the administration of the great sacrament of the Christian mystery in the case of sickness.

A collection of Prayers for the Sick and Prayers for Use by a Sick Person brings this section of the Prayer Book to its close. These prayers are a rich resource for coming to terms with sickness and living with it in the power of the cross.

Death

Death is the one inevitable fact of natural life. Each passing moment brings us closer to that end. From the moment we are born we approach the grave. Awareness of that fact colors every aspect of human existence. In the face of death, Christianity proclaims its faith: "the communion of saints, the forgiveness of sins, the resurrection of the body, and the life everlasting." In the face of death, Christians hear that message as good news, as their Gospel.

"THE LAST ENEMY TO BE DESTROYED IS DEATH"

Death is the enemy of the natural life. The point does not need to be labored. Death forcibly tears the one who dies out of the network of relationships in which he or she lived. For those left behind, those broken relationships mean uncompleted business, love frustrated, guilt unreconciled. The jagged edges are painful. We face death as an unknown adventure. No matter how expectantly we approach it, it surely evokes some anxiety in most of us. Sometimes, it is true, death comes as a blessed relief from suffering. As such, it looks like a relative good. But as the end of life and the separation from all we love and enjoy, it speaks an irrevocable "no" to human existence.

In the words of St. Paul, death is "the last enemy" (1 Cor. 15:26). We can dream about conquering most of the other things that hinder the fulfillment of life. Poverty, slavery, sickness—all such things, in the course of time, can be made to yield to human efforts. But on the basis of human resources alone, death seems unconquerable.

Christian hope in the face of death is based on what God has done. Jesus' resurrection from the dead is the first installment of a new life that we shall ourselves, by the mercy of God, inherit. Several biblical images make the point plain. Christ is the first fruit of the crop. The full harvest is all the people of God. Christ is the first-born from the dead. All the people of God will share that new birth in God's good time. Easter, the central Christian celebration, proclaims God's triumph over death in the case of Jesus of Nazareth. At every Christian burial, we appropriate that triumph anew, for each child of God whom death overtakes.

When a person dies, the church has really no other ministry than to affirm the resurrection. On the resurrection is based the strength and confidence that the church tries to give to those who mourn, the assurance of pardon in the face of unresolved guilt, the hope of the presence of God to those who enter that unknown land.

The resurrection is a corporal event. It involves bodies, and it involves the bodies of all God's people together in the society of his kingdom. Whatever else our resurrection bodies may or may not give us, we shall be recognizable individuals and we shall have the capacity for experience. At least that much seems clear from what we know of the resurrection of Jesus himself—and all our knowledge is based on that. We shall be our true selves in the resurrection—purified, transformed, but unmistakably *selves*; and we shall see and touch, know and love each other in the communion of saints.

This hope and expectation is what Christian liturgies seek to proclaim when a person dies.

LITURGICAL SERVICE

The current Book of Common Prayer makes a series of provisions for Ministration at the Time of Death—prayers and a litany for use when a person is near death or has just died, prayers for a vigil before the funeral, prayers when the body is received in the church. The burial service itself, as we have learned to expect, is embodied in a service of the Word like that of a regular Eucharist, with special readings, extensive use of psalms (as is traditional), and special intercessions. Among the familiar lessons are the passage in Romans which ends, "I am sure that neither death nor life, nor angels, nor principalities, nor things present, nor things to come, nor powers, nor height, nor depth, nor anything else in all creation, will be able to separate us from the love of God in Christ Jesus our Lord" (Rom. 8:38-39); St. Paul's description of the resurrection; "The trumpet will sound, and the dead will be raised imperishable, and we shall be changed" (1 Cor. 15:52); and from St. John, "In my Father's house are many rooms . . ." (Jn. 14:2). Among psalms traditionally read at a burial service are Psalms 46, 23, and especially Psalm 90.

Holy Communion may follow this proclamation of the word. There is provision for the consecration of a grave and a service for committal of the body to its final resting place.

The only item that requires further comment is the way the body is handled in Christian burial.

Nothing in the Bible prescribes what to do with a dead body. As in the case of marriage, the New Testament contains neither a liturgy for the burial of the dead nor the description of one. What the Prayer Book provides is based on long-standing tradition; and as we also found in the case of marriage, some of its features may be expected to change, from time to time, and to vary in different cultures.

According to the usual custom among us, a body is brought to the church in a closed coffin, preferably covered by a pall. It is taken to the chancel steps in a procession led by the officiant, as the familiar words are said or sung. "I am the resurrection and the life, saith the Lord. . . ." The older custom, according to which the family followed the coffin in this procession, has largely disappeared. At the end of the service, the officiant commends the dead person to God: "Acknowledge, we humbly beseech you, a sheep of your own fold, a lamb of your own flock, a sinner of your own redeeming. . . ." Then the coffin is carried in procession out of the church, while some of the new anthems or an appropriate hymn is sung.

If the body is to be buried, a congregation of family and friends gather at the side of the grave for the interment: "We commit his body to the ground, earth to earth, ashes to ashes, dust to dust. . . ." Prayers follow. Provision is also made for burial at sea or in a mausoleum (pp. 485, 501).

Cremation is becoming more common. Until a generation or so ago, a feeling was widespread that cremation would somehow affect the resurrection of the body and was not appropriate in Christian burial. In the Episcopal church there has never been a rule forbidding cremation, and in the face of the growing convictions that, on the one hand, one's resurrection body cannot be simply a reassembly of the atoms of one's present body and, on the other, that cremation has considerable practical advantages, prejudice against it is disappearing. It is being used more and more widely.

18

Pastoral Offices (II):
For Reconciliation and Commitment

In this second chapter on the Pastoral Offices, our interest shifts. Marriage, birth, sickness, and death are universal, natural human experiences that need Christian interpretation. Repentance and commitment, however, are evoked by the Gospel itself. It might even be said that they are unnatural. In times of moral crisis, the Gospel itself may convince us that we have been disobedient to God. It offers forgiveness to guilty consciences. Thus we are brought to repentance and confession of sin. In times of decision, the Gospel itself calls us to be obedient to God. It promises us strength and fulfillment. Thus we are brought to confession of faith and commitment to service. Among the Pastoral Offices of the current Prayer Book, the services for Reconciliation of a Penitent deal with the former situation and the services of Confirmation and Commitment to Christian Service with the latter.

Confession and Absolution

SIN AND FORGIVENESS IN THE NEW TESTAMENT

Forgiveness of sins is inseparable from the Gospel. In a certain sense, it is the Gospel. Christ died for sinners. His new life means our reconciliation with God. From the very beginning, baptism, our initiation into the Christian mystery, has been understood as a baptism "for the forgiveness of your sins" (cf. Acts 2:38). A large part of Jesus' ministry while he lived among us was to forgive sins. We remember the story of the woman caught in adultery (Jn. 8:1–11), the healing of the paralytic (Mk. 2:1–5), the parable of the Prodigal Son (Lk. 15:11–32), and many other incidents. Jesus did not come to call righteous people to himself but to call sinners to repentance (Mk. 2:17).

What is more, he dealt with sinners individually. Each of these incidents of forgiveness, which we remember and love, is a personal encounter with the Lord. There is something profoundly private about the forgiveness of sin.

The eighteenth chapter of St. Matthew is widely considered to be a book of church discipline for a very early Christian community.[1] It tells us how one early Christian church handled the transgression of its members. We read that if a member commits a sin, the person offended is to go to him privately and try to come to an agreement. If the offender will not listen, then one or two Christians are to go with the wronged person. If that does not work, then it is to be taken up in the whole congregation. If nothing succeeds in bringing the sinner to repentance, he is to be excommunicated. "Let him be to you as a Gentile and a tax collector" (Mt. 18:17).

But if the sinner asks forgiveness, he is to be assured of it. For Christ has entrusted to his church the power to forgive sin: "Whatever you bind on earth shall be bound in heaven, and whatever you loose on earth shall be loosed in heaven. Again I say to you, if two of you agree on earth about anything they ask, it will be done for them by my Father in heaven" (Mt. 18:18–19). Peter could not endure this teaching. "How often shall my brother sin against me, and I forgive him?" he asks. "As many as seven times?" Jesus assured him that seven times is only the beginning. His answer, "seventy times seven times," is a memorable way of saying that God's forgiveness of his children is endless, and that our forgiveness of our neighbors should be also.

This passage indicates several aspects of confession and forgiveness in the church that have influenced the development of the practice of private confession. For one thing, it indicates that even private transgressions are in some way the concern of the whole church; in the second place, it indicates that church members, like Peter, when they take sin seriously are slow to understand how free and full God's forgiveness is; in the third, it indicates that the forgiveness of God is endless. From the beginning, Christians have felt tension between the seriousness of sin and the free gift of grace.

SIN AND FORGIVENESS IN THE EARLY CHURCH

As we have seen in our discussion of baptism, forgiveness of sin was not full or free in the Christian communities of the first few centuries beyond the New Testament period itself. The early church quickly became a society of perfectionists. It took sin very seriously. One became a Christian by baptism. Former sins were forgiven. If one committed sins after baptism, however, there was no recourse. The end of the world was expected. Final judgment was at hand. One waited for it, keeping one's self free from sin and ready for judgment. As time went on and the kingdom did not arrive, baptism was often postponed until death approached. Christians of all people, it was held, could not afford to come to the judgment of God with sins on their conscience.

This situation proved intolerable. Early in the third century, Tertullian wrote about steps taken in the church to deal with sins committed after baptism. A rigorous program of public confession and penance was established, which, after enduring, a sinner could be received back into the communion of the church. This provision was available only one time. There was one more chance after baptism. "The second plank to salvation," Tertullian called it.

In this case, as in the New Testament, we notice that private transgression became the affair of the whole church. Yet the church, human institution that it is, failed to realize that the forgiveness of God knew no limits. Even the "second plank" is no real answer to the problem of the sins which Christians commit after they are baptized. To make a long story short, the whole penitential system, involving private confession, penance, and priestly absolution, was developed before the Middle Ages to deal in a pastoral way with this problem. The details of the system will not concern us here. Its origin is, in any case, obscure. Certain features of it, however, bear upon our own service of reconciliation.

1. The priest alone became the person who heard confession and pronounced absolution. In the early days of the church, the community was small. The trust level must have been high. When the church grew large, these circumstances changed. It became practically impossible to require a member to confess sin in public. The risk was too great. Confession was made to the priest, who nevertheless stood for the whole congregation in this matter. His declaration of forgiveness was spoken not only in the name of God but also on behalf of the people.

It is a matter of some interest to observe that in more recent years, small groups have again sought to institute public confession: Methodist cottage groups in the eighteenth century, and the twentieth century Oxford (Buchmanite) Group, to name but two. It is psychologically a powerful act. Sin is a mark of alienation not only from God but also from neighbors. To confess and receive forgiveness in public not only restores both vertical and horizontal relationships, but also *symbolizes* that restoration in a dramatic way. Powerful as the measure is, however, the practice seems always to founder on the untrustworthy quality of much community life as soon as the community grows large.

2. A second aspect of the medieval penitential system was its personal nature. Individuals were recognized in the depth and uniqueness of their personhood. Personal sin became the concern of the whole church through confession and absolution.

3. Its third feature was theologically perhaps its most important. It embodied the endless forgiveness of God. No limits were put on the number of times a penitent might ask and find mercy, if only his or her contrition were honest.

The corruptions of the penitential system, which led to its rejection by the sixteenth-century reformers, are well known. Private confession became a requirement rather than an option. When confession was required, the process all too often became trivial and mechanical. There also grew up a finely calculated system of punishment having to do with the length of time a soul would have to spend in purgatorial fire for each specific transgression. There was also a scheme of rewards for prayer, related to a shortening of that time. Even more open to corruption was the granting of such rewards in return for gifts of money to the church. It is another example of a principle we have observed before: the corruption of the best—the most pastorally sensitive extension of the Gospel—being the worst.

In any case, the English reformers, like their Lutheran and Calvinist counterparts, dismantled the system. They proclaimed a Gospel of forgiveness. They insisted that God's grace was freely available to all repentant sinners. Confession was to be made in public once more, though this time through the medium of general confessions. Individuals were expected to acknowledge their individual sins in their hearts as they said the words together in public. Absolution was full and free, and pronounced at every regular service, both in the Daily Offices and in the Eucharist. Every Eucharist was understood as an occasion for receiving forgiveness anew, and was celebrated "that we, and all thy whole Church, may obtain remission of our sins, and all other benefits of his passion" (BCP, p. 335). The words appear in all English and American Prayer Books.

Thus the Anglican tradition has not been negligent regarding the necessity for repentance and the importance of hearing and appropriating the word of God's forgiveness. This tradition has made individual sin an affair of the church, and it has affirmed the boundless mercy of God. On the other hand, private dealing with personal sin has been lacking, except in the case of the ministry to the sick. In that case, both English and American books have urged the sick person to make confession to a priest; and English Prayer Books, unlike American, have even provided a form for absolution. The pastoral experience of many priests in recent decades, however, has led them to see the psychological wisdom of making some provision for a person to confess sins privately, not simply on a sickbed, but in all cases where general confession does not deal adequately with a troubled conscience. Moreover, the corruptions that destroyed the earlier penitential system are no longer serious temptations for Episcopalians. Hence the current Prayer Book includes two forms for the Reconciliation of a Penitent. We shall examine them in the light of the foregoing discussion.

THE RECONCILIATION OF A PENITENT

Forms One and Two for the Reconciliation of a Penitent are the only Pastoral Offices designed primarily for private use. The services establish the context within which a contrite and penitent sinner can unburden his conscience to a confessor, usually a priest. The two meet alone.

The first of the two forms provides only the barest skeleton of an encounter. The penitent asks for the priest's blessing. The priest urges a true and humble confession. The penitent confesses particular sins and asks for God's mercy. The priest may offer counsel and comfort, and pronounces absolution. The penitent says, "Thanks be to God." The priest concludes, "Go in peace, and pray for me a sinner."

Form Two is longer. It provides some appropriate words from Scripture for both penitent and priest, and sets the individual's confession of sin into the framework of a formal prayer. It gives the priest an explicit opportunity to ask the one confessing sins to "turn again to Christ as your Lord," and to "forgive those who have sinned against you." It is a fuller, and by its eloquence perhaps a more moving, rite. There is, however, no essential theological difference between the two forms.

Both forms contain the same two alternative absolutions for the priest. As both absolutions make clear, and as our historical survey has already established, Christ conferred power to forgive sins upon his *church*. The priest, by virtue of the authority conferred at ordination, exercises this power *in the name of the church*. The first of the two absolutions expresses this authority in a striking way: " . . . by his authority committed to me, I absolve you from all your sins." The second absolution is not so direct. "Our Lord Jesus Christ . . . absolve you through my ministry by the grace of the Holy Spirit."

The former version, a translation of an ancient Latin formula, is a powerful affirmation that the power to forgive is focused and embodied in the priest. It is not, however, the priest's own power. Both statements of absolution are clear about that point. It is Christ's power. The Lord forgives. But the bold, incarnational quality of the first absolution, "*I* absolve you . . ." makes it liturgically and psychologically the more powerful one. A person deeply troubled by sin may need to know that some living, present, flesh-and-blood person forgives. Otherwise the forgiveness of God may remain abstract and remote. If God forgives and no person forgives, is forgiveness real?

The second form provides that the priest may touch the penitent when absolution is pronounced. Touch is just as important and just as significant in the case of absolution as in the case of healing the sick. One is claimed for the kingdom of God in both cases. Blessing and healing energy flow.

If the services of a priest cannot be obtained to pronounce this embodied word of forgiveness or to touch the sinner with the reconciling power of God, it belongs to the ministry of any Christian person to state the great evangelical fact of God's forgiveness. It is crucial to do so when someone is in deep distress of conscience. The Reconciliation of a Penitent is available for such a situation, with the use of the Declaration of Forgiveness instead of a formal absolution. When there is a critical need, deacons or lay persons, as well as priests, can use this pastoral office as an instrument of their ministries.

Confirmation and Commitment to Christian Service

HISTORICAL REVIEW

In our previous discussion of confirmation, we found that this service was originally an integral part of baptism. In Rome, it was separated from water baptism itself and kept as the bishop's prerogative when the bishop delegated the power to baptize to his presbyters. Subsequently, the separation of baptism and confirmation became the custom of Western Christianity, though not of Eastern Orthodoxy. Once separated, confirmation came to be regarded as a rite for receiving the strengthening power of the Holy Spirit as a person approached maturity, the age "of perfection."

The relation between baptism and confirmation, however, was never quite forgotten. One of the implications of that connection was the once-and-for-all character of confirmation. There can obviously be only one rite of initiation. If confirmation is part of it, it can be administered only once. For this reason, the possibility of a special rite for receiving the strengthening power of the Holy Spirit, a rite that would be available not once but as many times as desired, has not been even discussed until recent years.

One reason that the lack of such a repeatable rite has not been serious or acutely felt is similar to the reason that the absence of a special rite for confession and absolution did not impair the pastoral ministry of our church more than it did: the general adequacy of the Eucharist for such a need. Not only is every Eucharist celebrated so that "we, and all thy whole Church, may obtain remission of our sins," as we pointed out in our discussion of reconciliation, but also it is celebrated so that we may be "filled with thy grace and heavenly benediction, and made one body with him, that he may dwell in us and we in him," as the same eucharistic prayer continues (BCP, p. 336).

CONFIRMATION AND THE MINISTRY OF THE LAITY

The developing idea of the ministry of the laity has led to a new understanding of confirmation, however. This development has been both indirect and slow.

Thirty or forty years ago, confirmation was sometimes presented as the "ordination of the laity." Every lay person was encouraged to take up Christian ministry with as much seriousness and dedication as a deacon, priest, or bishop; and it was suggested that confirmation, a once-for-all occasion, paralleled the service in which ordained clergy were designated and empowered for their special ministries. Hence, "ordination of the laity."

This interpretation has considerable plausibility, and some people still entertain it. It has been widely abandoned, however, under the growing appreciation of the centrality of baptism, which we have described in our earlier chapter on rites of initiation. The older confirmation service has been reunited with the rite of water baptism in the current Prayer Book. At the same time, baptism itself has come to be understood as the ordination of laity. If another rite was required, in addition to baptism, in order to make lay ministries authentic, two levels of lay persons would be created, one ordained for ministry, one not. Such a structure would undercut the very notion of the ministry of the laity: namely, that every Christian by virtue of being a Christian—that is, by virtue of being baptized—undertakes mission and ministry.

REAFFIRMATION OF BAPTISMAL VOWS AND COMMITMENT TO CHRISTIAN SERVICE

If the older confirmation service has been rejoined to baptism, and baptism itself is the ordination of the laity, what then is the significance of confirmation as it appears in the current Prayer Book? As we have already tried to indicate, it is a rite for receiving the strengthening power of the Holy Spirit at critical times in a person's life. Confirmation proper is administered the first time one makes a mature confession of faith in Christ. Subsequently, at significant moments, one may make a new confirmation of faith and receive afresh the strengthening power of the Spirit.

One such special occasion, after confirmation, is when a baptized person who has made such a commitment in another denomination is received into our fellowship. It is appropriate for such a person to reaffirm the baptismal covenant, say again the baptismal creed, and receive the laying on of hands by the bishop. There are some other times too when it is appropriate to do these things. Something may happen to move one so profoundly or to challenge one so deeply that participation in the Eucharist, with no particular notice taken of this special situation, does not do psychological justice to the occasion. One needs a more sharply focused liturgical act in order to express a needy Christian's request for the strengthening gift of God's grace and the receiving of it.

This understanding, which developed only in the twentieth century, is analogous to the understandings of confession and absolution developed in the third century. What began as a once-for-all liturgy, never to be repeated, became, through a new liturgical rite, a new expression of the full and free availability of God's grace. God's forgiveness is boundless. That realization led to the development of the office of Reconciliation, in addition to baptism. Similarly, God's strength is boundless. This realization led to the development of the service for Reaffirmation of Baptismal Vows, after baptism and confirmation.

The current Prayer Book envisions two kinds of occasions when a service of commitment would be appropriate: a more formal and a less formal. The more formal service is the Reaffirmation of Baptismal Vows, which is one facet of the confirmation service itself. The bishop is the officiant. The formal way to request and receive a special accession of God's grace for a special purpose is to renew allegiance to the baptismal covenant and receive laying on of hands by the bishop.

The less formal way to proceed is by the rite provided for Commitment to Christian Service. In this case, the seeker prepares a statement of intention to be read in the course of a Eucharist. The statement is to include a reaffirmation of baptismal promises. In the services, the priest accepts the statement and prays that the seeker may receive the gift of the Spirit needed to make those intentions actual in the new and challenging situation.

Both of these services, like the two forms for Reconciliation of a Penitent, involve a dialogue between the officiant and the one who seeks strength through the rite. In one case, the seeker confesses sin and hears assurance of pardon. In the case of Reaffirmation of Baptismal Vows or Commitment to Christian Service, the seeker confesses faith and hears assurance of God's sustaining direction.

The current book itself makes no effort to distinguish between the occasions on which Reaffirmation would be the more appropriate service and those on which Commitment to Christian Service would be more apt. That determination is a pastoral matter and must be worked out in each case between the one seeking this ministry and the pastor.

The words of administration are nearly the same in each case. When a person reaffirms baptismal vows, the bishop says:

> "N., may the Holy Spirit, who has begun a good work in you, direct and uphold you in the service of Christ and his kingdom."

At a service of Commitment, the priest's sentence of administration runs,

> "May the Holy Spirit guide and strengthen you, that in this, and in all things, you may do God's will in the service of the kingdom of Christ."

These services, then, are not ordinations to lay ministry. They are special empowerments for special ministries or to meet special needs at particular times in one's life of service.

19

Episcopal Services

In the Episcopal Church certain liturgical acts can be performed only by a bishop. We have already discovered that in the beginning of the church's life, bishops presided at all liturgical functions. They were not the *sole* actors; we have been quite insistent on that point. Nevertheless, the bishop had a chief and irreplaceable role at every service. As the church grew, bishops, by common agreement, began to allow their priests (presbyters) to preside at most meetings of the church in one area of the diocese—the parish. (We might observe as a matter of general interest that the words *diocese* [Greek *dia-oikia*] and *parish* [Greek *para-oikia*] were administrative units of the later Roman empire, adopted for convenience by the church. Nothing in the New Testament corresponds to them.)

It came to be regarded as a matter of course that priests should be the chief celebrants at parish baptisms and Eucharists. The corresponding delegation of confirmation was not universal, as we have seen. Different traditions developed in Eastern Orthodoxy and in Western Catholicism.

The function of ordaining other bishops, however, as well as priests and deacons has never been delegated; and there are several other functions, having to do with the induction of an already ordained person into a new area of ministry and with the consecration of new church buildings, which our Anglican tradition reserves to bishops. Liturgies for these occasions—Ordination of a Bishop, Ordination of a Priest, Ordination of a Deacon, Celebration of a New Ministry, and Consecration of a Church or Chapel—appear as Episcopal Services in the current Prayer Book.

Strict logic might have dictated that the confirmation service, at which in our tradition only bishops preside, should appear in this group also. The importance of confirmation in the development of each individual Christian's life, however, and its relationship to other Pastoral Offices, which we tried to establish in the last chapter, makes it preferable to place confirmation among Pastoral Offices. Logic also might require the Litany for Ordination, which appears as an Episcopal Service, to be located elsewhere; for a bishop need not read it at an ordination service, and in fact rarely does. In this case, sheer convenience is the deciding factor. It is an invariable part of ordination rites.

Holy Orders

We shall consider the ordination first. Three services are provided for the three orders—bishop, priest, and deacon—which, as the Preface to the Ordination Rites in the current Prayer Book indicates, "since the time of the New Testament . . . have been characteristic of Christ's holy catholic Church" (p. 510). These orders are customarily called "holy orders." What is their significance?

In the discussion of liturgy in this book, we have emphasized over and over again the importance of the ministry of every Christian person. By baptism, one is commissioned a minister in Christ's church and sent out on a mission into the world. The ministry of the laity has been a strong and pervasive theme in a great deal of recent discussion about the nature and work of the church. The 1973 statement of the Anglican-Roman Catholic International Commission on the subject of ministry (the so-called Canterbury Statement),[1] for example, takes as its point of departure that in both traditions "there exists a diversity of forms on ministerial service" (para. 12), some ordained, some authorized in other ways, some not recognized by any overt ecclesiastical action. "All Christian ministry, whose purpose is always to build up the community, flows and takes its shape from the life and self-offering of Christ" (para. 13). Every selfless action of service, care for the hungry, sick, and aged, efforts for racial, political, and social justice, work for peace and mutual forgiveness, though not narrowly ecclesiastical ministries, are nevertheless rooted in the life and ministry of our Lord.

What is more, the current Book of Common Prayer, as we have seen in our discussion of other services, makes a large place for lay persons in the conduct of public worship. There are relatively few liturgical roles they do not assume. Lay persons preach. They are often as good or better pastors than ordained persons are. They teach. They are called to positions of significant leadership and decision making. The questions have been asked with some force: Then why should there be ordination at all? Do we need holy orders?[2]

HISTORICAL REVIEW

The best approach to these questions is to keep in mind the development of holy orders through the course of Christian history.

The New Testament Period

In the New Testament, the orders of bishop, priest, and deacons are not the only special ministries mentioned, or even the most prominent. Jesus called twelve men to be apostles, those "sent out" to preach the Gospel, teach, and heal. St. Paul's letters mention the apostles as well as prophets, teachers, and several others (cf. 1 Cor. 12:28–30). We have already noticed the function of prophets and teachers in connection with the emerging service of the Word.

These most primitive ministries need not concern us. The remarkable fact is that they did not last very long, perhaps not beyond the New Testament period. From the *Didache*, that remarkable document at least as early as some books of the New Testament, we learn that prophets, like apostles, were traveling ministers: charismatic, Spirit-filled, as were all the persons on St. Paul's list. But as charismatic worship did not continue, neither did these particular ministries. Prophets settled down, as the *Didache* shows, in various local churches and assumed roles of leadership.

The fact is, however, that among all the various Christian ministries, two underlying functions are clearly evident: oversight and service. The Greek word for oversight is *episcope*, literally a "looking over" or a "seeing to." The Greek word for service is *diakonia*. *Episcope* and *diakonia*—we might say, *responsibility* and *service*. All ministries had these two qualities. Within the New Testament, they came to be centered or focused in two offices, those of bishop and deacon. It would be an oversimplification, however, to say that bishops were concerned only for overseeing the church and deacons only with serving it. Both were involved in both aspects of ministry, as were the charismatic persons we have already discussed, and the laity as well. But bishops, through their office and leadership, gave particular focus and emphasis to oversight and responsibility; deacons focused on and emphasized service.

There is a third order in holy orders—the priesthood. We examined the development of priesthood in an earlier connection. It will be recalled that there is no order of Christian priests in the New Testament itself. Christ is the only priest. He was accorded that title, as we saw, because his life and death accomplished what the priests of old Israel were supposed to have accomplished by their sacrifices and did not. In the course of the third century, the title *priest* was given to bishops, and eventually it fell to presbyters, also, because bishops and presbyters presided at the Eucharist, which made Christ's sacrificial death present to the worshiping community and its effects available to the church.

The third order, then, is really the order of the presbyters, or elders. It is clear that at a very early date, some Christian communities were headed by groups of presbyters, or elders, on the analogy of the Jewish synagogue. St. Paul appointed elders in various churches on his missionary journeys (Acts 14:23), and the leadership of the church in Jerusalem comprised "apostles and elders" (Acts 15:6). The title was at first probably descriptive. The persons who exercised authority may in fact have been older and more mature. Before long, however, qualities of leadership undoubtedly appeared among younger members of the church, and the descriptive title *elder* came to apply to those in whom the community found these qualities of leadership without necessary reference to age.

The relation between the order of presbyters and the other orders is not clear. The process by which one bishop emerged in a local community as having some preeminence and status different from that of the elders was probably not the same everywhere. A prophet who settled down in the way the *Didache* describes would probably have such special status. Or the elders might in some places have elected a presiding officer, in the fashion of the synagogue.

It is not clear, either, that bishops were always ordained by other bishops. In fact, there is some evidence to suggest that the bishops of Alexandria were ordained by fellow presbyters until a fairly late date. The idea that every bishop was ordained by other bishops in direct succession from the apostles themselves cannot be proved by existing evidence. It can be demonstrated, however, that the periods of persecution in the early centuries forced the church to become united and cohesive. The role of the bishop was decisive in achieving the unity necessary to survive. After this fairly early date, bishops in Catholic churches have been ordained by other bishops in a line unbroken from generation to generation. This institution is known as the *"historic episcopate."* The provisions in the current Prayer Book for the ordination of bishops preserve this venerable and providential institution.

Medieval Developments

As we have seen, bishops acquired the title of *priest* during the late second century, and well before the beginning of the Middle Ages presbyters acquired it. As the church gradually expanded, presbyter-priests came to be more than merely the representatives of delegates of the bishop. In large urban centers, it is true, the bishop remained a familiar figure. But in vast rural areas, particularly in northern Europe, the bishop was rarely seen, and his ministry was more theoretical than real. Laity were often recent converts, uneducated and untrained in the Christian faith. The *diaconate* also began to wane. Deacons had played a major part in the life of the church in early centuries. In Rome, they administered the church's financial affairs. But during the Middle Ages, the diaconate became merely a step to priesthood.

As a result of all these developments, priests became, de facto, the only functioning ministers. They often had full responsibility for the pastoral oversight of a large area. Small towns would have had only one ordained pastor, and in view of the importance of the sacraments in the church's life, that pastor would be a priest. Apart from bishops, only priests were authorized to celebrate the Eucharist. (At the Council of Nicaea in 325, bishops had already decided not to extend this authorization to deacons.) By necessity, perhaps more than by design, the priesthood became an omnivorous order that in the course of several centuries consumed all other ministries. By the late Middle Ages, the dominance of the priestly ministry was so great that theologians named the priesthood as the highest order of the ordained ministry. The bishop was perceived as a kind of administrator-priest to whom certain sacramental acts were reserved.[3]

This emerging interpretation was almost exactly the antithesis of the historical development. At the beginning, the fundamental ministry of Christ was entrusted to the *laos*, the laity, the people of God. Special functions of leadership were assumed by bishops, elders, and deacons. Priesthood was a theological concept, applied first to the people of God as a whole, and subsequently to bishops and presbyters.

By the end of the Middle Ages, however, priesthood was considered the highest ministry, exercised by bishops and presbyters in descending order. Grace trickled down from on high to the church. A hierarchy, a sacred ladder, reaching from God through those in holy orders to the laity had been created. The laity were not considered to be ministers at all. Our popular use of the word *minister* still reflects this idea. The higher on the ladder one stood, the holier, the closer to God one was. The reversal of the biblical view was nearly complete.

A second medieval development also helped to distort the New Testament idea of ministry: the church acquired temporal power. It exercised jurisdiction; it used courts of law, legal procedures, and punitive force to gain and hold its control of the population of Europe. The church could probably not have avoided this responsibility after the fall of the Roman Empire. There was a power vacuum. It had to be filled in order to preserve even a minimal amount of civil peace and order. The ordained clergy of the church and its monks and nuns formed a body of able, educated men and women in a single unified organization. The prior existence of this ecclesiastical structure made this development possible. The responsibility of *episcope* made it obligatory. Bishops became the chief administrators for kings, and priests constituted a local civil service throughout the Holy Roman Empire.

But what a contrast this arrangement of things made to the view of ministry that Jesus himself expressed: "The kings of the Gentiles exercise lordship over them," he said on one occasion, "and those in authority over them are called benefactors. But not so with you; rather let the greatest among you become as the youngest, and the leader as one who serves" (Lk. 22:25–26). In fact, this acquisition of temporal power is a further example, perhaps the best example in Christian history, of the principle that the corruption of the best is the worst. The Inquisition stands as a perpetual reminder that the church, considered as a human institution, did not gracefully resist the temptations of power.

The Protestant Reformation in England

The sixteenth-century Reformation aimed to correct these abuses along with other distortions that had crept into Christian life and teaching, and that we have noticed in other connections. In England, under the leadership of Archbishop Cranmer, the threefold ministry of bishop, priest, and deacon, with the bishop as its source, was boldly reasserted in theory. Nevertheless, the practice of the times continued to give a preponderant importance to the priesthood and to the three orders as a "stepladder" upward to sacred power. This point of view is dramatically evident in the concluding prayer that Cranmer himself composed for the ordination of deacons. The prayer asks that the newly ordained deacons "may so well behave themselves in this *inferior* Office, that they may be found worthy to be called unto the *higher* Ministries in thy Church" (BCP 1928, p. 535; emphasis added). The hierarchical concept of the ordained ministry that the phrase so vividly expresses still prevailed.

What is more, the idea of the ministry of the laity, the concept that ministry belongs to the whole body of the church, was not recaptured. In the rubrics of English and American Prayer Books, strictly interpreted, "minister" almost invariably means the rector or curate of a parish. In ordinary English usage to this day, *minister* means *ordained minister*.

The churches of the Reformation were effectively shorn of temporal power in the sixteenth century. The king or queen of England was designated "Supreme Governor of the Church of England" when crowned. Whatever political power the Church of England had previously exercised had now been absorbed by the state. Nevertheless, like other Reformation churches, the Church of England was established by law. As we noted in chapter 7, loyalty to the established church was an important sign of allegiance to the sovereign. To this day, ties between church and state have still not been completely severed in England. In the United States, such ties were broken for all religious bodies at the time of the American Revolution, and a wall of separation erected.

HOLY ORDERS IN TODAY'S CHURCH

Not until the present century, however, did the church begin to recover the fuller understanding of ministry that underlies this whole volume. This new understanding is more clearly grounded than the former one, we believe, on New Testament models of ministry and on the pattern of the first centuries. It determines the approach to holy orders that is expressed in the current Prayer Book.

Ordination and Leadership

If ministry belongs to the whole church, and if all Christians, both lay and ordained, are ministers, ordination cannot designate those who are *more* faithful or *more* committed to Christian faith. All Christians in their own way are to be as faithful and as committed to their life in Christ as possible, and that life *is* their ministry. The Canterbury Statement is helpful. "Like any human community, the Church requires a focus of leadership and unity, which the Holy Spirit provides in the ordained ministry" (para. 7). The purpose of the ordained ministry is to serve the people of God by providing this focus. Ordination designates the service of leadership, a concept that reflects the tension in the idea of leadership that we have found in the Gospel itself. "Let the greatest among you become as the youngest, and the leader as one who serves."

Three Qualities of Leadership

From this perspective, the significance of the three orders of ordained ministry becomes apparent. They are related to the three crucial dimensions of the life of the people of God in the world: *episcope* (responsibility), *hierateuma* (priesthood), and *diakonia* (service). The church is in the world to serve it, to mediate between the world and its Creator, and to have oversight, responsibility, for it. Deacons serve as a focus of leadership in the function of serving, priests in the function of mediating, bishops in the function of overseeing.

In other words, the ordained ministry does not perform these functions on behalf of the church or instead of the church. Deacons do not serve so that the other Christian people don't have to serve. Ordained deacons serve in order to *enable* the church to serve better. Priests do not mediate in order that other Christians can be relieved of their commission to represent God to the world and the world to God. Priests function to make the priesthood of all believers possible. Bishops are not responsible for the church so that the church as a whole does *not* need to be responsible for the rest of the world, but in order that every Christian, in the particular way open to him or her, may exercise the basic Christian ministry of responsible oversight.

Furthermore, these ministries are not mutually exclusive. A lay person exercises all three from time to time in an unspecialized form. A bishop has the *special* ministry of *episcope*, and special liturgical functions are reserved to bishops to express their characteristic ministry of oversight. Bishops are the presiding ministers at the liturgy and at church councils when they are present. They ordain all other ministries. But they also may function as priests and deacons. Similarly, a priest has the *special* ministry of priesthood. Special liturgical functions are reserved to priests, to express their characteristic ministry of mediation. They preside at the Eucharist, for example, and pronounce absolution. But priests share *episcope* and *diakonia* in an unspecialized way. They are responsible servants of Christ.

By the same token, a deacon has the *special* ministry of service. The liturgical function that best expresses the deacon's role of service is that of assisting. Deacons most characteristically assist at liturgies. They do not normally preside. Very few liturgical acts by tradition are reserved to them. The reading of the Gospel at the Eucharist, and the singing of the *Exsultet* at the Great Easter Vigil are the only two in the current Prayer Book. Bishops and priests may do all that a deacon can do. In fact, it is because bishops remain servants throughout their ministries that the notion of their overseeing the church does not distort the idea of Christian ministry so much that episcopal oversight becomes a contradiction in terms.

The Purpose of Ordination

In the second paragraph of the Preface to the Ordination Rites in the current Prayer Book, the following sentence appears:

> The persons who are chosen and recognized by the Church as being called by God to the ordained ministry are admitted to these sacred orders by solemn prayer and the laying on of episcopal hands.

This sentence sets forth three considerations pertinent to the ordained ministry. First, the personal vocation or calling by God of the one who seeks holy orders. Those who desire to be ordained must be convinced, to the best of their abilities, that God has chosen them for this special ministry. Second, the whole church recognizes the call. Third, persons so called and recognized are admitted to their order by prayer for the power of the Holy Spirit and the laying on of hands, claiming and blessing the person who is ordained for this special ministry. Each of these aspects of ordination deserves further examination.

The road toward ordination begins with a call. The call to ordained ministry is often misconceived in a narrow and individualistic sense. All Christians are called to ministry, as we have insisted again and again. The call to an ordained ministry has to be understood against the background of this wider vocation or calling (the two words mean the same thing), which comes to the whole church. Some persons are called to minister to Christ as lawyers, some as nurses, some as carpenters, some as priests. All minister by service, priesthood, and *episcope*. *All* are called.

The call to ministry is both inward and outward. One called to any ministry will have a deep inner conviction about that call. But there must be an objective as well as a subjective side to it. The church must recognize and validate the call. Recognition of ordained ministries is especially important, for these ministries, after all, belong to the whole church. The whole process leading to ordination—involving consultation with one's parish priest, with the Commission on Ministry, the vestry, the diocesan standing committee, and the bishop—is a process of examining and testing one's inner call. Without such objective confirmation, a *sense* of vocation to ordained ministry—or any other ministry—may be nothing more than self-deception. The inward call must find some objective authentication. If none is found, there is in fact no call at all. The Canterbury Statement puts it this way: "those who are ordained are called by Christ in the Church and through the Church" (para. 14). Holy orders pertain to the life *of the Church*. They cannot stand apart from the community from which they draw their meaning.

Persons with a genuine call to holy orders must be specially empowered for their special ministry. This is accomplished when bishops lay hands upon candidates for any of the holy orders with solemn prayer. This moment is the focus of the whole process by which one comes to holy orders. It is the liturgical proclamation of the church's authorization. This proclamation communicates the nature of Christ's own ministry so powerfully, and holy orders are such an essential expression of the nature of the whole church, with its *episcope, hierateuma,* and *diakonia,* that holy orders is generally reckoned by Anglicans to be a sacramental act.

There is nothing automatic or mechanical about the relation between the laying on of hands and the coming of the Holy Spirit. The Spirit empowers a person for one of these specialized ministries in answer to the prayer of the church. God, who is faithful to his promises, who always answers prayer, gives on these occasions the gifts that are asked in his Son's name, for the sake of the Son's ministry. The inauguration of the president of the United States provides a helpful analogy to ordination. A candidate for the presidency begins with a strong conviction that he is "called" to the office, that by natural gifts, abilities, and interests, he would fill it well. This inner sense of fitness has to be confirmed and authenticated by the response of the people to his campaign. He has to be elected. Even after his election, however, he is not yet the president. He cannot function as president. He must be inaugurated in a solemn ceremony that focuses the meaning of his election, proclaims the fact of it, and officially empowers him to act. Not until he is sworn in by the Chief Justice is he really the president of the United States. Yet that final moment is the culmination of the prior process, and would be both meaningless and powerless without what had gone before it.

Ordination Is for the Whole Church

When the church gathers to ordain a person to oversight, mediation, and service, the action pertains to the entire Christian community. Within a local parish, the gifts of lay persons are recognized for the parish itself. Sometimes the members of a congregation perceive potential for leadership in a person even before the person realizes its implications. At ordination, on the other hand, the church publicly recognizes gifts for ministry—not just for the local parish but for the universal church. Many times over, the vocation of a person ordained in one place is exercised in some distant land. Such a change of scenery does not require new authorization or empowerment. One is not ordained every time one moves. The church in one place simply *recognizes* the persons ordained in another area, when assurance is given that their ordination was properly performed. The ordained ministry belongs to the universal church and ought to be recognized by the universal church.

When the church is divided into denominations and sects, one of the most crippling results of the fracture is the inability to have a universally recognized ministry. The restoration of such a ministry is one of the chief goals of any plan to reunite the fragments of the church.

The bishop is perhaps the chief symbol and agent of this universal ministry. At the beginning, bishops were the chief pastors of local Christian communities. In the course of time, they had to delegate the ministry of Word and Sacrament to presbyters. Nevertheless, the various local communities in a diocese found their unity in their bishop. The bishop was also the agent through whom the boundaries of the local community were transcended. He took the concerns of each local community and placed them within the wider perspective of the diocese. Moreover, through a continuing relationship with other bishops in the "college of bishops," each diocesan bishop could lay local concerns before the whole church and represent in each locality the common life that the people of a diocese shared with Christians the world over. This episcopal collegiality expressed itself not only in the fact that every bishop had a place in synods and councils of wider regions, but also in the custom of having bishops from neighboring dioceses join in the laying on of hands at the ordination of a new bishop.

ORDINATION RITES IN THE CURRENT PRAYER BOOK

The ordination services in the current Prayer Book express the understanding of holy orders that we have sought to establish in the foregoing discussion. Each service takes place in the context of the Eucharist, a feature which, by this time, we find familiar.

In an attempt to discourage the hierarchical, stepladder interpretation of holy orders, the services have been arranged in the sequence bishop, priest, deacon, rather than the reverse. This arrangement has the additional advantage of suggesting the fact, also prominent in our earlier discussion, that the bishop is the source of the other orders. All is inherent in his presiding office. The other orders have acquired their functions as bishops have assigned and deployed them.

Each rite consists of three parts, in addition to the proclamation of the Word of God and the celebration of the Eucharist. The three parts of the ordination services are the Presentation, the Examination, and the Consecration.

The *Presentation* at the very beginning of each service, before the Ministry of the Word, establishes the fact that the church has properly and canonically recognized the call of those who are to be ordained, the candidates' acceptance of the authority of the Episcopal Church, and the willingness of the congregation to assent to the ordinations. This element of the service corresponds to the church's recognition of the call of the candidates.

The *Examination* of the candidates for each order occurs after the Ministry of the Word, before the Creed. It make explicit the fact of the candidates' call, and it puts them on record as agreeing with the church's understanding of the office they are about to assume. The particular duties and responsibilities of each order are set forth in the exhortation that introduces the respective Examinations.

Bishops, for example,

> are called to guard the faith, unity, and discipline of the Church; to celebrate and to provide for the administration of the sacraments of the New Covenant; to ordain priests and deacons and to join in ordaining bishops; and to be in all things a faithful pastor and wholesome example for the entire flock of Christ. (p. 517)

A priest is

> to proclaim by word and deed the Gospel of Jesus Christ, and to fashion your life in accordance with its precepts. You are to love and serve the people among whom you work, caring alike for young and old, strong and weak, rich and poor. You are to preach, to declare God's forgiveness to penitent sinners, to pronounce God's blessing, to share in the administration of Holy Baptism and in the celebration of the mysteries of Christ's Body and Blood, and to perform the other ministrations entrusted to you. (p. 531)

A deacon is

> to study the Holy Scriptures, to seek nourishment from them, and to model your life upon them. You are to make Christ and his redemptive love known, by your word and example, to those among whom you live, and work, and worship. You are to interpret to the Church the needs, concerns, and hopes of the world. You are to assist the bishop and priests in public worship and in the ministration of God's Word and Sacraments, and you are to carry out other duties assigned to you from time to time. At all times, your life and teaching are to show Christ's people that in serving the helpless they are serving Christ himself. (p. 543)

Those words are perhaps the best description of the way our church understands holy orders today.

The *Consecration* occurs immediately after the Creed. It is in the form of a prayer by the ordaining bishop. In the case of the ordination of a bishop, the ordainer is the Presiding Bishop or someone appointed by him. Hands are laid on the candidates during this prayer of consecration, which includes the words, "Make him a bishop [or priest, or deacon] of your Church." In the case of a bishop, at least two other bishops join the Presiding Bishop in the laying on of hands, in accordance with an ancient custom noted earlier. In the case of a priest, fellow priests lay their hands on the head of their new colleague, along with the bishop. In the case of a deacon, only the bishop lays hands on the candidate, in recognition of the status of the deacon as the bishop's assistant.

After the Consecration, the peace is exchanged in each case and the Eucharist proceeds.

To make actual the conception of ministry embodied in these services requires a transformation in the mind of the church. We need to recognize the interdependence of all forms of oversight, mediation, and service. No member of the church, clergy or lay, has all the gifts of ministry. Yet the church needs them all. We need to hear again St. Paul's teaching about the diversity of Christ's gifts to his church and the cooperative use of those gifts "to equip the saints for the work of ministry, for building up the body of Christ, until we all attain to the unity of the faith and of the knowledge of the Son of God, to mature manhood, to the measure of the stature of the fulness of Christ" (Eph. 4:12–13).

Celebration of a New Ministry

Since bishops are the source of ordination, it is appropriate not only that they should ordain men and women to holy orders, but also that they should induct persons into new ministries within their diocese. The order for the Celebration of a New Ministry is "for use when a priest is being instituted and inducted as the rector of a parish. It may also be used for the installation of deans and canons of cathedrals, or the inauguration of other ministries, diocesan or parochial" (BCP, p. 558).

The service is built around the Proclamation of the Word at Eucharist. In addition to the Eucharist, there are two parts to the action: the Institution and the Induction. The *Institution* expresses the acceptance of the new minister by the people among whom he or she is to work. The *Induction* is represented by a series of presentations—Bible, water for baptizing, a stole, a book of prayers, keys, a book of canons, bread and wine, and perhaps other things to signify special ministries. Their acceptance by the new minister indicates acceptance of the responsibilities of the new office. The mutual recognition of people and their new minister, in the presence of the bishop and with his prayers, constitutes the celebration of a new ministry consistent with the understanding of the church expressed in the ordination rites.

The Dedication and Consecration of a Church

This service provides for the dedication and consecration of a church and its furnishings. Such an event is of major importance and is a matter of concern and rejoicing for the whole church. It is therefore appropriate that the celebrant at this service should be the bishop, who represents the whole church to the local community. By dedication, the building and its furniture are given to God and set aside for the use of his people. By prayer of consecration, they are made holy, as the Lord's.

At the beginning of the service, the door is opened for a procession. The bishop marks the threshold with the sign of the cross. Font, lectern, pulpit, and altar are separately dedicated, to make the church the focus of Word and Sacrament. Then the service moves into the Eucharist, the church's usual and regular way of giving thanks to God on every occasion.

20

EPILOGUE
Living the Liturgy

We have now reached the end our study. In retrospect, we can see that three themes have been woven into nearly all the previous chapters. These three themes may be said to constitute the warp of this book. The other material—the biblical and liturgical details, the theological interpretations—are its woof. Obviously both warp and woof are essential to any woven texture. But the warp is basic. These three themes constitute the underlying message of the foregoing pages. It may be helpful to mention them at the end, so that readers can see for themselves how much these ideas have influenced and shaped the whole of the study.

These three themes are: (1) the interdependence of liturgical worship and obedient life in the world—the people of God live their liturgy continuously; (2) the interdependence of corporate and individual worship—the individuality of Christian worshipers is heightened by their participation in the liturgy of the whole people; and (3) the richness and variety that is possible in Christian worship—the joyful unity of the people of God is not secured by uniformity of worship but by mutual love, trust, and faith; variety need not impair Christian unity.

The greatest shortcomings in Christian thought and charity often occur when well-intentioned Christians fail to acknowledge one of two mutually dependent sides of the truth. The themes we have identified might serve as illustrations of the point. They require that an even balance be kept between two emphases that at first glance might seem to be mutually exclusive.

1. Liturgy and Life

We have insisted, perhaps too frequently, that liturgy and life belong together. The title of the book, *Liturgy for Living*, holds them together. The New Testament, as we saw, uses the word *liturgy* exclusively to refer to the way Christians *live*. Only gradually was the word liturgy applied to church services and to the text of Christian *prayers*.

Once made, however, this identification of liturgy *only* with services of worship proved to be the stronger one. It has almost crowded out the older and original sense of the term—a life lived in the world, obedient to the sacrificial example of Jesus himself. When liturgy means a service of worship disconnected from the context in life that originally gave it its meaning, serious distortion occurs. In reaction against such a distortion of true worship, Christians have sometimes rejected liturgical worship altogether, in favor of purely worldly ethical obedience. The decade of the tumultuous sixties offered many examples of that rejection.

In this book we have sought to restore the mutual connection between liturgy and life. We have proposed the term *intensive liturgy* to describe what happens when Christians assemble to worship God, and the term *extensive liturgy* to describe what happens when Christians leave the assembly to conduct their daily affairs. The two are mutually dependent. By its intensive liturgies, the church encounters Christ as present in Word and Sacrament. Under these forms, Christians appropriate his example and the power he makes available. To describe a liturgy in such terms, however, is to make its incompleteness obvious. One appropriates an example and its power only for a purpose. One leaves the intensive liturgy to live in accordance with the model and in the strength of the grace it supplies.

As our intensive liturgies drive us into the world to do our extensive liturgies, so our extensive liturgies brings us back week by week to the Christian assembly, to seek God's presence once more under the embodied forms of Word and Sacrament. For the world is stronger than we are. By our own strength, we cannot long live up to Christ's example, nor can we get along without a renewal of spiritual power. Failures are frequent. Discouragement is always close. Need alone would return us to the unfailing source of renewal, given expression and made accessible by the liturgy of the church.

Not only need brings us back, to be sure; thanksgiving also brings us back. Our extensive liturgies are not only the story of failure, although failures are many; they are also the stories of success and triumph. To keep the record straight, and to make sure that we give God the credit due to God alone, we return to give him thanks.

To need and thanksgiving, among the motives that drive Christians to worship in their intensive liturgies, should be added adoration and joy. Finally, worship is an end in itself. Finally, liturgy is play. It is endless joy to add our voices to the praises on which God's people enthroned the Lord; and it is our final fulfillment to adore God for his beauty and majesty, to be "lost in wonder, love, and praise."

2. Corporate and Individual Worship

We have also insisted, perhaps too often, that liturgy is not merely a private affair between each individual and God. Neither is it a transaction between priest and God, which lay persons are privileged to watch, and from which they benefit, but in which they do not play an essential role. By way of contrast to both these views, caricatures (though recognizable ones) of Protestant and Catholic distortions of worship, we have insisted in this volume that worship is an affair of all the people of God, clergy and laity together, each in their own order.

In each section of our study, we have tried to show how this all-encompassing conception of worship has been given liturgical expression. We have also gone to some lengths to indicate that corporate worship does not mean the end of individual worship but rather enhances it. Worship is not corporate *instead* of being individual. It is corporate *so that it can be* truly individual.

The Christian body is composed of separate selves. Yet individuals become who they are not in isolation from their relationships with other individuals but because of those relationships. When we are redeemed by Christ, we cannot be extracted from our associations. God *saves* the world; he does not simply rescue individuals *from* the world.

Thus when we live our liturgies, either intensive or extensive, we do so as individual persons who are members of the body of Christ. Our participation in the congregation deepens our individuality. On the other hand, our individual lives, deepened and redeemed, forgiven and empowered by God, *together* compose the Church, the agent of God's will in the world. We worship both as individuals and as a corporate body. Both individual and corporate dimensions are essential to true Christian worship.

3. The Richness and Variety of Christian Worship

The third thread that has made up the warp of this book is the richness and variety of Christian worship. Anglicans have not believed for a long time, if we ever did, that unity is to be equated with uniformity. At least from the time of Queen Elizabeth I in the sixteenth century, the Church of England has been conceived as a "roomy" church. One major contribution of the Catholic revival of the nineteenth century was to introduce an even larger range of liturgical options, although sometimes at the cost of unity and harmony within our fellowship.

The current Book of Common Prayer attempts to strike a delicate balance between a core of common and irreplaceable texts on the one hand, and variety of expression and style on the other. It rests on the assumptions that the need of the emerging English nation in the sixteenth century for a stable and uniform state church has long since passed, that books are easily obtainable, and that literacy is common. The church can therefore afford to encourage far more variation than it could at the beginning.

Yet Anglican experience has taught us also the value of fixed prayers and a uniform translation of the psalm that can sink deep into our hearts, leaving an invaluable store of strength, beauty, and wisdom. Some invariable liturgical forms and unchanging words are of incalculable value in the formation of Christian lives. The church must preserve the liturgical heritage in which generations of Anglicans have found their identity.

In the resulting balance in the current Prayer Book between the fixed and the optional, between the changing and the invariable, between freedom and order, the American Episcopal church hopes that all its people in a number of different styles will be able to worship God with the freedom of the primitive Christians, with the splendor of the medieval church, with the sober dignity of the Reformation, and with a simplicity and grace all its own.

The Lord is in his holy temple. Come, let us adore him.

Notes

For complete bibliographical data, see the Bibliography of Works Cited.

Chapter 2: Worship and Liturgy

1. Quoted in the Oxford English Dictionary, ad loc.
2. The Quran, Surah xcvi. 3–4.
3. *The Hymnal 1940*, Hymn 337.
4. There are other biblical words for worship, although the others are not as significant for our present discussion as the ones we have considered already. The Aramaic word *segad* in Daniel (which has Aramaic sections as well as Hebrew) is translated as worship. It also means to bow down or to do obeisance. The Hebrew *'abad*, which usually means serve, is sometimes translated *worship*, much as the English word *service* sometimes denotes a service of worship or the service of God in a religious context. *Eusebeō* and *sebomai* mean to do reverence or to be pious. *Latreuō*, which contributes such words as idolatry to the English language, is used four times to mean public worship or ritual. *Threskeia*, a religious observance, appears once, and *therapeuō* (to serve or to heal) is used once. By contrast, *shachah*, the usual Hebrew word, appears over a hundred times in the Old Testament, and *proskyneō* some fifty-nine times in the New.
5. See, for example, 2 Sam. 19:19 LXX.

Chapter 4: Features of Liturgy

1. James Muilenberg, "The History of Israel's Religion," in *The Interpreter's Bible*, vol. 1, p. 344.
2. See Tertullian *On Baptism* xvii (ANF 3:672); and Cyprian *On the Unity of the Church* xvii (ANF 5:427).
3. "A constant element of preparation for sacrifice was the prayer which set forth the purpose of the particular *thusia* (sacrifice) to be offered." Royden K. Yerkes, *Sacrifice in Greek and Roman Religion and Early Judais*, p. 101.
4. Paul Tillich, *Systematic Theology*, vol. 1, p. 127.
5. See Henri Nouwen, *Reaching Out*, p. 88.
6. *The Hymnal 1940*, Hymn 301.
7. For further discussion of this point, see W. Eichrodt, *Old Testament Theology*, vol. 1, p. 423.

Chapter 5: Implications and Consequences of Liturgy

1. *The Hymnal 1940*, Hymn 80.

Chapter 6: The Background of the Prayer Book

1. *Didache* ix. 1 (AF 2:323).
2. *Didache* ix. 3 (AF 2:323).
3. *Didache* x. 2 (AF 2:323).
4. *The Hymnal 1940*, Hymn 195; emphasis added.
5. Pliny's "Letter to Trajan," in H. Bettenson, ed., *Documents of the Christian Church*, p. 6.
6. See, for a comprehensive treatment, Archdale A. King, *Rites of Western Christendom*.

Chapter 7: Anglican Prayer Books

1. *The First and Second Prayer Books of Edward VI* (Everyman's Library), p. 215. Here and in the quotations that follow the spelling has been modernized.
2. Ibid., p. 241.
3. Ibid., p. 252.
4. Ibid., p. 269.
5. Quoted in F. F. Procter and W. H. Frere, *A New History of the Book of Common Prayer*, p. 56.
6. The rubric on p. 573 of the 1928 Prayer Book reads: "Then shall the Instituted Minister kneel at the Altar. . . ."
7. First Prayer Book of Edward VI, p. 212.
8. Second Prayer Book of Edward VI, p. 381.
9. BCP 1928, p. 80; emphasis added.
10. Second Prayer Book of Edward VI, p. 390.

Chapter 8: Holy Baptism

1. *Manual of Discipline* viii. 13–14.
2. Justin Martyr *First Apology* lxi (ANF 1: 183).
3. Hippolytus *Apostolic Tradition* 21. 3 (Easton ed., p. 45).
4. Ibid., 16. 25 (p. 43).
5. Ibid., 21. 9 (p. 45).
6. Ibid., 22. 1 (p. 47).
7. Ibid., 22. 2 (p. 47).

Chapter 9: Confirmation

1. Tertullian *On Baptism* vii (ANF 3:672).
2. Ibid., viii (ANF 3:672).
3. J. D. C. Fisher, "History and Theology," in *Confirmation Crisis*, p. 36.
4. Ibid., p. 35.

5. Thomas Aquinas, *Summa Theologica,* pt. III, q. 72, arts. 7–8 (English Dominican ed., vol. 1, p. 18).

6. Thomas Cranmer, *Miscellaneous Writings and Letters,* p. 80.

7. Marion Hatchett, *Sanctifying Life, Time and Space,* p. 117.

8. Jeremy Taylor, *The Whole Works,* vol. 5, pp. 616–17.

9. Cf. Gregory Dix, *The Theology of Confirmation in Relation to Baptism*; Geoffrey W. H. Lampe, *The Seal of the Spirit*; and Lionel S. Thornton, *Confirmation, Its Place in the Baptismal Mystery.*

10. John Calvin, *Institutes,* iv. 19.4 (LCC 2:1451–52).

11. *The First and Second Prayer Books of Edward VI* (Everyman's Library), p. 404.

12. See *Confirmation Crisis,* p. 10.

Chapter 10: The Word of God and the Bible

1. J. B. Phillips, *The Gospels in Modern English,* p. 189.

2. Jer. 2:1; Ezek. 3:16; Hos. 1:1; Jl. 1.1; etc. Or "The Word came to Jeremiah from the Lord" (Jer. 11:1), or "Thus saith the Lord" (Am. 1:3, 6, 9, 13). There are many variants.

3. See, for example, Karl Barth, Church Dogmatics, I/l, pp. 136ff; and Paul Tillich, *Systematic Theology,* vol. 1, pp. 158–59.

4. Cf. George T. Ladd, *The Doctrine of Sacred Scripture,* vol. 2, pp. 76–77.

Chapter 11: The Word of God in the Liturgy

1. Cf., for example, G. von Rad, *Old Testament Theology,* vol. 1, pp. 355–459.

2. Cf. Ibid., especially vol. 1, pp. 192ff, and vol. 2, pp. 104ff.

3. The book of Esther on the Feast of Purim, and the Song of Solomon on Passover.

4. Justin Martyr *First Apology* lxvii (ANF 1:185–86).

5. *Apostolic Constitutions* II. Vii (ANF 7:421).

6. The Liturgy of St. James (ANF 7:539).

7. Hippolytus *Apostolic Tradition* 35–37 (Easton ed., pp. 54–55).

8. Pliny's "Letter to Trajan," in H. Bettenson, ed., *Documents of the Christian Church,* p. 6.

9. See J. A. Jungman, *The Liturgy of the Word,* pp. 42f.

10. See P. Batiffol, *History of the Roman Breviary,* pp. 132–33.

Chapter 12: Morning and Evening Prayer in Today's Church

1. J. N. D. Kelly, *Early Christian Creeds,* pp. 1–3.

2. John Calvin, *Institutes,* IV. 17.43 (LCC 2:1421f.)

3. In England. In the United States, Ante-communion ended after the Gospel.

Chapter 13: The Holy Eucharist (I): The Proclamation of the Word of God

1. Augustine *Confessions* IV. 14 (LCC, p. 8)

Chapter 14: The Holy Eucharist (II): The Holy Communion

1. Gregory Dix, *The Shape of the Liturgy*, p. 50; J. Jeremias, *The Eucharistic Words of Jesus*, chap. 1, pp. 15–18.
2. Cited in G. Dix, *The Shape of the Liturgy*, pp. 52–53. Cf. also H. L. Strack and P. Billerbeck, *Kommentar zum Neuen Testament aus Talmud and Midrash*, vol. 4, p. 628.
3. Justin Martyr *First Apology* lxvii (ANF 1:185–86).
4. Hippolytus *Apostolic Tradition* 4.3 (Easton ed., p. 35).
5. Ibid. 4. 4-8 (pp. 35–36).
6. Ibid 4. 9-10 (p. 36).
7. Ibid. 4. 11 (p. 36).
8. Ibid. 4. 12-13 (36).
9. Ibid. 4. 12 (p. 36).

Chapter 15: The Holy Eucharist (III): Theories about the Eucharist

1. *The Hymnal 1940*, Hymn 199, *Pange lingua*, verse 4.

Chapter 16: The Christian Calendar

1. *The Hymnal 1940*, Hymn 122.
2. *The Hymnal 1940*, Hymn 153.
3. *Didache* viii. 1 (AF 3:321).
4. *Apostolic Constitutions* viii. 333 (ANF 7:495).
5. *The Hymnal 1940*, Hymn 94.
6. A. A. MacArthur, *The Evolution of the Christian Year*, pp. 41–43.

Chapter 17: Pastoral Offices (I): For Marriage, Birth, Sickness, and Death

1. Ignatius to *Polycarp* v (AF 1: 273).
2. Tertullian *To His Wife* ii. 8 (AF 4:48).
3. W. K. L. Clarke and Charles Harris, *Liturgy and Worship*, p. 461.

Chapter 18: Pastoral Offices II: For Reconciliation and Commitment

1. See David Hill, *The Gospel of Matthew*, p. 272; and Walter Grundman, *Das Evangelium nach Matthäus*, p. 411.

Chapter 19: Episcopal Services

1. *Ministry and Ordination: A Statement on the Doctrine of the Ministry Agreed by the Anglican-Roman Catholic International Commission, Canterbury, 1973* (New York: Morehouse-Barlow, 1973).
2. See Arnold B. Come, *Agents of Reconciliation*.
3. Thomas Aquinas, *Summa Theologica*, pt. III, q. 40, art. 5 (English Dominican ed., vol. 19, p. 68).

Glossary of Liturgical Terms

Ablutions: ceremonial washings, as, for example, the cleansing of the chalice after communion.

Absolution: the declaration by a bishop or priest of forgiveness by Christ of persons who have repented and confessed their sins.

Abstinence: a penitential practice in which certain foods are not eaten (meat, for example), or only a small quantity of food is eaten.

Administration: the giving of the sacramental gifts to a communicant.

Advent: the liturgical season of the four Sundays prior to Christmas; the name is derived from the season's focus on the second coming of Christ at the end of time. The First Sunday in Advent is reckoned as the beginning of the Christian year.

Affusion: a method of baptism in which water is poured on the candidate. See Aspersion and Immersion.

Agape: the Christian "Love-Feast" or common religious meal eaten in connection with the Eucharist in the early centuries of the church.

Agnus Dei: an ancient hymn to Christ as the "Lamb of God"; it originated in the East and was introduced into the West at Rome late in the seventh century to accompany the breaking of bread before communion.

Alb: a narrow-sleeved, full-length white vestment; originally widely used as secular dress in Rome, it became the basic liturgical garment. It was replaced by the surplice in the later Middle Ages for most noneucharistic offices and has been in wide general use within Anglicanism since the nineteenth century.

Alleluia: a liturgical acclamation of praise, especially characteristic of the period from Easter to Pentecost, and in association with the chant prior to the Gospel; it became the custom in the West to eliminate it during Lent. The word is derived from the Hebrew *Hallelujah*, which means "Praise Jahweh!"

Ambo: a raised platform or desk from which a reading from Scripture is proclaimed.

Anamnesis: in the eucharistic prayer, the passage immediately following the Words of Institution, in which the "memorial" of Christ's death, resurrection, and ascension, and sometimes his return in glory, is made.

Anaphora: the usual Orthodox title for the eucharistic prayer; the title is derived from the "offering" or Oblation of the eucharistic gifts, which are "lifted up."

Anointing: a rite in which consecrated oil is placed upon persons or things as a sign of God's sustaining presence; an anointing may complement the water rite of baptism or may be administered in unction as a sign of God's healing grace. The title *Messiah*, often applied to Jesus, means "the Anointed One" and is an expression of his divine authority. In the Old Testament, associated with the Spirit (Is. 61:1), or with kingship (1 Sam. 10:1) and priesthood (Lev. 8:12).

Ante-communion: the first part of the rite of Holy Communion through the Gospel (American BCP) or the Prayers of the People (English BCP); the title is normally used when the eucharistic prayer and communion do not follow. *See* Liturgy of the Word, *Pro-Anaphora*.

Anthem: The English form of the word *antiphon*; a musical setting for the choir of a text from Scripture, or any appropriate liturgical text.

Antiphon: a phrase appointed for use before (and after) a canticle or psalm that indicates the theme of the liturgical celebration; for example, a number of antiphons are provided in the BCP, pp. 42–44, 80–82, for use with the invitatory.

Apostles' Creed: a profession of faith associated with baptism in the Western church from the third or fourth century; this brief summary of the Christian faith was taken into the Daily Offices during the Middle Ages, and from thence passed into Anglican Morning and Evening Prayer. (Cf. BCP, pp. 53–54, 66; pp. 96 and 120 give the ICET version.)

Ascension: the fortieth day of the paschal season, the Thursday after the Sixth Sunday of Easter; the ascension of Christ into heaven marked the end of his appearances to the disciples after the resurrection; the liturgical feast commemorates the event and also the Lordship of Christ who now reigns "at the right hand of the Father." (Cf. Mk. 16:19, Acts 1:1–11.)

Ash Wednesday: the first day of Lent, occurring forty days (exclusive of Sundays) before Easter; so named because of the custom of imposing ashes upon the heads of the people as a sign of penitence. (Cf. BCP, pp. 264–69.)

Aspersion: a method of baptism in which the candidate is sprinkled with water. See Affusion and Immersion.

Athanasian Creed: a profession of faith composed about the fifth century, once widely used in the West; it is still required on certain occasions in the Church of England. (Cf. BCP, pp. 864–65.)

Banns: the public announcement of a forthcoming marriage during an assembly for worship.

Baptism: the sacramental action by which a person is made a member of the church through water (used for immersion, affusion, or aspersion) and the invocation of the Holy Trinity. The water rite is usually complemented by a laying on of hands, an anointing, or a signing with the sign of the cross.

Benedicite, omnia opera: a canticle from the Apocrypha (Song of the Three Young Men, verses 35–65), traditionally associated with Morning Prayer (cf. BCP, canticles 1 and 12, pp. 47–49, 88–90). In the Roman Catholic Breviary, this canticle is used on Sundays at Lauds.

Benediction: a blessing.

Benedictus: a canticle from the New Testament (Lk. 1:68–79), traditionally associated with Morning Prayer. (cf. BCP, canticles 4 and 16, pp. 50–51, 92–93.) In the Roman Catholic Breviary, this canticle is used daily at Lauds.

Benedictus es, Domine: a canticle from the Apocrypha (song of the Three Young Men, verses 29–34; cf. BCP, canticles 2 and 13, pp. 49, 90). This canticle was introduced for use at Morning Prayer in the American BCP 1928.

Benedictus qui venit: a liturgical acclamation based upon Mt. 21:9, and itself a citation of Ps. 118:26. It has been appended to the *Sanctus* since the fifth century: "Blessed is he that cometh. . . ." (Cf. BCP, p. 424.)

Betrothal: a free consent to future marriage between a man and woman; in the liturgy of marriage, the introductory part certifies these consents. (Cf. BCP 1928, p. 47.)

Bidding Prayer: an invitation to the people calling them to pray for a series of proposed intentions: e.g., the church, the state, special needs, the deceased. (Cf. BCP 1928, p. 47.)

Bishop: an order of the ordained ministry of the church; the chief pastor and administrator of a diocese. The word comes from Greek *episkopos*, "overseer."

Black-Letter Days: minor commemorations as distinguished from major festivals of the Church Year. *See* Red-Letter Days.

Breviary: the liturgical book that contains the appointed psalms, hymns, and readings for the Roman Catholic Divine Office; corresponds to the material for Morning and Evening Prayer in the BCP.

Burial Rite: the liturgical rite made up of psalms, readings, and prayers appointed for the burial of the dead. *See* Requiem.

Byzantine Rite: the principal liturgical family among the various Eastern rites; it originated in Constantinople.

Canon: a fixed order or rule, as, for example, a set form of prayer such as the eucharistic prayer, or the list of books accepted as Sacred Scripture.

Cantemus Domino: the song of Moses (Ex. 15:1–6, 11–13, 17–18), a canticle for the Daily Offices especially suitable for Easter season, introduced in the current revision of the BCP.

Canterbury Statement: a theological statement on the question of the Ministry of the Church, agreed by the Anglican-Roman Catholic International Commission in 1973.

Canticle: a "song" derived from Scripture, which is used in the church's worship.

Cassock: a long garment, usually black, worn originally to keep warm, and now customarily worn under any vestments to be used in the liturgy.

Catechesis: instruction in the Christian teaching, used especially in connection with the prebaptismal preparation of adults in the early church.

Catechism: a form of instruction usually based upon questions and answers. (Cf. BCP, pp. 845–62.)

Catechumen: a person who is undergoing Christian formation prior to baptism.

Censing: the ceremonial use of incense in a liturgical rite, usually associated with the offering of prayer.

Ceremonial: the actions that are necessary or customary for the celebration of a liturgical rite.

Chaburah: among the Jews, a group of friends; our Lord and his disciples formed such a group. It is widely held that the Last Supper was a *chaburah* meal, characteristic of such groups.

Character: the concept in medieval theology of an indelible aspect to certain sacrament—namely baptism, confirmation, and ordination—which means that they cannot be received more than once by the same person and, having been received, cannot be lost (though they may be rendered ineffective).

Chasuble: a liturgical vestment originally derived from the outdoor cloak worn by men and women in Roman society; its shape was similar to that of a tent, from which its name (*casula*, "little house") developed; it is often worn by the celebrant of the Eucharist as the principal garment.

Chrism: olive oil mixed with balsam (an aromatic resin) and consecrated by a bishop for use at baptism, confirmation, ordination, and various episcopal blessings.

Christmas: the liturgical feast of the birth of Christ celebrated on December 25; the choice of the date probably rests upon Christian opposition to the pagan feast of the "Birth of the Unconquered Sun" kept on this date into the fourth century. There is no record of the actual date of Jesus' birth.

Chrysom: a white garment put on after baptism.

Church Orders: various early Christian writings dealing with the life and worship on the church; these Orders influenced the fixing of liturgical forms and today offer valuable information on the early stages of church history. Among these writings are the *Didache*, the *Apostolic Tradition* of Hippolytus, and the *Apostolic Constitutions*.

Collect: a short form of prayer, originally intended either to summarize or "collect" the intercessions of the faithful (*collectio*), or designed to be said at a place where the faithful had gathered (*collecta*) in order to proceed to the place where the liturgy was to be celebrated on that day. *See* Stational Liturgies

Commixture: the dropping of a particle of the consecrated bread into the chalice. *See Fermentum.*

Common: a set of appointed scriptural readings equally appropriate to various feasts of the same type. (Cf. BCP, "The Common of Saints," pp. 925–27.) *See* Proper.

Common Prayer: public worship, as contrasted with private prayer; the Book of Common Prayer in its various forms within the Anglican tradition is intended as a single comprehensive basis for corporate worship.

Communion: the act of receiving the eucharistic gifts, or that part of the liturgy during which this action takes place; among Anglicans, the title "Holy Communion" has traditionally been applied to the entire eucharistic rite.

Compline: a pattern of prayer at the time of going to bed.

Concelebration: the celebration of the Eucharist by one of more bishops or priests in addition to the presiding celebrant. A concelebration may involve the assisting clergy in the recitation of the Great Thanksgiving, but the original pattern was based upon physical proximity to the principal celebrant rather than verbal participation.

Confession: usually an acknowledgment of sin, either in general terms in public worship or in specific terms in private, before a bishop or priest who declares the words of absolution. The word is sometimes used to indicate a profession of faith.

Confirmation: a rite that developed from the bishop's laying on of hands upon a candidate at baptism, later separated from that water rite. In Anglican practice, confirmation has come to be generally understood as a laying on of hands by the bishop at the time a person makes a mature profession of Christian faith by reaffirming baptismal vows.

Consignation: a signing or "sealing" with the sign of the cross as, for example, upon the forehead at baptism.

Consubstantiation: a theory of the sacramental presence of Christ in the Eucharist in which his body and blood and the bread and wine coexist in the sacred elements. *See* Real Presence, Receptionism, and Transubstantiation.

Cope: a decorated liturgical cape used especially in processions and on other solemn occasions.

Course Readings: a system of appointed psalms and scriptural readings read from day to day in the order in which they appear in the Bible.

Credence: a small table usually near the altar upon which bread, wine, and water are placed for use in the Eucharist.

Creed: a summary statement of the basic doctrines of Christianity. *See* Apostles' Creed, Athanasian Creed, and Nicene Creed.

Crosier: the crook-shaped pastoral staff carried by bishops.

Customary: a book containing a description of the rites and ceremonies of a particular diocese, cathedral church, or monastery, known also by the title "Consuetudinary."

Daily Offices: services of psalms, readings, canticles, and prayers provided for certain times of each day throughout the year: e.g., Morning and Evening Prayer in the Book of Common Prayer.

Dalmatic: the liturgical vestment traditionally associated with deacons; because it is a festal garment, it is not worn in penitential seasons.

Deacon: an order of the ordained ministry of the church; the title is derived from the New Testament word for "servant" or "minister"; deacons are traditionally associated with the bishops as their chief administrative assistants.

Decalogue: the Ten Commandments (Ex. 20:1–17), used in Anglican worship from the Reformation period.

Deprecations: intercessions, especially for deliverance from evil.

Dignus es: Song to the Lamb (Rev. 4:11; 5:9–10, 13), a canticle for the Daily Offices introduced in the current revision of the BCP.

Diocese: the territorial division for the pastoral oversight and administration of the church, under the authority of a bishop; the name is derived from one of the administrative divisions of the late Roman Empire. *See* Parish and Province.

Diptychs: the lists of the names of the living and the dead who are to be remembered in the intercessions of the Eucharist; the name is derived from two wax tablets folded together on which the names were inscribed.

Disciplina arcani: the "Discipline of the secret" involved the withholding of instruction concerning the basic elements of Christian faith until after baptism; the practice remained in force through the fifth century.

Dismissal: the phrase at the end of the Eucharist that signals the sending forth of the faithful; during the early centuries, persons not yet baptized were dismissed after the Scripture readings and homily.

Doxology: an ascription of glory to God; in Christian worship, addressed to the persons of the Holy Trinity, and often appended as a concluding formula to a prayer or hymn.

Easter: the feast of the resurrection of Christ, celebrated liturgically for fifty days ending with the Day of Pentecost. Eostre was the Anglo-Saxon goddess of spring.

Eastern Rite: the general designation of the various liturgical families of rites that developed principally in West Syria (especially Antioch and Jerusalem), Egypt (especially Alexandria), East Syria (Persia), and finally Constantinople. In later centuries, these rites spread far beyond their places of origin. The most frequently used Eastern Rite is that attributed to St. John Chrysostom, one of the Constantinopolitan, or Byzantine, liturgies.

Eastward Position: the custom of the celebrant of the Eucharist standing so that his back is toward the people with the altar near the back wall. This position became common in the West from the eight or ninth century as the participation of the laity ceased to be normative.

Ecce Deus: the First Song of Isaiah (Is. 12:2–6). "Surely it is God who saves me," a canticle for the Daily Offices introduced in the current revision of the BCP.

Effeta: a ceremony of the medieval rite of baptism in which the priest moistened the ears and nose of the candidate with saliva (cf. Mk. 7:34). From the Aramaic word meaning "be opened," it designates a prayer for the opening of the baptized person to the Gospel.

Elevation: in the eucharistic prayer, the custom of lifting up the consecrated elements during the Words of Institution; the practice was introduced from the late twelfth century as the result of a dispute about the Real Presence.

Ember Days: four sets of three days of special prayers during the course of the year. They seem to have originated in connection with the four seasons or with the planting and harvesting of crops.

Embolism: the expansion of the phrase "deliver us from evil" of the Lord's Prayer into an extended petition prior to the doxology. From a Greek word meaning "something thrown in," it designates an insertion into an established text.

Epiclesis: the Invocation in the eucharistic prayer, often centered on the activity of the Holy Spirit to change the bread and wine into the body and blood of Christ; the prayer may also invoke the Spirit to accomplish the benefits of communion among the communicants.

Epiphany: (the Greek word means "showing forth") the feast of the "manifestation" of Christ, celebrated on January 6, and originally concerned with the commemoration of the baptism of Christ; later the association with the Magi was emphasized in the West.

Episcopal Services: the liturgical rites celebrated by the bishop, and including the rites of Ordination, the Celebration of a New Ministry, and the Consecration of a Church or Chapel. (Cf. BCP, pp. 509–79.)

Espousal: the rite by which a man and a woman contract marriage; in the espousal, the exchange of promises of lifelong fidelity that constitute the marriage takes place. (Cf. BCP, p. 427.)

Eucharist: the primary act of Christian "thanksgiving" in which is celebrated and commemorated the central events of Christian faith; the rite in which the church obeys the command of Christ at the Last Supper, "Do this in remembrance of me."

Eucharistic Prayer: the principle prayer of the Eucharist. *See* Great Thanksgiving, *Anaphora.*

Evensong: the title of the evening office in the BCP 1549, now frequently applied to Evening Prayer when it is chanted.

Exhortation: a form of bidding or admonition addressed to the people; for example, with reference to their attendance at the Eucharist. (Cf. BCP, pp. 316–17.)

Exorcism: a form of prayer for the casting out of any evil power that may be present in persons or things.

Exsultet: the "Paschal Proclamation" which is traditionally sung by a deacon at the blessing of the paschal candle at the Easter Vigil; the name is derived from the first word of the Latin text, meaning "rejoice."

Extreme Unction: *see* Unction.

Feria: an ordinary weekday on which no special liturgical commemoration occurs.

Fermentum: the name given to the fragments of the eucharistic bread sent by the bishop to the presbyters assigned to parish churches as a sign of the unity of all Eucharists with that of the bishop.

Form: the authorized words integral to the sacramental rite. *See* Matter.

Fraction: the breaking of the eucharistic bread prior to the administration of communion; "the breaking of bread" was a primitive name for the Eucharist. (Cf. Acts 2:42.)

Gallican Rite: the family of liturgical rites of the church in Gaul, gradually replaced by the Roman Rite that Charlemagne imposed on the Holy Roman Empire for the sake of unity.

Gloria in excelsis: the "Greater Doxology" beginning with the phrase "Glory to God in the highest"; first used as a morning hymn among the Eastern Orthodox, the text passed gradually into the Eucharist in the West as a hymn on feast days.

Gloria Patri: the "Lesser Doxology" beginning with the phrase "Glory to the Father. . ." which is commonly used at the end of psalms and canticles.

Godparents: the sponsors or witnesses at a baptism who undertake special responsibilities toward the candidate.

Good Friday: the day on which the crucifixion of Christ is commemorated, occurring two days before Easter; the liturgical celebration of the day developed during the fourth century as part of a new emphasis on the historical events in the life of Christ (cf. BCP, pp. 276–82). The Eucharist is not normally celebrated on Good Friday.

Gradual: appointed psalm verses to be sung or read between eucharistic readings, usually after a reading from the Old Testament and before the Epistle.

Great Bible: the edition of the English Bible prepared by Miles Coverdale and issued in 1539.

Great Entrance: in Byzantine Rite, the procession with the bread and wine to be consecrated at the Eucharist. *See* Little Entrance.

Great Thanksgiving: the principal prayer of the Eucharist in which thanksgiving is offered to God the Father on the basis of Christ's command, in remembrance of his saving acts, and through invocation of the Holy Spirit, as the context for consecration of the gifts of bread and wine to be the body and blood of Christ. *See Anaphora,* Eucharistic Prayer.

Great Vigil of Easter: the nocturnal service that traditionally opens the celebration of Easter; the liturgical rite usually includes an introductory blessing of fire, the blessing of the paschal candle, the *Exsultet,* scriptural readings, psalms, canticles, and the rite of baptism; the vigil ends with the celebration of the first Eucharist of Easter. (Cf. BCP, pp. 284–95.)

Holy days: festivals of the Church Year for which appointed collects and readings are provided in the authorized liturgical books.

Holy Saturday: the day before Easter Sunday, and the day that commemorates the resting of Christ's body in the tomb; the Eucharist is not normally celebrated on Holy Saturday, but late in the day or at night the Great Vigil of Easter terminates in the celebration of the first Easter Eucharist.

Holy Week: the week preceding Easter, during which the liturgical rites focus on the events associated with the passion of Christ.

Homily: a sermon, usually an exposition of the appointed Scripture reading at the Eucharist.

Hours of Prayer: a name given to the monastic pattern of the Divine Office, made up of Matins, Lauds, Prime, Terce, Sext, None, Vespers, and Compline.

Humble Access: a prayer of preparation of Holy Communion that begins: "We do not presume to come to this Thy Table." (Cf. BCP, p. 337.)

ICET: The International Commission of English Texts, an organization of scholars involved in the preparation of contemporary English versions of a number of common liturgical texts for ecumenical use.

Immersion: a method of baptism in which all or part of the candidate's body is lowered into the water. *See* Affusion and Aspersion.

Imposition: ordinarily used in reference to a laying on of hands; sometimes used in reference to the placing of ashes on worshipers' foreheads on Ash Wednesday. (Cf. BCP, p. 265.)

Incense: aromatic gums and spices that are burned to produce a fragrant smoke; it was used in the worship of the Jewish temple and taken into Christian worship in the early sixth century; it is held to symbolize prayer rising to God. (Cf. Rev. 8:3.)

Institution: the installation of a new rector into the pastoral care of a parish.

Institution Narrative: *See* Words of Institution.

Intention: the purpose of doing what the church intends to do, as in a sacramental act, or the specified reason for which an intercession is made.

Intercession: prayer on behalf of others.

Intinction: a method of administering Holy Communion in which the bread is moistened in the wine so that both of the sacred elements are received together.

Introit: originally, a portion of the Psalter sung during the entrance of the clergy at the beginning of the Eucharist; now applies to an entrance hymn as well.

Investiture: the clothing of a candidate at ordination with the distinctive vestments of the new office.

Invitatory: a psalm or canticle that is said or sung near the beginning of Morning or Evening Prayer as an invitation to the act of praise; the invitatory immediately precedes the appointed psalm or psalms. (Cf. BCP, pp. 42–46, 63–64, 80–83, 117–18.)

Invocation: a prayer that calls upon God; specifically, a prayer that calls upon God to accept and consecrate the eucharistic gifts. *See Epiclesis.*

Jubilate Deo: Psalm 100, " O be joyful in the Lord," a canticle used in Anglican Morning Prayer since 1552, appointed as an invitatory in the current revision of the BCP.

Jus liturgicum: the authority of a bishop to regulate the liturgical norms of a diocese; although significant during medieval times, it has been limited during recent centuries by general church controls over texts and rubrics.

Kiddush: in Jewish liturgical practice, a prayer of "sanctification," which is the meaning of the word in Hebrew.

Kyrie eleison: "Lord have mercy" (in Greek), and known as the "Lesser Litany"; it appears prior to the reading from Scripture in the Eucharist, where it is a vestige of an ancient litany. (Cf. BCP, p. 324, 356.)

Kyrie pantocrator: a Song of Penitence (Prayer of Manesseh 1–2, 4, 6–7, 11–15), a canticle for the Daily Offices especially suitable for Lent and other penitential occasions, introduced in the current revision of the BCP.

Laity: From the Greek word *laos*, "people"; all the baptized members of the church, usually distinguished from the ordained clergy.

Lauds: from the Latin word for "praise," Lauds was the title of the monastic hour of prayer that was sung at dawn; the name derived specifically from the Psalms of Praise (148–150) that ended this morning office.

Lection: a passage from Scripture appointed to be read at a liturgical service.

Lectionary: a table of appointed psalm and Scripture readings for use at regular services.

Lent: the forty-day period (exclusive of Sundays) prior to Easter, beginning on Ash Wednesday; the period developed in connection with the preparation of candidates for baptism and penitents for reconciliation at the end of Holy Week. Lent is traditionally associated with Jesus' forty days of fasting and temptation in the wilderness.

Litany: a form of prayer that consists of a series of petitions to which the people make such fixed responses as *Kyrie eleison* or "Hear our prayer."

Little Entrance: in the Byzantine Rite, the procession with the Gospel book before the reading of the Gospel. *See* Great Entrance.

Little Hours: the short monastic offices of Terce (the third hour—9 A.M.), Sext (the sixth—noon), and None (the Ninth—3 P.M.); the names were derived from the hours of daylight reckoned from 6 A.M., although the Little Hours were often shifted to other times for convenience.

Liturgical Colors: a sequence of colors for use at various feasts or seasons of the Church Year for vestments and altar hangings; used in the West with great flexibility until the later Middle Ages. The Eastern church still does not prescribe a fixed pattern.

Liturgy: the word is used in two senses: (1) in reference to all authorized services of the church (as distinct from acts of private devotion); (2) specifically as a title of the Eucharist.

Liturgy of the Word: the name applied in general to the first part of the Eucharist, but essentially referring to the readings from Scripture and the sermon. *See* Ante-communion and *Pro-Anaphora.*

Magna et mirabilia: The Song of the Redeemed (Rev. 15:3-4), "O ruler of the universe," a canticle for the Daily Offices introduced in the current revision of the BCP.

Magnificat: the traditional first canticle of Evensong as well as that of Roman Catholic Vespers; its text is the song of praise sung by the Blessed Virgin Mary and recorded in Lk. 1:46-55.

Maniple: an item of liturgical vesture that came to be worn over the left arm by the celebrant at the Eucharist; it is now falling into disuse.

Manual: a handbook of pastoral offices used by a priest; in the Roman Rite it is known as the Ritual.

Manual Acts: the gestures of the celebrant at the Eucharist, especially those indicated by the rubrics in the eucharistic prayer in connection with the Institution Narrative.

Mass: the common medieval title for the Eucharist, probable derived from the Latin phrase at the conclusion of the liturgy: *Ite missa est*, "Go, you are dismissed." The word often appears in various combinations, e.g.:
High Mass: a sung celebration of the Eucharist, the celebrant being assisted by other ministers and choir.
Low Mass: a celebration of the Eucharist without music, usually by one celebrant.
Solemn Mass: a High Mass at which incense is also used.

Matins: originally, and still in monastic community, the Vigil Office of psalms and readings performed during the night; as *Mattins*, a title for Morning Prayer in the BCP 1549, and still retained in popular use.

Matrimony: the Christian sacrament of marriage in which the natural union of man and woman in a permanent bond is proclaimed as the framework of mutual sanctification. (Cf. BCP, pp. 423-38.)

Matter: the physical element of a sacrament, as, for example, the water in baptism, bread and wine in the Eucharist or the laying on of hands in ordination. *See* Form.

Maundy Thursday: the Thursday before Easter Sunday; the word *maundy* is derived from *mandatum* (Latin), meaning "commandment," and refers to the new commandment of Christ that his disciples love one another (Jn. 13:34). This text was sung in connection with the washing of the feet associated with this day. Other liturgical aspects of Maundy Thursday have included the commemoration of Christ's institution of the Eucharist at the Last Supper, the consecration of oils, and the reconciliation of penitents.

Memorial: a collect added after the appointed collects, in order to bring to mind some special event, person, or concern.

Minister: as a technical term, a person authorized to perform liturgical or spiritual functions in the church. Such responsibilities are often distinguished in particular context; for example, celebrant: the principal liturgical minister at the Eucharist, who is always a bishop or priest; officiant: the liturgical minister for various offices, such as morning or Evening Prayer, and not necessarily a person in Holy Orders. As a general term, one who helps or serves another in any way in the name of Christ.

Minor Oblation: a phrase sometimes used, albeit ambiguously, in reference to the presentation of the bread and wine at the altar during the Offertory, and thus prior to the Oblation in the eucharistic prayer.

Missal: in Roman Catholic usage, the liturgical book containing all the texts of the Eucharist for the entire Church Year in a single volume for the use of the celebrant; the Missal developed as priests came to take over the ministries of others at the liturgy.

Miter: the liturgical headdress often worn by bishops; the miter (or British: mitre) was first used in outdoor processions and was used indoors from the eleventh century.

Mozarabic Rite: the name given to the liturgical family that developed in Spain from the early medieval period; these forms were closely related to those of the Gallican Rite. Increasing domination by the Roman Rite led to its abolition in the eleventh century except in a few authorized places (e.g., Toledo Cathedral).

Mystery: another name for *sacrament*, especially in the Eastern church. The word refers in origin to an act of God in which his presence, though hidden from those who do not believe, is revealed to the faithful.

Nicene Creed: the title given to a version of the creed issued in 325 at the Council of Nicaea. It ended with the phrase, "We believe in the Holy Spirit." It was extended by the Council of Constantinople in 381 to cover the remaining affirmations about the Spirit, the church, etc. The Nicene Creed was slowly taken into the Eucharist (cf. BCP, pp. 326–28). Technically, the creed of the Eucharist is the Niceno-Constantinopolitan Creed.

Nocturn: a group of psalms sung in the monastic vigil office of Matins.

None: the hour of prayer said at the ninth hour of the day (3 P.M.), but often anticipated and hence the origin of the English word *noon*.

Nunc dimittis: the canticle known as "The Song of Simeon" (Lk. 2:29–32) and traditionally associated with either Evening Prayer or Compline. (Cf. BCP, pp. 66, 120, 135.)

Nuptial: pertaining to the liturgy for marriage, as Nuptial Eucharist.

Oblation: the act of offering the eucharistic gifts to God.

Offertory: the action in the Eucharist in which the bread and wine, and the alms, are presented at the altar.

Office: usually used in regard to Morning or Evening Prayer, but may also refer to other liturgical forms, such as the Burial Office.

Orans: a standing posture for prayer in which the arms are outstretched and the hands uplifted; the basic posture for prayer among the Jews at the time for Christ, and among Christians for many centuries.

Order: the structural form of a liturgical service; may also refer to one or another of the ordained ministries.

Ordinal: the volume or section of a liturgical volume that gives the rites of ordination for bishops, priests, and deacons.

Ordination: the sacramental designation and authorization of persons for the ordained ministries of the church.

Ornaments Rubric: a rubric of the English BCP that regulates the vestments to be worn by the clergy and the ornaments to be used in the church.

Pall: a cloth covering of two basic types: (1) a small linen cloth, stiffened with cardboard or plastic, which is used to cover the chalice; (2) a very large cloth, of white, purple, or black material, which covers the coffin at a funeral.

Palm Sunday: one of the names for the Sunday before Easter Sunday, and thus the first day of Holy Week; the name is derived from the custom of a procession of the people carrying palms in commemoration of Christ's entry into Jerusalem.

Parish: an ecclesiastical division for pastoral oversight; originally a geographic division of a diocese, it now usually refers to a congregation of baptized persons ministered to by a rector.

Pascha nostrum: "Christ our Passover," a canticle consisting of 1 Cor. 5:7–8; Rom. 6:9–11; and 1 Cor. 15:20–22, appointed as an invitatory at Morning Prayer during the Easter season (Cf. BCP, pp. 46, 83.)

Paschal Season: the fifty-day period between Easter Day and Pentecost.

Paschal candle: the large candle traditionally lighted at the Great Vigil of Easter, which burns at all liturgical services through the Day of Pentecost. (Cf. BCP, pp.285-97.)

Passion Sunday: one of the names for the Sunday before Easter Sunday, and thus the first day of Holy Week; the name is derived from the custom of reading one of the Passion Gospels at the Eucharist of the day. (e.g., Mt. 26:36—27:54, etc.; cf. BCP, pp. 270-73. *See* Palm Sunday.) In BCP 1928, but not earlier, the name of the *second* Sunday before Easter.

Pastoral Offices: a category of shorter rites including, for example, confirmation, marriage, reconciliation of a penitent, and other offices. (Cf. BCP, pp. 411-507.) *See* Manual.

Pater noster: Our Father: the Latin name and first two words of the Lord's Prayer.

Patronal Feast: the feast day of a parish, observed on the date of the saint for whom the parish is named.

Pax: the "peace"; the Latin title for the Kiss of Peace.

Peace: the exchange of greeting in the name of the Lord within the fellowship of those gathered for the Eucharist. (Cf. BCP, pp. 332, 360.)

Penitential Psalms: Psalms 6, 32, 38, 51, 102, 130, 143; associated with the Fridays of Lent in the late Middle Ages, and with Ash Wednesday in the English BCP.

Pentecost: the fiftieth day after Easter Day and the last day of the Paschal Season; the day of special commemoration of the outpouring the Holy Spirit upon the Apostles.

Petitions: intercessory phrases, especially used in reference to the series of intercessions in a litany.

Phos hilaron: an ancient evening hymn sung at the lighting of the vesper lamp; now an optional invitatory at Evening Prayer. (Cf. BCP, pp. 64, 118.)

Pie: in medieval England, the book of directions for the liturgy, and later censured in the BCP of 1549 for its excessive complexity.

Pontifical: a handbook of offices of which the bishop is the minister, including, for example, the rites of Ordination and the Consecration of a Church. (Cf. BCP, pp. 509–517.) *See* Episcopal Services.

Post-communion Collect: the prayer in the Eucharistic rite, which comes immediately after communion and refers to the sacrament just received.

Prayers of the People: the general intercession of the Eucharist; originally it occurred immediately after catechumens were dismissed from the liturgy.

Preces: responsive petitionary phrases, as, for example, those that precede the collect of the day at Morning and Evening Prayer. *See* Suffrages.

Preface: the opening section of the eucharistic prayer, immediately following the dialogue between the celebrant and the assembly; the content of the preface centers upon thanksgiving to God the Father, and often includes a variable element (the *Proper Preface*) that refers to the particular feast of season; the preface terminates in the *Sanctus*. (BCP, pp. 333–34, 361–362, 377.)

Presbyter-Priest: an order of the ordained ministry of the church; originally a body of "elders" (comparable to that of Jewish synagogues) presided over from the second century by a bishop; with the expansion of the church, the bishops began to delegate sacramental and teaching authority to the presbyters who thus came to share the bishop's sacerdotal ministry; the English word *priest* is derived from *presbyter*.

Prime: the hour of prayer said at the first hour of the day (6:00 A.M.) in the monastic cycle of prayer; in recent years, because of its originally private character, it has fallen out of use.

Primer: a collection of elementary religious instruction and devotional material printed in various forms during the late Middle Ages.

Pro-Anaphora: the parts of the liturgy prior to the eucharistic prayer, and thus coinciding in a general sense with the Liturgy of the Word.

Procession: a liturgical movement of participants prior to, in the course of, or following the liturgy itself, including the clergy and their assistants but also possibly the choir and people as well; a procession implies movement from one place to another, and thus has a utilitarian basis.

Proper: appointed readings, prayers, psalms, or other elements appropriate to the celebration of a particular feast, season, or special occasion. *See* Common.

Province: an ecclesiastical unit made up of a group of neighboring dioceses, headed by an archbishop or, in the American Episcopal Church, by a president.

Psalter: the collection of the 150 psalms.

Quaerite dominum: the Second Song of Isaiah, (Is. 55:6–11), "Seek the Lord," a canticle for the Daily Offices introduced in the current revision of the BCP.

Real Presence: the doctrine that the eucharistic bread and wine are objectively identified with the true blood and blood of Christ. *See* Consubstantiation, Receptionism, and Transubstantiation.

Receptionism: a theory of the sacramental presence of Christ in the Eucharist which teaches that although the bread and wine remain unchanged, they are the means by which the communicant who receives in faith participates in the benefits or Christ's presence. *See* Consubstantiation, Real Presence, and Transubstantiation.

Red-Letter Days: important feasts of the Church Year, each provided with proper collects and Scripture readings. *See* Black-Letter Days.

Reproaches: the name of a text sometimes sung on Good Friday centering on a phrase conceived as being addressed from Christ on the cross to his people: "O my people, what have I done to you, or wherein have I wearied you? Answer me." The *Trisagion* forms the responsory.

Requiem: a Eucharist celebrated for the repose of a dead person.

Reservation: the keeping of the consecrated bread and wine after a celebration of the Eucharist for the subsequent administration of communion to those who are sick or unable to be present.

Responsory: a short phrase sung by the choir of congregation as a refrain to a psalm or after a reading.

Rite: the prescribed order and text for a public liturgical action, or a general designation for the liturgical provisions of a church, as, for example, the Byzantine Rite.

Ritual: pertaining to the performance of a liturgical rite, including both text and ceremonies.

Rogation Days: traditionally the three days preceding the feast of the Ascension on which prayers for the harvest were offered; in the latest revision expanded to include prayer for commerce and industry, and for stewardship of creation. (Cf. BCP, pp. 258–259.)

Roman Rite: the principal liturgical family of Western Christendom until the Reformation; the liturgy of the Roman Catholic Church.

Rubrics: the ceremonial directions of the church as authorized in the BCP; these were once printed in red (Latin: *ruber*) a fact from which their name is derived.

Sacerdotal: pertaining to the ministry of ordained bishops and priests.

Sacramentary: a liturgical book that contains the texts needed by the celebrant at the Eucharist.

Salutation: the greeting, "The Lord be with you."

Sanctorale: the calendar of saints' days. *See* Temporale.

Sanctus: the acclamation based upon Isaiah 6:3 that has been part of the eucharistic prayer since the third century: "Holy, holy, holy, Lord God of Hosts."

Sarum Rite: the liturgy of the English Cathedra of Salisbury during the later Middle Ages, and a major source for the First Book of Common Prayer (1549). *See* Use.

Scrutiny: in the early rites of initiation, an examination of the candidates prior to baptism.

See: the official seat (*sedes*) or throne (*cathedra*) of a bishop; thus the place where the cathedral is located is known as the bishop's see.

Sermon: an address to a liturgical assembly in the context of worship, usually presented by a person in Holy Orders, and based upon the appointed Scripture readings or an appropriate religious theme.

Sext: the hour of prayer appointed for the sixth hour of the day (noon) in the monastic cycle of prayer.

Sponsors: the witnesses at the baptism of an adult who attest to the character of the candidate and who engage themselves for special responsibility toward the candidate.

Stational Liturgies: the parish liturgies in Rome, especially during Lent, which were presided over by the pope. In early years, the whole Christian congregation of Rome would proceed to a different place or station each week to commemorate a different person or event. *See* Collect.

Stole: a long, thin liturgical vestment worn around the neck and shoulders by bishops and priests, and by deacons over the left shoulder; the stole is restricted to the ordained clergy.

Subdeacon: considered in the Middle Ages as the lowest of the three major orders (along with deacon and priest); the subdiaconate was abolished in the sixteenth century in Anglicanism at the same time the episcopate was reaffirmed as the primary ordained ministry.

Suffrages: the individual petitions of a litany; short petitionary phrases used as versicles and responses. (Cf. BCP, pp. 55, 67–68, 97–98, 121–22.) *See* Preces.

Surplice: a wide-sleeved, white vestment, often made of linen and worn over a cassock; it originated as a loose-fitting version of the alb. *See* Alb.

Surge illuminare: the Third Song of Isaiah (Is. 60:1–3, 11a, 18–19), "Arise, shine," a canticle for the Daily Offices introduced in the current revision of the BCP.

Sursum corda: the Latin words for "Lift up your hearts," and hence the name given to the dialogue between celebrant and people that opens the eucharistic prayer.

Te Deum: a fourth-century Latin hymn, "We praise thee, O God," used in the Breviary as a festal conclusion to Matins, and in Anglican Prayer books after 1549 as a canticle at Morning Prayer.

Temporale: the calendar of the seasons of the church except for the material contained in the *Sanctorale*. See *Sanctorale*.

Tenebrae: a night office of psalms and readings, monastic in origin, used on Wednesday, Thursday, and Friday nights of Holy Week; the word means "shadows," and is derived from the darkness in which the office is recited as the traditional fifteen candles are successively extinguished in the course of the service.

Terce: the hour of prayer appointed for the third hour of the day (9 A.M.) in the monastic cycle of prayer.

Thurible: a metal vessel for the burning of incense in a liturgical context; the thurible is suspended from chains that permit it to be swung; it is also known as a censer.

Transubstantiation: a theory of the sacramental presence of Christ in the Eucharist based upon philosophical premises of the late Middle Ages in which the substance (the essential reality) of the bread and wine are converted into the substance of the body and blood of Christ. *See* Consubstantiation, Real Presence, and Receptionism.

Triduum Sacrum: "the three sacred days," a name applied to the final three days of Holy Week commemorating the Last Supper, the passion and death of Christ, and his resting in the tomb.

Trisagion: a canticle primarily associated with the Byzantine and other Easter rites, in which the words "Holy God, Holy and Mighty, Holy Immortal One, have mercy upon us" are repeated; in the West, traditionally retained on Good Friday, and introduced among Anglicans in the current revision of the BCP. (Cf. pp. 324, 356.)

Unction: an anointing with holy oil or chrism, and generally associated with the ministry of healing and accompanied by the laying on of hands. (Cf. BCP, pp. 455–57.)

Use: a ritual pattern associated with a particular region, usually a modification of details of one of the major liturgical families; e.g. what is often referred to as the Sarum Rite is actually the Roman Rite as celebrated in the Use associated with Salisbury Cathedral.

Venice Statement: a theological statement on the question of Authority, agreed by the Anglican-Roman Catholic International Commission in 1976.

Venite: the traditional invitatory at Anglican Morning Prayer, "O come, let us sing unto the Lord"; its content varies: Psalm 95 entire (English book); Pss. 95: 1–7a; 96:9, 13 (earlier American books and Rite I, BCP, pp. 44–45); Ps. 95:1–7 (Rite II, BCP, p.82).

Versicles: short verses, often taken from the Psalter, which are usually recited antiphonally between officiant and the people who reply with *responses*.

Vespers: (Greek: *hespera*, "evening"); the title for the monastic hour of prayer that was sung at the end of the day; Lauds and Vespers are the oldest and most important of the hours of prayer, as the times of corporate praise at the beginning and end of day. In Anglicanism, Evening Prayer corresponds to Vespers in basic structure; furthermore, both forms are characterized by the singing of the *Magnificat* as the evening canticle.

Vestments: the clothing appropriate to persons performing liturgical actions. In England, governed by Ornaments Rubric; in the United States, there are no rubrics or canons governing their use, except a minimum description at ordinations.

Vigil: a night office, associated especially with the eve of an important feast, such as the Great Vigil of Easter.

Votive: a term applied to prayer or celebrations of the Eucharist that are celebrated for a special purpose, occasion, or theme, rather than in accordance with the Church Year; examples of votives would include a Nuptial Mass or a Requiem.

Western Rite: the general designation of the family of rites that developed in western Europe, but especially those associated with the church at Rome that extended its influence far beyond central Italy.

Westward Position: the custom of the celebrant of the Eucharist standing at the altar so that he faces the people across the altar during the liturgy.

Windsor Statement: a theological statement on the question of the Eucharist agreed by the Anglican-Roman Catholic International Commission in 1971.

Words of Institution: the words used by Christ in instituting the Eucharist at the last Supper; although there are many variants in the various eucharistic prayers of East and West, one form or another of the words of Institution appears in almost every known Anaphora; in the Roman Rite, the consecration of the bread and wine has been traditionally linked to the Words of Institution, whereas the Eastern Rites give this significance to the Epiclesis. Most sacramental theologians today emphasize the importance of the entire Eucharistic prayer in the act of consecration.

Bibliography of Works Cited

ABBREVIATIONS

AF   The Apostolic Fathers. Loeb Classical Library. London and Cambridge, Mass.: Harvard University Press, 1912 ff.

ANF   The Ante-Nicene Fathers. Edited by Alexander Roberts and James Donaldson, revised by A.C. Coxe. 10 vols. Grand Rapids, Mich.: Eerdmans, 1957 ff.

LCC   The Library of Christian Classics. Philadelphia: Westminster, 1950 ff.

I. The Bible

The Holy Bible (Revised Standard Version).

II. Official Publications of the Church

The First and Second Prayer Books of Edward VI. Everyman's Library, London: Dent, 1949.

The Book of Common Prayer, 1928.

The Hymnal 1940.

Lesser Feasts and Fasts, rev. ed. New York: Church Pension Fund, 1975.

The Book of Common Prayer, 1976.

III. Ancient and Medieval Works

Apostolic Constitutions, ANF, vol. 7.

Augustine, *Confessions and Enchiridion*. Translated and edited by Albert C. Outler. LCC, vol. 7. Philadelphia: Westminster, 1955.

Cyprian, *On the Unity of the Church*, ANF, vol. 5.

Dead Sea Manual of Discipline. Edited by W. H. Brownlee. New Haven, Conn.: American Schools of Oriental Research, 1951.

Didache, AF, vol. 2.

Hippolytus, *The Apostolic Tradition of Hippolytus*. Edited by B. S. Easton. Cambridge: Cambridge University Press, 1934.

Ignatius, *To Polycarp*, AF, vol. 1.

Justin Martyr, *First Apology*, ANF, vol. 1.

Tertullian, *On Baptism*, ANF, vol. 3.

Tertullian, *To His Wife*, ANF, vol. 4.

Thomas Aquinas, *Summa Theologica*. Translated by Fathers of the English Dominican Province. 2d and rev. ed. London: Burns, Oates and Washborne, 1921–1935.

IV. Reformation and Post-Reformation Writings

Calvin, John. *Institutes of the Christian Religion*. Edited by John T. McNeil. 2 vols. LCC vols. 20 and 21. Philadelphia: Westminster, 1960.

Cranmer, Thomas. *Miscellaneous Writings and Letters*. Cambridge: The Parker Society, 1848.

Pusey, E. B. *Scriptural Views of Holy Baptism* (Tracts 67–69). In Tracts for the Times, vol. 2. London: Rivington, 1839.

Taylor, Jeremy. *The Whole Works*. 10 vols. London, 1847–1854.

V. Modern Works

Batiffol, P. *History of the Roman Breviary*. London: Longmans, Green, 1912.

Barth, Karl. *Church Dogmatics*. 13 pts. Edinburgh: T. & T. Clark, 1936.

Bettenson, H., ed. *Documents of the Christian Church*. London: Oxford University Press, 1943.

Clarke, W. K. L., and Harris, Charles. *Liturgy and Worship*. London: S.P.C.K., 1932.

Come, Arnold B. *Agents of Reconciliation*. Philadelphia: Westminster, 1960.

Dearmer, Percy. *The Parsons' Handbook*. Rev. and rewritten by Cyril E. Pocknee. New York: Oxford University Press, 1965.

Dix, Gregory. *The Shape of the Liturgy*. London: Dacre Press, 1945.

The Theology of Confirmation in Relation to Baptism. London: Dacre Press, 1948.

Edwards, O. C. and Bennett, R. *The Bible for Today's Church*. New York: Seabury, 1979.

Eichrodt, Walther. *Old Testament Theology*. 2 vols. Philadelphia: Westminster, 1961.

Eliade, Mircea. *The Sacred and the Profane: The Nature of Religion*. New York: Harcourt Brace & World, 1959.

Fisher, J. D. C. "History and Theology." In *Confirmation Crisis*, pp. 19–42. New York: Seabury, 1968.

Grundman, Walther. *Das Evangelium nach Matthaus*. Berlin: Evangelische Verlagsanstalt, 1968.

Hatchett, Marion. *Sanctifying Life, Time and Space*. New York: Seabury, 1976.

Hill, David. *The Gospel of Matthew*. London: Oliphants, 1972.

Jeremias, Joachim. *The Eucharistic Words of Jesus*. New York: Scribner, 1966.

Jungmann, Josef A. *The Liturgy of the Word*. London: Burns and Oates, 1966.

Kelly, J. N. D. *Early Christian Creeds*. New York: Longmans, Green, 1950.

King, Archdale A. *The Rites of Western Christendom*, 4 vols.: vol. 1, *Liturgy of the*

Roman Church; vol. 2, *Liturgies of the Religious Orders*; vol. 3, *Liturgies of the Primatial Sees*; vol. 4, *Liturgies of the Past*. London: Longmans, Green, 1955–1959.

Ladd, George T. *The Doctrine of Sacred Scripture*. New York: Scribner, 1883.

Lampe, Geoffrey W. H. *The Seal of the Spirit*. London: Longmans, Green, 1951.

MacArther, A. A. *The Evolution of the Christian Year*. London: SCM, 1953.

Muilenburg, James, "The History of Israel's Religion." In *The Interpreter's Bible*, vol. 1. Nashville, Tenn.: Abingdon, 1952.

Nouwen, H. *Reaching Out*. Garden City, N.Y.: Doubleday, 1975.

Otto, Rudolf. *The Idea of the Holy*. New York: Oxford University Press, 1931.

Phillips, J. B. *The Gospels in Modern English*. London: Geoffrey Bles, 1952.

Procter, F. F., and Frere, W. H. *A New History of the Book of Common Prayer*. London: Macmillan, 1908.

Strack, H. L. and Billerbeck, P. *Kommentar zum Neuen Testament aus Talmud und Midrasch*, Munich: C. H. Beck, 1928.

Thornton, Lionel S. *Confirmation, Its Place in the Baptismal Mystery*. London: Dacre Press, 1954.

Tillich, Paul. *Systematic Theology*, 3 vols. Chicago: University of Chicago Press, 1951–63.

von Rad, Gerhard. *Old Testament Theology*. 2 vols. New York: Harper & Row, 1962.

Yerkes, Roydon K. *Sacrifice in Greek and Roman Religion and Early Judaism*. New York: Scribner, 1952.

Bibliography for Further Reading

Part One—The Meaning of Worship

Bell, Catherine. "Ritual, Change, and Changing Ritual." *Worship* 63:1 (1989).

Bouyer, Louis. *Liturgical Piety*. Notre Dame, Ind., 1955.

Bradshaw, Paul F. *The Search for the Origins of Christian Worship*. N.Y., 1992.

Chauvet, L. M. *Symbol and Sacrament: A Sacramental Reinterpretation of Christian Existence*. Collegeville, Minn., 1995.

Chupungco, A.J. *Handbook for Liturgical Studies*, I. Collegeville, Minn., 1997. (This is the first of a projected five volume series covering all basic questions in liturgical studies.)

Collins, Mary. *Worship: Renewal to Practice*. Washington, D.C., 1987.

Douglas, Mary. *Natural Symbols*. New York, 1970.

Geertz, Clifford. "Religion as a Cultural System." *The Interpretation of Cultures*. New York, 1973.

Hoffman, Lawrence. "How Ritual Means: Ritual Circumcision in Rabbinic Culture and Today." *Studia Liturgica* 23 (1993), 78–97.

Huizinga, J. *Homo Ludens*. Boston, 1950.

Jennings, Theodore W. "Ritual Studies and Liturgical Theology: An Invitation to Dialogue." *Journal of Ritual Studies* 1:1 (1987), 35–56.

Jones, Cheslyn, Geoffrey Wainwright, Edward Yarnold, and Paul Bradshaw eds. *The Study of Liturgy*. N.Y., 1992.

Kelleher, Margaret Mary. "Liturgy: An Ecclesial Act of Meaning." *Worship* 59 (1985), 482–97.

Langer, S. *Philosophy in a New Key*. Cambridge, 1942.

Lathrop, Gordon. *Holy Things: A Liturgical Theology*. Minn., 1993.

Mitchell, Nathan. "Revisiting the Roots of Ritual: Basic Directions in the Field of Ritual Studies." *Liturgy Digest* 1:1 (1993), 4–36.

Pieper, J. *In Tune with the World*. N.Y., 1965.

Procter-Smith, Marjorie. *In Her Own Rite: Constructing Feminist Liturgical Tradition*. Nashville, 1990.

Rahner, Hugo. *Man at Play*. N.Y., 1967.

Rahner, Karl. "The Theology of Symbol." *Theological Investigations*, vol. 4. Baltimore, 1966, 221–52.

Schmemann, Alexander. *For the Life of the World*. N.Y., 1973.

Searle, Mark. "New Tasks, New Methods: The Emergence of Pastoral Liturgical Studies." *Worship* 57 (1983), 291–308.

Von Allmen, J. J. *Worship: Its Theology and Practice.* N.Y., 1965.

Weil, Louis. "The Gospel in Anglicanism." *The Study of Anglicanism*, ed. S. Sykes, J. Booty, and J. Knight. London, 1998, 55–83.

——. "Prayer, Liturgical." *The New Dictionary of Sacramental Worship*, ed. Peter Fink. Collegeville, Minn., 1990, 949–59.

Part Two—Liturgy and the Book of Common Prayer

Cuming, G. J. *A History of Anglican Liturgy.* N.Y., 1982.

Dix, Gregory. *The Shape of the Liturgy.* London, 1945.

Hatchett, M. J. *Commentary on the American Prayer Book.* N.Y., 1980.

——. *Sanctifying Life, Time and Space: An Introduction to Liturgical Study.* N.Y., 1976.

Marshall, P. V., and Lesley Northup. *Leaps and Boundaries: the Prayer Book in the 21st Century.* Harrisburg, Pa., 1997.

Meyers, R. A., ed. *A Prayer Book for the 21st Century.* Liturgical Studies 3. N.Y., 1996.

Proctor, F. F., and W. H. Frere. *A New History of the Book of Common Prayer.* London, 1908.

Shepherd, M. H. *The Oxford American Prayer Book Commentary.* N.Y., 1950.

——. *The Worship of the Church.* N.Y., 1952.

Stuhlman, B. *Occasions of Grace: An historical and theological study of the Pastoral Offices and Episcopal Services in the Book of Common Prayer.* N.Y., 1995.

Weil, Louis, ed. *Unbound! Anglican Worship beyond the Prayer Book.* Papers delivered at a symposium on the liturgy at the Church Divinity School of the Pacific, Berkeley, Calif., January, 1999. *Anglican Theological Review* 82:1 (Winter 2000).

Part Three—Christian Initiation

Dunn, James D. G. *Baptism in the Holy Spirit.* Studies in Biblical Theology, 2d Series, No. 15. London, 1970.

Fisher, J. D. C. *Christian Initiation: Baptism in the Medieval West.* London, 1965.

——. *Christian Initiation: The Reformation Period.* London, 1970.

Holeton, D. R., ed. *Growing in Newness of Life: Christian Initiation in Anglicanism Today.* Toronto, 1993.

Jeremias, J. *Infant Baptism in the First Four Centuries.* Philadelphia, 1960.

Johnson, M. E. *The Rites of Christian Initiation: Their Evolution and Interpretation.* Collegeville, Minn., 1999.

——. ed. *Living Water, Sealing Spirit. Readings on Christian Initiation.* Collegeville, Minn., 1995.

Kavanagh, A. *The Shape of Baptism: The Rite of Christian Initiation.* N.Y., 1978.

——. *Confirmation: Origins and Reform.* N.Y., 1988.

Lampe, G. W. H. *The Seal of the Spirit.* London, 1967.

Meyers, R. A. *Continuing the Reformation: Re-Visioning Baptism in the Episcopal Church.* N.Y., 1997.

Mitchell, L. L. *Baptismal Anointing.* London, 1966.

Stevick, D. B. *Baptismal Moments; Baptismal Meanings.* N.Y., 1987.

Turner, P. *Confirmation: the Baby in Solomon's Court.* N.Y., 1993.

Turner, T. J. "Confirmation, Membership and Ministry." *Welcoming the Baptized: Anglican Hospitality Within the Ecumenical Enterprise.* Grove Books/GROW, no. 34. Nottingham, London, 1996.

Whitaker, E. C., ed. *Documents of the Baptismal Liturgy.* London, 1960.

Part Four—Regular Services: Divine Offices, Holy Eucharist

A. DIVINE OFFICES

Bradshaw, Paul F. *Daily Prayer in the Early Church.* London, 1981.

Campbell, S. *From Breviary to Liturgy of the Hours.* Collegeville, Minn., 1995.

Dugmore, G. W. *The Influence of the Synagogue upon the Divine Office.* Westminster, Md., 1964.

Guiver, G. *Company of Voices.* N.Y., 1998.

Lamb, J. A. *The Psalms in Christian Worship.* London, 1962.

Salmon, P. *The Breviary Through the Centuries.* Collegeville, Minn., 1962.

Taft, R. *The Liturgy of the Hours in East and West.* Collegeville, Minn., 1986.

B. HOLY EUCHARIST

Childs, B. S. *Memory and Tradition in Israel.* London, 1962.

Crockett, W. R. *Eucharist: Symbol of Transformation.* N.Y., 1989.

Jeremias, J. *The Eucharistic Words of Jesus.* N.Y., 1966.

Kilmartin, E. J. *The Eucharist in the West: History and Theology.* Collegeville, Minn., 1998.

LaVerdiere, E. *The Eucharist in the New Testament and the Early Church.* Collegeville, Minn., 1996.

Leon-Dufour, X. *Sharing the Eucharistic Bread: the Witness of the New Testament.* N.Y., 1987.

Leonard, J. K., and Nathan D. Mitchell. *The Postures of the Assembly during the Eucharistic Prayer.* Chicago, 1994.

Porter, H. B. "Episcopal Anaphoral Prayers." *New Eucharistic Prayers,* ed. Frank Senn. N.Y., 1987, 63–73.

Power, D. N. *The Eucharistic Mystery: Revitalizing the Tradition.* N.Y., 1993.

Stevenson, K. *Eucharist and Offering.* N.Y., 1986.

Williams, R. *Eucharistic Sacrifice: The Roots of a Metaphor.* Grove Liturgical Study, no. 31. Nottingham, London, 1982.

Part Five—Other Liturgies
Pastoral Offices and Episcopal Services

A. MARRIAGE

Brueggemann, W. "Covenanting as Human Vocation." *Interpretation* 33:2 (1979).

Palmer, P. F. "Christian Marriage: Contract or Covenant?" *Theological Studies* 33 (1972), 617–65.

Phillips, J.M. "A Critique of the Rite of the Celebration and Blessing of a Christian Marriage." *A Prayer Book for the 21st Century*, ed. Ruth A. Meyers. Liturgical Studies 3. N.Y., 1996, 110–29.

Schillebeeckx, E. *Marriage: Saving Reality and Human Mystery.* N.Y., 1965.

Stevenson, K. *Nuptial Blessing: A Study of Christian Marriage Rites.* N.Y., 1983.

B. RECONCILIATION

Countryman, W. L. *Forgiven and Forgiving.* Harrisburg, Pa., 1998.

Dallen, James. *The Reconciling Community: the Rite of Penance.* N.Y., 1986.

Dudley, M. and Geoffrey Rowell, eds. *Confession and Absolution.* Collegeville, Minn.,1990.

Hyde, C. *To Declare God's Forgiveness.* Wilton, Conn., 1984.

Kennedy, R. J., ed. *Reconciliation: the Continuing Agenda.* Collegeville, MN, 1987.

Leech, K. *Soul Friend.* London, 1977.

Smith, M. L. *Reconciliation: Preparing for Confession in the Episcopal Church.* Cambridge, Mass., 1985.

C. HEALING

Brooke, Avery. *Healing in the Landscape of Prayer.* Cambridge, Mass., 1996.

Fink, P., ed. *Anointing of the Sick: Alternative Futures for Worship*, vol. 7. Collegeville, Minn., 1987.

Condon, K. "The Sacrament of Healing." *Sacraments in Scripture* ed. T. Worden. Springfield, Ill., 1966, 172–86.

Dudley, Martin, and Geoffrey Rowell, eds. *The Oil of Gladness: Anointing in the Christian Tradition.* London, 1995.

Empereur, James. "Anointing." *The New Dictionary of Sacramental Worship.* Collegeville, Minn., 1990, 49–56.

Gusmer, C. *And You Visited Me: Sacramental Ministry to the Sick and Dying.* N.Y., 1984.

———. *The Ministry of Healing in the Church of England.* Great Wakering, U.K. 1974.

Kelsey, M. T. *Psychology, Medicine and Christian Healing.* San Francisco, 1988.

Ramshaw, E. *Ritual and Pastoral Care.* Philadelphia, Pa., 1987.

Smith, D. H. *Health and Medicine in the Anglican Tradition.* N.Y., 1986.

Part Six—Ministry and Holy Orders

Audet, J. P. *Structures of Christian Priesthood.* N.Y., 1968.

Brown, R. E. *Priest and Bishop.* N.Y., 1970.

Congar, Y. M. J. *Lay People in the Church.* Westminster, Md., 1957.

Countryman, W. L. *Living on the Border of the Holy: Renewing the Priesthood of All.* Harrisburg, PA, 1999.

Doohan, L. "Laity, Theology of the." *The New Dictionary of Sacramental Worship,* ed. Peter Fink. Collegeville, Minn., 1990, 636–44.

Holmes, U. T. *Ministry and Imagination.* N.Y., 1981.

Lathrop, G. *Holy People: A Liturgical Ecclesiology.* Minneapolis, Minn., 1999.

Moberly, R. C. *Ministerial Priesthood.* London, 1897, reprinted 1969.

O'Meara, T. *Theology of Ministry.* N.Y., 1999.

Schillebeeckx, E. *The Church with a Human Face.* N.Y., 1985.

Internet Resources

Online materials on liturgy

http://www.gtu.edu/library/LibWorship.html
http://www.osb.org/liturgy
http://divinity.library.vanderbilt.edu/bibs/liturgics.htm#

Online Liturgical Resources

http://www.wabashcenter.wabash.edu/Internet/liturgy.htm
http://www.nccbuscc.org/liturgy/current/index.htm
http://www.bostontheological.org/libraries
http://www.nd.edu
http://www.evansville.edu
http://www.catalog.litpress.org
http://www.csbsju.edu/library
http://www.music.princeton.edu/chant_html/liturg.html

Early Christian sources

http://www.iclnet.org/pub/resources/christian-history.html
http://www.evansville.edu
http://www.ccel.org
http://www.fordham.edu

Index

A

Absolute, The, 9-11

Absolution, 111, 112, 126, 186-190

Accumulated Services, 117

Advent, 138, 166; First Sunday in 138, 159, 163, 166

Anamnesis (Memorial), 135, 144, 147

Anglican communion, 1, 3, 28, 37, 51, 57, 74, 117, 151, 154, 168, 170, 194; separation of Baptism and Confirmation within, 82-84, 190-191

Anointing 80, 81, 83, 87, 182-183

Ante-communion, 117

Apocalypses, 103-104, 105

Apocrypha, 98

Apostolic Constitutions, 45, 46, 105, 139

Apostolic Fathers, 98

Apostolic Tradition , 45, 46, 71, 76, 80, 83, 84, 106, 133, 134-136, 139-146

Aquinas, St. Thomas, 82, 150-151

Aristotle, 150-151

Articles of Religion, 98

Ash Wednesday, 162, 166

Augustine, St., 122, 153

B

Baptism, 19, 22, 49-50, 52, 54, 55, 66-89, 126, 190-193; and Catechesis, 84; Development of Liturgy of, 73-75, 80; Early Liturgical Patterns of, 70-77; and Holy Spirit, 66, 72, 78, 83; Infant, 76-77. 88; of Jesus, 68-70, 78-79; Jewish, 66; of John, 66-68 in Current Prayer Book,75-76; as

Ordination of Laity, 191; Separation of Confirmation from 80-82, 190-191

Basil, St., Liturgy of, 46

Benedict, St., of Nursia, 107-108

Bible, 12, 13-15, 20-21, 24, 26, 27, 28-29, 32-33, 39-40, 42, 44, 45, 52, 66, 69, 76, 78-79, 95-100, 128-129, 157, 160, 181, 185; King James Version,57, 79; Limits of Old and New Testaments, 97-99; Marriage in, 17; Scripture in Christian worship,103-109; significance of, 99-100; sin and forgiveness in,186-187; Word of God and the 93-100, 102-103, 121

Blessing Prayer of, 134, 138, 139-142

Bread and wine, distribution of, 136, 147

Breaking of the Bread, 136, 147

Breviary, 47, 108, 121

Burial of the Dead, 54, 126

C

Calvin, John, 3, 84-85, 96-97

Canterbury Statement (1973) of Anglican-Roman Catholic International Commission, 195, 199, 201

Canticles, 113, 114

Catechesis, 84, 85, 87

Catechism, 57, 75; Confirmation and, 84-85

Child, birth or adoption of, 179-180

Christian calendar, 155-170; day, 155-156; month, 158-159; week,